That's a Pretty Thing to Call It

That's a Pretty Thing to Call It

Prose and Poetry by Artists
Teaching in Carceral Institutions

Edited by Leigh Sugar

NEW VILLAGE PRESS • NEW YORK

Published in the United States by New Village Press
bookorders@newvillagepress.net
www.newvillagepress.org
New Village Press is a public-benefit, nonprofit publisher
Distributed by NYU Press
First Edition: October 2023

Paperback ISBN: 978-1-61332-211-6
Hardcover ISBN: 978-1-61332-212-3
eBook Trade ISBN: 978-1-61332-213-0
eBook Institutional: 978-1-61332-214-7

Library of Congress Control Number: 2023942197

Cover Illustration: Kimberly Pappas, Flowers, The Mind of the Brush, 2020, Acrylic, 11 x 14 in, with permission from the Prison Creative Arts Project, University of Michigan.

For Etheridge Knight, Spoon Jackson, Judith Tannenbaum,
Buzz Alexander, Janie Paul, Mary Heinen, and all the
artists and teachers who held the torch before us.

the years fall
like overripe plums
bursting red flesh
on the dark earth
                    —ETHERIDGE KNIGHT

There is nothing
that has nothing to do with this
                    —SOLMAZ SHARIF

Contents

Hybrid/Mixed Genre *83*

Poetry *155*

Foreword

I.

You're cross-legged on the floor, then your legs are laid straight in front of you, then you're cross-legged again. You're sweating through your shirt. Your knuckles have started to swell from being pressed against the ground. The flex-cuffs restraining your hands behind your back bite into your skin. You've been here, in this goddamn dayroom, for three hours. A quote you recently wrote downplays on loop in your mind: "You put me in here a cub. But I will go out a roaring lion and will make all hell howl."[1] You are one of sixty in this brightly lit room, not counting the Special Response Team sentinels, their black cargo pants tucked into combat boots, tasers and bean-bag rifles gripped tight. This is a training exercise—there have been no riots, no killings, no hunger strikes. This is a training exercise. An education, one might say. You've been told that there will be no use of the bathroom, no standing, no moving. While your cell is being ransacked by the young trainees, your watchers discuss what they will eat after this. They laugh and pat each other on the back and call each other *brother*. These are the lives we find ourselves waking to. Your shoulder aches and you try to laugh as your watchers had laughed. Laugh, because—look what you've become.

Later, after that small corner of madness recedes, you make a note about the day's events, but *it's hard to translate a muscular language to a verbal one.*[2] The note is non-descriptive, an overview with the final imperative to never forget the cuffs and the bodies and the hard floor, the bright lights, the sweat and the undercurrent of strange violence. You want to write more about this but wonder if the inexpressible can truly be contained within the expressed. You wonder about that, too: being contained. You often forget because, in the house of your life, days like this are simply rooms you take no pleasure in visiting. Most days the house seems small and stuffed with old photographs. You do not forget that these rooms exist, but that most visitors will be horrified that such rooms are not permanently locked and separated from the rest. You find it hard to explain

---

1. Carry Amelia Nation. "Chapter VIII." Essay. In *The Use and Need of the Life of Carry A. Nation*, 148–48. Charlottesville, Virginia: F.M. Steves, 1909.
2. Cortney Lamar Charleston. "It's Important I Remember That They Don't Have the Tools to Critique Me." *Poetry Foundation*, June 2019. www.poetryfoundation.org

that separation has not been an option you've had the luxury of choosing for years now, and you still stumble over words, trying to get them to stay a while, maybe have a meal and some coffee, just for a bit, but they keep looking and looking and looking at the door. They want to talk about it and understand it. You try to explain so they can understand, to make sense of it for them and for you, but you cannot, and they cannot. So, you open the door and step inside as they pack up their knapsack and step out to their crisp walk home, all the while thinking about you and the doors in your small house. When you leave the room there is no body around to call you by name, and so you begin to forget even that because aren't numbers easier, more efficient? *But you have to remember the name / they gave you first. The one you came with.*[3]

II.

Late summer. The volunteer creative writing instructor gazes out of the barred window as the group takes notes on Ginsburg's *Howl*. "The grounds here I can't believe how beautiful they are, all the flowers," the instructor says quietly. A few group members set down their pens and look out to the yard. "You must take a lot of pride in that. I mean, visitors must be impressed." A few loose mutters of agreement, pens returning to work.

No good deed goes unpunished—or something like that. Language is filled to the brim with tropes like this. Whether this particular body of meaning is a savage American creature or some universal truth bestowed upon us by a cup, somewhere, runneth over, I have no idea. But if punishment is on the table, so to speak, then we may as well examine it, or at least give it a name.

One might accuse those who teach Arts in Corrections of trafficking in redemption songs, which seems to be an ironic, and thus cruel, form of punishment. I am far from a sadist, no matter what the penal system wants you to believe, but I cannot say that I find zero glimmers of truth in this accusation. I wonder often if writing has offered me a form of freedom or if I am simply putting my cage on loan to another zoo.

When I ask my friend J.L. Wine III for his thoughts surrounding Arts in Corrections—*Don't be afraid to offer criticism*—he tells me that I'm over-thinking the whole thing, that our stories "need to be heard." Another friend, Justin Schneider, is more amicable to my frustrations but still offers

---

3. Patrick Rosal. "Brooklyn Antediluvian." In *Brooklyn Antediluvian: Poems*. New York: Persea Books, 2016.

what I've come to think of as the company line: "If it helps us, then what is there to complain about?" As much as I want to shout *reckless capitalism* or *institutionalization* (synonyms?), they are not wrong. Quickly, I have become confused about who is more prideful about their flowers.

Inner conflict: I do not believe that art is enough. As much as I believe Nam June Paik when he says "an artist's job is to bite the hand that feeds them," I am not sure who's hand to bite or, in a cage already, how much I can afford to bite at all.[4] So, if we are to be capitalists (were we ever not?), then I must ask: through art, what have we gained? Our voices? The ability to speak and write with confidence is certainly a gain a measurable one at that - but if our voices are to reach and cause some brand of paradigm shift in the minds of those with our lives in their palms, then we need more than writing workshops. What would be enough, anyway? Freedom? Money? Love?

What does it matter that I can analyze the poems of others, that I can attempt to write my own? *If poetry can't be applied to how one moves through this world then I see very little worth in it, which is where it started // for me.*[5] Words are not the same thing as me offering you half of a peanut butter and jelly sandwich cut corner-to-corner, lately the first image that comes to mind when I think of intimate care, what I might call appreciation, or even love.

Yet another friend, Robert Leonard King II, who will soon be released, spouts the benefits that creative writing workshops have poured into his life, but he provides a caveat: "I felt like I was peddling my own pain to entertain these university types, so I started to write for my own peace." I can't say that I have found anything I can identify as *peace*, but I can attest—as I am sure many others can—to a brief calm, as if a field has cleared and I can see for miles, after I write a poem or read the work of others in which I might find pieces of my self.

The moment lasts ten breaths, and in that silence // I imagine that I can see spirits, I can know myself, and I will not fear / the betrayals of my body and love and earth, and the machinations // of self-made emperors and pontificates. It will be winter soon.[6]

And so much for trafficking.

---

4. Sophie Heawood. "Grayson Perry's First Exhibition in Years Is Deliciously Provocative—and Utterly Brilliant." *British Vogue*, September 24, 2019. www.vogue.co.uk.

5. Charleston, "It's Important I Remember . . ."

6. Kwame Dawes, "Before Winter." *The New Yorker*, September 23, 2019.

III.

Martín Espada: "It is important to convince people that their lives are the stuff of poetry."[7] This could be another trope, but I prefer to see it as a call to reclamation. A reclamation of story, of body and all its aches, of violence wrought and a once seemingly impossible light still breaking through to a raucous morning.

It's important I remember that they don't have the tools to criticize me, a woman tells Cortney Lamar Charleston in his poem of the same title.[8] The woman is speaking about poetic craft but Charleston understands what is being said, what must be heard: *that there is more to me or anyone // alike than being menace or miscreant, minstrel or misanthrope, or / murdered as all four would be with equal fanfare.* I have the urge to write a dissertation on Charleston's poem, to teach it, give his words as a gift to everyone I encounter, and perhaps one day I will, but I digress—you should read the poem. For now, I will simply appreciate the song, for in it I can begin, again and for the first time, to *know myself, and I will not fear / the betrayals.*[9]

All this to say, I think Espada is right: a life—any life—can be the stuff of poetry. The inverse is also true: poetry can be the stuff of lives. Perhaps, through some form of crooked osmosis, a poetics can help me reclaim the contents of my days, eventually carrying me to a threshold where I *believe whatever / I do next will surpass what I have done.* How funny to remember that *poetry was a dead white thing in my life once.*[10]

IV.

You still don't know how to make sense of it, how you were cuffed and herded into a room full of other bodies to service a very specific method of education. The bruises on your knuckles, your damp shirt, your aching shoulder, all these cells and locks and fences. Winter now, and that day has dissolved amongst the thousands of other days you've been down. You almost forget.

You've been asked to write a foreword for an anthology of work by people who have taught arts in corrections. You agree, then debate with yourself for months over whether or not you should tell the editor to find

---

7. Gabriel Thompson, Gabriel and Martín Espada. Against Oblivion. Interview. *Poetry Foundation*, May 1, 2018. www.poetryfoundation.org.

8. Charleston, "It's Important I Remember that the Moral Arc of the Universe Bends"

9. Dawes, "Before Winter."

10. Charleston, "It's Important I Remember . . ."

someone else. What is there to say? *You have to make peace with the chaos but you cannot lie.*[11] You are alone. You have just met the half-way point of a sixteen-to-forty-year sentence. You have written some poems. You sign paperwork with your number first, then your name if it's asked for. You are the opposite of free. *What's free? Free is when nobody else can tell us what to be.*[12] And make sense of this: you don't want to see violence, but you don't *not* want to see violence, and that's the quickest line to understanding what you've become. You've written some poems about this.

Still there is a nagging, a pull toward *something*. You read and re-read a poem you've cut out of a magazine in hopes you might be reminded of what you have learned, who you are. You begin to piece words together into sentences, sentences into paragraphs and sections. You begin to doubt that any of this, whatever *this* is, has ever been about redemption or reclamation or even reason. Perhaps all along it's been about memory, about recollection—of your name, your many pains, and all the words left unspoken—so that once all this bullshit is said and done, once the doors are opened or at least unlocked and cells no longer hold you, once you can slice a peanut butter and jelly sandwich corner-to-corner and share it with your child or lover or brother, then you can finally rest; even if only for ten breaths, and know that you are still, even now, becoming more than the struggles you've overcome. Maybe you will accept, after so long, that words were enough, even if only because they had to be. Maybe you will remember all the poems and songs that made you, and if that happens, promise me one thing: *promise that you'll sing about me.*[13]

Justin Rovillos Monson, Freeland, Michigan
November 2019

11. Ta-Nehisi Coates. Essay. In *Between the World and Me*, 71–71. New York: Spiegel & Grau, 2015.

12. Meek Mill ft. Jay-Z and Rick Ross. *What's Free*. CD. *Championships*. STREETRUN-NER and Tarik Azzouz, Atlantic Records, 2018.

13. Kendrick Lamar. *Sing About Me, I'm Dying of Thirst*. CD. *Good Kid, M.A.A.D. City*. Atlanta, Georgia: Interscope Records, 2013.

Introduction

The popular perception is that art is apart. I insist it is a part of. Something not in dispute is that people in prison are apart from. If you can accept—whatever level of discipline and punishment you adhere to momentarily set aside—that the ultimate goal should be to reunite the separated with the larger human enterprise, it might behoove us to see prisoners, among others, as they elect to be seen, in their larger selves. If we go there, if not with our bodies then at least our minds, we are more likely to register the implications.[14]

So reads an excerpt from *One Big Self*, the late poet C.D. Wright's stunning book-length poetry sequence written after several visits to three state prisons in Louisiana over the course of a year. Along with her friend, photographer Deborah Luster, Wright entered the facilities to "produce a record of Louisiana's prison population through image and text." She emerged from her experiences at the East Carroll Parish Prison Farm, the Louisiana Correctional Institution for Women, and the Louisiana State Penitentiary at Angola with a newfound urgency, in her words:

[n]ot to idealize, not to judge, not to exonerate, not to aestheticize immeasurable levels of pain. Not to demonize, not to anathematize. What I wanted was to unequivocally lay out the real feel of hard time.[15]

Like Wright, the artists included in this anthology have entered "correctional facilities" and come away with an urgency to express "the feel of hard time" not in terms of numbers, nor from the perspective of an incarcerated person (those of us who've never been incarcerated can never know that), but from the perspective of a person who, by some stroke of luck or grief, found themselves in the strange position of choosing to enter prison to share their art with people who can't choose to leave.

Much has been written about mass incarceration, and in recent years the crisis has been at the forefront of this country's collective consciousness.

---

14. C.D. Wright, *One Big Self* (Port Townsend: Copper Canyon Press, 2007), xiv.
15. Wright, xiv.

The landscape of "hard time" is commonly represented through data: as of March 2022, there are nearly two million people in jails and prisons in the United States, a number that reflects a significant reduction since the start of the COVID-19 pandemic due to system slowdowns (though this number is quickly rebounding).[16] When those on probation and parole in the US are included in this corrections-involved statistic, the number jumps to nearly 6 million.[17] At a rate of 573 per 100,000 people—over 1.75 times that of Russia—the US incarcerates more of its people per capita than any other country in the world.[18] Comparable nations, such as Canada, the UK, and France, incarcerate citizens at rates 5 to 10 times *lower* than the US.[19] These numbers reflect harsh sentencing laws and policies—particularly those associated with the War on Drugs, which began officially in 1982—as well as increasing sentence lengths and cutbacks on parole releases.[20] Mass incarceration disproportionately affects poor folks and people of color, populations that often overlap due to systemic and institutional racism and socioeconomic inequality. And this is by no mistake; the US prison system as we know it exists as a direct descendent of American slavery.

Statistics alone, while staggering, cannot fully characterize the incarceration epidemic. Hunger for a fuller, more humane characterization of imprisonment and its reaches drives this book.

This is a collection of writing by artists who have taught creative arts to people who are incarcerated or otherwise involved in the criminal legal system. Contributions were selected from submissions responding to a national call, as well as from targeted outreach to specific individuals involved in the prison arts community. I accepted poetry and prose, fiction and nonfiction. This project is unique in its polyvocality: it gathers accounts from artists from across the country (and one international submission) working across different mediums, demonstrating the range of experiences one can have when entering these institutions. Locations represented here

16. Wendy Sawyer, and Peter Wagner. "Mass Incarceration: The Whole Pie 2022." *Prison Policy Initiative*, March 14, 2022. www.prisonpolicy.org/

17. Sawyer and Wagner, 2022.

18. "Russian Federation." *World Prison Brief*, January 31, 2022. www.prisonstudies .org/

19. Emily Widra, and Tiana Herring. "States of Incarceration: The Global Context 2021." States of Incarceration: The Global Context 2021. *Prison Policy Initiative*, September 2021. www.prisonpolicy.org/

20. "Fact Sheet: Trends in U.S. Corrections." *The Sentencing Project*, May 2021. www .sentencingproject.org/

include California, Colorado, Connecticut, Florida, Illinois, Kansas, Kentucky, Massachusetts, Michigan, Minnesota, New York, Pennsylvania, South Carolina, Texas, Vermont, Virginia, Washington, Washington D.C., and Greece. Also, because the writers come from a range of theoretical and institutional/organizational backgrounds, they approach this work from various perspectives. Some view arts in corrections as rehabilitative for the incarcerated participants, some view it as therapeutic, others approach from an academic perspective, and others, like myself, understand bringing arts workshops to prisons as an outlet for—to use Judith Tannenbaum's words—"human beings desiring real communication," desiring to bridge the literal and figurative chasm created by institutional boundaries. This inclusivity resists a single narrative of "prison work."

Despite these best intentions to create a fully inclusive collection, the prison arts community is vast, and no single book can capture the entire landscape. Several artists I reached out to were unable, for various reasons, to participate in the project. Additionally, my professional network is limited; there are many prison arts workers creating incredible, world-changing works who are not featured here. Please know that their absence is not a statement on the quality or impact of their work, but an inevitable consequence of being a single editor with my own limitations in time, resources, and social capital.

Poet and lawyer Reginald Dwayne Betts, who was himself incarcerated for eight years, describes the prison system in this country as "the business of human tragedy." A superficial understanding of this statement might assume that the *tragedy* applies only to those incarcerated. This is not the case. The tragedy extends to all involved in the criminal legal system: people living in jail or prison, their immediate family, their children, their friends, their teachers, their co-workers, their community; the people who work inside prisons—officers, counselors, medical staff, administrators; those who enter from the outside—lawyers, teachers, clergy, programming volunteers, students. And victims of crime. And non-incarcerated students learning about prison. And those who never enter at all but read an article in the news or hear a story on the radio. And any person wanting to learn about prison beyond what is depicted in mainstream media.

The list is infinite, which is to say: we are all included—indicted, even—in this tragedy.

When we create art with people in prison, we not only affirm the value, the relevance, the importance of their experience—of their humanity—but we also have our own experiences. After several years spent facilitating creative writing workshops inside prisons in Michigan and teaching yoga to incarcerated children in Seattle, I noticed my own writing shift; start to reflect in tone and content the simultaneous devastation and brilliance I saw on my weekly sojourns to prison. I felt alone in my experiences, and alone in my writing. My poems and essays had nowhere to go, and I felt doubly concerned about the impetus to even *put* this writing somewhere. I worried over my fear of aestheticizing trauma, of turning an unjust and inhumane system into an object of beauty by publishing beautiful writing on this topic. Inherent to these concerns was a hyper-awareness of my own subjectivity. I am a white woman with access to generational wealth, healthcare and education, and as a result have privileges that many people who are incarcerated do not. *Perhaps*, I thought, *it is not my place to write on this. Perhaps I should instead focus all my energy on bringing the voices of incarcerated artists beyond the prison gates. Perhaps by writing and sharing my experiences, and those of other non-incarcerated artists, I am somehow continuing to speak for a group of people already silenced by an oppressive and silencing system.*

I learned, through my conversations with other practitioners, that I am not alone in these fears (For a great interrogation of these concerns, see Judith Tannenbaum's included piece "In the Very Essence of Poetry There is Something Indecent," where she writes of her doubt, which taunts, "You're exploiting your students' lives for your poems!"). I also learned, in the process of constructing this anthology, that these concerns guided me towards a stronger collection, as it became increasingly important to seek out pieces by artists who had different experiences in—and orientations to—their prison work, due to coming from backgrounds different from my own (particularly with regards to race, sexuality, gender, and socio-economic status, identities that have major influence on how a person navigates the prison system, whether as a volunteer, employee, or prisoner). Further, while these concerns reflect my first and foremost principle in this work to *do no harm*, I also had to remember and internalize what I told the incarcerated writers in the workshops I facilitated: that words matter; that stories matter. At a 2016 lecture in Seattle, multi-media/multi-disciplinary artist C. Davida Ingram said: "We need access to beauty because without it, people die." The writing in this collection recognizes—and resists—a system that works at all levels to deny the humanity of those it involves. It brings these stories to light.

This book is for non-incarcerated students learning about arts in prison, practitioners looking to share their skills and knowledge with incarcerated students, people concerned with questions surrounding access and privilege in the arts, incarcerated artists interested in the experience of those who enter the facilities to teach, and anybody curious to encounter the prison industrial complex from a human/creative, rather than policy/statistical, perspective.

While each included writer's experiences vary, some themes appear again and again, and their frequency starts to assemble a portrait of what one might encounter as a prison arts teacher. Some interrogate their own assumptions about the students and officers, as in the excerpt from "In the Very Essence of Poetry There Is Something Indecent," where Judith Tannenbaum must confront her own biases as she navigates San Quentin prison as both a teacher to incarcerated students and colleague of those tasked with maintaining the "law and order" of the facility. Ambivalence is expressed in many pieces here, as in Anna Plemons' "Showing Up," where she questions the ethics of her presence in the prison classroom, worrying about her role in "trafficking . . . transformational narratives," and in Katharyn Howd Machan's poem "On Learning That My Daughter's Rapist Has Been Taught to Write a Poem," where she must confront the realization that the work she so believes in is offering opportunities to an individual who has inflicted harm on her family. Other writers describe intense identification with the incarcerated folks they're interacting with. In "One of the Girls," Amani Sawari intimates being mistaken for one of the incarcerated girls she worked with. And Christopher Soto, in "The Children in Their Little Bulletproof Vests," demonstrates there are no convincing reasons why he ended up on one side of the bars versus the other: the teenage "incarcerated boys" in the poetry workshop are "Fathers & / Brother & / Boyfriends." The list of identities could describe anyone, suggesting the speaker feels simpatico with the participants. Indeed, he clarifies his role not as a teacher, but peer, saying they learned to write "together." Michael Torres, too, writes about this phenomenon in *Teaching at the Prison in December,* noting the writers in his workshop "remind me of nicknames and handshakes / from back home."

Other common feelings and themes include anger, as in Renny Golden's *Ode to Cook County Jail*; reverence, as in Ellen Bass's *Bringing Flowers to Salinas Valley State Prison* and Caits Meissner's *Praise Poem*; the therapeutic potential of fun and laughter, as in Pat Graney's stories *Bicycles* and *Home*; dark humor and irony, as in Ian Demsky's *Already There* and Jill McDonough's *Prison Education*; and intense investigation and interrogation of place, as in the excerpts from *Exit, Civilian* by Idra Novey. Fear and cautious optimism appear, too. In her poem *Saturdays at Reynolds Work Release*, Paisley Rekdal repeatedly states she was "not afraid" during her weekly teaching sojourns to the work release home where some men recently released from prison lived before gaining full freedom, though the repetition operates more as reassurance than fact; the opening sentence that spans nearly six stanzas is mimetic of an adrenalized mind. By the end of the poem, though, the reader senses the fear is not of the men Rekdal worked with, but rather of the larger system that brought these unlikely characters together in the first place. Karla Robinson writes about working with "young woman" in a similar setting in her poem *Reprieve: A Testimony*, though this piece offers a quiet hope that the teacher's belief in these incarcerated children may, in fact, make a difference in their lives. Some pieces, such as those by Erin Wiley, don't even seem to be about prison at all. These poems enact the mind of a prison teaching artist in both its struggle to translate what it's witnessing into words and its inevitable joys in sharing the humor and impossibility of language with fellow writers.

All of that is here—ambivalence, self-identification, anger, reverence, humor, irony, gratitude, fear, struggle, joy—because *here* is our shared world: it is a world that holds both the free and the imprisoned, the jailers and the jailed. Holding these pieces compiled together, I reflect again on C.D. Wright's words:

> *The popular perception is that art is apart. I insist it is a part of. Something not in dispute is that people in prison are apart from.*[21]

We can sense, in this collection, exactly what prison tries to prevent us from sensing: we are all—prisoner, teacher, volunteer, officer, observer, family, friend, witness—connected. We are in this together.

---

21. Wright, *One Big Self,* xiv.

Editor's Note on Language

After speaking with writer, activist, and organizer Victoria Law early in the creation of this project, I resolved to stop using the term *inmate* in conversation and writing. Law pointed me to an open letter by Eddie Ellis, founder of CUNY's Center for NuLeadership on Urban Solutions—a human justice policy, advocacy, and training center founded, directed, and staffed by academics and advocates who were formerly incarcerated—in which he notes that the term "inmate" makes it easier for a person to become, linguistically, a "thing."[22] This "thingification" is a necessary step in any oppressive model. He emphasizes the potential for language to serve as a tool for progress and re-humanization. After learning about this and other initiatives, and my subsequent decision to change my own language, I faced a quandary: What to do about the word inmate when it appeared in submissions to this anthology?

Initially, I contacted the contributors whose pieces featured the word, asking them to change their language to honor my decision. Some writers responded with gratitude for sharing about efforts to remove the word from the English lexicon, but others questioned the ethics of my decision. Many of them had *deliberately* chosen the word for its power, history, and connotation, and rejected my blanket request to use different terms. Their willingness to educate me led me to realize mine was an unethical edit. Some writers elected to change the word, while others elected to keep their original language. I am grateful to the contributors for their artistic integrity and patience with me as I navigated the editor's role.

For similar reasons, I editorially endorse—but do not impose—the terms "criminal legal system" and "prison" rather than "criminal justice system" or "correctional facility," and I present the contributors' work as it was received.

Finally, gendered terms such as "men's" or "women's" to describe prison and other institutional divisions reflect the binary language of the criminal legal system, not the fluid reality of sex and gender.

---

22. "An Open Letter to Our Friends on the Question of Language." *CMJ Center,* July 2017. The Center for nuleadersip on Urban Solutions. https://cmjcenter.org/

Editor's Note on the Nature and History of "Arts in Prison" Programs

Incarcerated people have been creating art since the inception of incarceration. That is, if it is true, as social scientists say, that storytelling and creativity are central tenets of humanness, then stories and art have *always* been woven and shared within and beyond prisons. The *making* exists outside of organizational and institutional structures built to catalogue, curate, and document it. It is a relatively recent phenomenon to even call this movement a field—a phenomenon one can't separate from similarly colonial initiatives to categorize and package the arts and histories of groups often marginalized from (and oppressed by) historically white and male academic institutions (as seen in the proliferation of fields such as Women's and Gender Studies; Black Studies; Latinx Studies; Jewish Studies; Disability Studies, etc.).

Countless anonymous-to-us incarcerated artists have created work in prison that will never be seen or formally acknowledged. Think of the drawings sketched on *kites* passed between cells; oral histories shared with bunkies; rhymes spit on the yard. Similarly, many coveted pieces of contemporary literature were written by incarcerated writers forming their words independent of an "arts in prison" organization (beloved pieces such as Martin Luther King Jr.'s *Letter from a Birmingham Jail* and Etheridge Knight's *Prison Poems* are but two examples). These are the creative practices and traditions that precede any and every organizational or institutional initiative to provide opportunities for prisoners to "make art."

I say this not to devalue or discount the work done by arts in prisons organizations, but to contextualize. These days, most of the facilitators and teaching artists included in this book would not be able to do the work we do without affiliating with organizations and institutions. It varies by location and carceral-institution-type (prison vs. jail; Federal vs. state), but for a non-incarcerated person to enter as a volunteer or teacher, we must first submit to rigorous background checks and orientations. In addition to managing the administrative aspects of these application processes, prison arts organizations also provide necessary orientation and training beyond the rudimentary provided by the overseeing corrections department. Furthermore, they provide structure and community for those of us doing this often lonely work, and in this community we learn from and support each other through the joys and challenges of teaching art in prison.

Prison arts organizations are often housed within universities and colleges, which can allocate funding and institutional support towards their missions. Some of the largest and most active of these include the Prison Creative Arts Project (University of Michigan); California Arts in Corrections (housed in various California state prisons); and the Alabama Prison Arts & Education Project (Auburn University). To the extent that such division is possible, I am focusing on programs that explicitly offer arts opportunities, rather than those known for their college-in-prison programs. Some prominent organizations, such as the Justice Arts Coalition, PEN Prison Writing Program, William James Prison Arts Association, Shakespeare Behind Bars, and Jail Guitar Doors, exist as entities unaffiliated with specific universities.

A comprehensive history of how these organizations—and the field of Arts in Prison in the United States in general—began and evolved, lies beyond the scope of this collection. Still, a broader understanding of the current arts in prison landscape and its evolutionary timeline is recommended. See Appendix, "Further Arts in Corrections Research and Resources," for guidance on beginning this learning journey.

Prose

Phil Christman

On Diction and Disprivilege:
How an obscure verb changed
the way I edit prisoners' writing

For T. Engel, 1980–2015.

"Indite"—I-N-D-I-T-E—is, or so the Shorter Oxford English Dictionary informs me, a transitive verb, from the Old French *enditier*. It means to put into words, to compose, or to put in writing, as in, a letter. It is now rare, as I have reason to know. I looked it up several times during the winter of 2013–14, as I finished editing *The Sky is On Fire, After All: The Michigan Review of Prisoner Creative Writing Volume Six*. The word appears in Benjamin Cloud's poem "Prison Letters," (published here, p. 172)—first line, "A nigga gets a lot of time to think"—that is not otherwise much dependent on obsolete Elizabethan verbs. I hesitated over the word as I transcribed Cloud's poem. I figured that what he meant was "indict," I-N-D-I-C-T, even though that construal did not make any sense within the context of the poem. But I had a vague half-memory of having encountered the word "indite" once or twice, somewhere back in grad school, so I went ahead and looked it up, just to be sure that I was right and the writer was wrong, and there it was: "indite," to put into words, compose, or to write, as in a letter.

I looked it up again about a month later, when the manuscript came back to me from our volunteer copyeditor, whose work is generally flawless, with, among others, this note: "I changed indited to indicted (assuming that's what was meant)." I changed it back. I sent the manuscript on to the director of my organization, who happens to be my wife. She changed it again. I changed it back again. From there it went to our brilliant typesetter/printer, Shon Norman of Dakota Avenue West, who made one more attempt at changing it back.

By now I was second-guessing myself. I was second-guessing myself on at least two fronts. One, I wondered how Benjamin Cloud, a working-class man who from other comments he has made about himself has not had a great deal of access to formal literary instruction, had come across this word—a word that appeared to have stumped several of the smartest people I know. As soon as I had this thought, I dismissed it, with good reason. It is condescending. It is classist. It is also unimaginative. Benjamin Cloud could easily have found "indite" in some battered old rhyming dictionary in the prison library, if his prison has one. Or he could have found it while reading through the dictionary for fun—something I've often known, among many other sorts of people, imprisoned and homeless people lacking other reading matter to do. You can almost always find a dictionary, and you can almost always learn something from it. In any case, I edit a magazine of prison literature, and I wanted to be the kind of editor who has faith in his writers' artistry, in the literacy of his litterateurs—in their curiosity, in their having the same kind of restless interest in new words that every writer has.

But even after this I continued to second-guess myself, because I knew that the faith I choose to exercise in the writers I publish is rare. Even for me it is often hard-won. It is always a choice, and often requires an exercise of will, a bracketing-off of what I think I know about the writer so that I can see whether there are less-than-obvious riches hiding here in plain sight. Many of the people who buy the *Michigan Review* do so out of humanitarian interest, or from the desire to read "raw" and "real" work, to bear some sort of witness to the "prison experience." I won't deny that these aesthetic categories have their uses. They have long helped the work of imprisoned people, poor people, racial and sexual minorities, and other marginalized people to gain a hearing from the privileged. Upper-middle-class white people go to see a movie like *Precious* not to admire the camera angles or the editing rhythm, and certainly not because we expect it to be fun, but because we feel it is, in some obscure way, "important" to "witness" its story. But in doing so, we shut ourselves off to the artistry, the craft, the intelligence, that may be displayed in its making. We shut ourselves off to the possibility of encountering a mind. (It may be that *Precious* has really cool camera angles. I'll never know, because all the reviewers ever wanted to talk about was how raw and painful it was, and I don't willingly subject myself to pain for its own sake, because I'm not a masochist.)

I don't mean to criticize one of the primary audiences of my own magazine. People read for their own reasons. But when the work of prison writers is appreciated primarily for being a vector of painful experience, or perhaps as a kind of number-free sociological knowledge, we risk overlooking the intelligence, craft, or awareness of literary tradition that writers may bring to the page. I think that sometimes formally educated, privileged audiences take that risk, not from snobbery or racism, but from the laudable desire not to project what they think may be a bourgeois, or white, or Western, or anyway somehow narrow and provincial concern for artistry onto people who may not share that concern. But many of them do share it. I share it, and I come from solid Midwestern working-class stock. If the love of good work for its own sake weren't in some sense a species-wide phenomenon, we would not have had, in our short and bloody history on this planet, so many examples of work that is, nevertheless, surpassingly, unnecessarily, gratuitously well-made. Being poor or oppressed doesn't always destroy the imagination—many oppressed peoples' lives would be easier, less bitterly unsatisfying, less haunted, if it did.

My dad is a janitor who reads Dostoevsky on his breaks. My mom is a Medicare biller who loves Anthony Trollope. Our society's collective unwillingness to imagine that such people exist creates an atmosphere in which, even if I believe Benjamin Cloud *meant* to write "indite," I'm *still* tempted to foist an unnecessary and absurd edit on the poem, simply because I don't think some of *his* readers will be able to read the word without assuming it's an error, one ultimately attributable to him, a man in prison, a black man—a man who hardly needs more strangers attributing errors to him. I find myself tempted to butcher his copy for his own protection!

Ultimately, of course, I didn't do so. I didn't do so because it would be a horrible violation of my role as editor and his role as writer. I also didn't do it because I chose to believe, in a position that was then new to me, in the idea that art-for-art's-sake is true all the way down, true not only for Oscar Wilde in his drawing room but for Oscar Wilde in his cell, and for everyone, from whatever social location, who inhabits that cell after him. But, as I say, this was all a choice. And I talk about it with such overweening, argumentative self-confidence in part because I spent a chunk of my first year as editor of this journal defending that choice. Not a few volunteers in the organization heard "I want to publish good work because it's good" as "I don't care about prisoners' feelings." One volunteer asked me pointblank whether I was trying to publish "just the best work," or whether I wanted to "represent" all the voices of Michigan prisoners. When I said that I wanted to publish the best work, she cried. And quit. The perception that caring about quality was too hard-nosed of an approach to take to a journal of prison writing was so strong that I began to worry that I was simply mean, or wrong.

All of that was a little over a year ago. Just a few weeks back, as I was putting the finishing touches on *The Michigan Review of Prisoner Creative Writing, Volume Seven,* I heard from T. Engel, as he preferred to be known, a writer whose surreal office story we were publishing. He thanked me effusively, and then he asked me an odd question. He asked whether we actually liked the piece, or whether we had published him as "a token." He went on to assure me that he writes avidly, that he reads obsessively and works hard at his prose. That moment was, for me, all the confirmation my choice of editorial philosophy ever needed. Because here is a guy, like so many women and men in Michigan prisons, who cares about making a good sentence. And I needed right then to be able honestly to say that I had published him for the same reason a free world writer would take for granted: because he'd written some.

Brian Daldorph

Antonio Sanchez-Day

For Antonio Sanchez-Day, 1974–2021.

Before leaving the Dance Ground Cemetery on the Potawatomi reservation in Mayetta, Kansas, I put the flowers my daughter had given me for Antonio Sanchez-Day on his grave and said goodbye to my friend. As I walked back to my car, I looked around at the Kansas prairie in early spring, the stand of trees at the center of the cemetery still bare, glad that Antonio was in a peaceful place at last. He'd been *taking on life,* as he'd say, for 46 years. He was tired of fighting all those demons within and without. March 2021: time for him to sleep.

I first met Antonio in 2013 at Douglas County Jail in Lawrence, Kansas, when he filed into the classroom at the tail end of a procession of orange jump-suited men. By that point, I'd been teaching my creative writing class at the jail for over a decade. Every Thursday afternoon, I'd watch the classroom fill up as writers took their places in the circle. For some, writing class meant a welcome couple of hours out of their cells. However, a lot of the guys who joined the class came to like their two hours together in the classroom, writing, telling stories, sharing jokes. Hey, if it lifted weary spirits, then that was a good thing, right? Might even be an opportunity to get some serious writing done.

At first, I didn't pick out Antonio in the class. Some guys come to class and make a big splash: they arrive with a poem or rap ready for us, happy to have an audience. They do their thing, and if it's good, they hear, *Hey, that's what's up,* and, *There it is. You got that, brother.*

But Antonio wasn't like that. Antonio—owl-faced and shaven-headed, with a distinctive tattoo, *Delores,* on his neck—was watchful. He'd sit back and listen to what everybody else had to say before sharing his work, most often a neatly written page that he'd later tell me was written and rewritten in his cell until it was *exactly* right.

One of the first poems he read in class was "Penitentiary Protocol," written, he said, for this cocky young guy he'd met who was going to prison for the first time claiming that doing time was no big deal. Antonio wanted him to know that prison meant menace and blood:

> *When you arrive, read the sign: "Leave all hopes*
> *And dreams behind." Forget all you have or had*

16

In the free world, it no longer matters . . . Learn to like the sight
And smell of blood, it surrounds you. Prepare to witness
The evil men do.

In 2013, when he first read that poem to us, Antonio was in Douglas County Jail waiting for his case to be heard. He knew that he'd have to go back to prison, and he began telling the class that he was going to do this time *differently.* He'd had enough time behind the walls.

Back in prison for two more years, he made monumental changes to his life, just as he'd told us he would. "Inactive" in gang business, he served his time working on his poetry, getting in touch with his Native American roots and religion, exploring the rich literature of Hispanic writers, and following the example of his main man, Jimmy Santiago Baca, himself a former prisoner and now one of the major voices in American poetry. During this prison "bid" (as he'd call it), he had to deal with temporary blindness, a condition caused by his diabetes. If you want to know about fear, then try thinking of being blind in prison with how many enemies lurking? Fortunately, *amigos* looked after him and two emergency operations restored his sight.

I met Antonio again in 2015 when he was released and moved back to Lawrence. He wanted to work, if possible, though he had serious health issues, including diabetes and kidney and heart troubles. But mostly he wanted to write, and that's what he did. He wrote and wrote, working on a first book. He also returned to the writing class circle in Douglas County Jail where he'd started his odyssey of self-recovery, but this time as an instructor, the only formerly incarcerated person allowed back into the class. He'd sit in the circle again and tell us his story. How he'd been bullied at school as the only Native/Hispanic kid in his class. How he'd joined a gang which had seemed like family. How he'd gotten involved in a street fight and hurt someone "real bad." The judge had sentenced him to ten years, a tough sentence meant to show other gang members that they'd be harshly dealt with in Lawrence, Kansas.

I'd been teaching the class for almost 15 years when Antonio joined me as a co-instructor, but I couldn't reach the guys in class in the same way Antonio could. "I've sat where you're sitting," he'd tell them. "If I can do it then anyone can. I'm just one bad decision away from being right back in trouble again." We listened to his poems and were drawn into the worlds he created, like the one about the man in the library who meets a former version of himself, or the one about how he and his friend stood back-to-back and fought against enemies gathered around like wolves, or the one about Chuey the chihuahua, Antonio's "wingman."

In October 2019, I drove with Antonio down to Wichita where he was giving a presentation at the Kansas Authors Club convention. He stood in front of the audience looking like a million dollars in his smart blue suit and Paris Left Bank beret and told us about his writing, how it had saved him and how he woke every morning thanking his gods for this gift. After his presentation, a tall guy—upright, maybe ex-military—came up to talk to him, said he'd been a cop for thirty years and that what Antonio had been talking about—the trauma of violence—was happening on the other side of the line too, for ex-cops. Though they'd been on opposite sides of the law, they heard each other. They connected.

In 2017, I interviewed Antonio for a book about the jail class. I asked him what he'd be doing in 10 years' time. Would he still be writing? Definitely, he said. He had so much more to write. He told me that he wanted to write more about his mother, Delores, who had been a huge influence on his life.

But what we didn't know then, but maybe should have seen, was that his time was running short. By that point, he was going in for dialysis three times a week, which deeply tired him each time. Then, there was the triple bypass surgery. In early 2021, Antonio had just gotten himself a dog called Scooby to love, when there was more bad news from the hospital: he was on the verge of total liver failure and, if that happened, he'd only have weeks left to live. When I heard this, I couldn't help thinking that this fighter would come through. He'd been fighting demons all his life, surely he'd fight them off one more time.

On a Sunday morning in early March 2021, I saw a Facebook post, written by his aunt, that Anthony Sanchez-Day had died at KU Med in Kansas City. I checked around, willing it not to be true. But it was. Antonio Sanchez-Day, RIP.

I drove to his funeral in Hoyt, Kansas, north of Topeka, at the Chapel Oaks Funeral Home, with two other jail class teachers; all of us had loved and respected our colleague and friend, Antonio Sanchez-Day. We met his family for the first time and saw how much he was loved, how much we were all grieving. After a short Catholic service, we formed a procession in our cars and drove on backroads through Indian Country to the cemetery. Antonio's ashes were buried next to his father's grave.

I think of Antonio during those last five or six years—out of prison, a free man, a respected man, a man who sat with judges and police chiefs on the Criminal Justice Coordinating Council and gave his advice, from the inside, about improving the criminal justice system. I think of the brilliant poems that illuminated experiences that most of us would never have, and yet they reached us all. I think of his magnificent first book of poetry, *I've been fighting this war within myself: The Poetry of Antonio Sanchez-Day*.

I grieve for my friend because there should have been so much more. I think of his spirit in that peaceful cemetery, and recall a few of the words he left behind for us:

Raindrops of sadness wash away the pain
help me forget as I dance in the rain . . .

Note from Brian about Antonio: When I met Antonio's family at his funeral, his aunt and stepfather asked if I'd look through the writing he'd left behind, a plastic crate full of files and ring binders of his work from over the years. It took me several weeks to read through his words and pick out material for a posthumous collection of his work. I include this piece here as part of my tribute to my friend. If only he'd been granted, by his Great Spirit, a few more years.

_____

Two Stories

I. BICYCLES

Joyce and I were stuck in the middle. Stuck in-between the open gates and the closed gates. We had brought in bicycles. Even though we'd cleared them—even though as volunteers we'd planned this part of the performance a month prior—eyebrows raised and security officers had to call back to the main desk at each checkpoint.

"Why are you bringing in bicycles?" The officers behind the glass, even the funny one, looked at us as if we'd been caught dragging in a fully gutted sheep, blood trailing behind us. "You can't bring those in. I gotta call up front." We also had duct tape. The duct tape ended up staying at the middle checkpoint but the bicycles got in. We wheeled them through the clanging gates, past the beginnings of a garden, past the smoking pit, past the cafeteria where inmates stood and stared, and into the gym. The sound the tires made on the new polyurethane floor as we entered the gym went *snick snick snick* as they peeled off the ground, free, wanting to be mounted, waiting to be ridden.

The women in the workshop were ecstatic. To them, we volunteers could do anything. We were champions, leaders, bringers of the bicycles. We wheeled them across the floor and carefully parked them against the far wall. They looked so lonely all of a sudden, the bicycles. Out of their element in the prison gym.

Before we could even get to the announcements for the class, women crossed the floor and jumped on the bikes. They squealed, rode fast, did wheelies, put on the brakes and flew. They zipped by, heads to the wind, dreams flying out of them at a million miles an hour. They made a trail clear-cut across the clean glass floor: a road of youth, of memory, a road outside the prison and outside themselves.

The bicycles transformed the space, the people, the entire performance. They sat against the wall like gymnasts waiting to compete. The performance became a period to endure before the bikes were ridden and a letdown after they were put away. Everyone in that gym lived through those bikes—the inmates, the audience, even the officers. It was like the bikes gave people a chance; people who'd thought they'd never done anything good in their lives, anything they could be proud of, got up, jumped on the bikes and rode. It was a miracle, something acutely brave and talented and dramatic. It had poise and flair and intelligence, like we were watching someone win a downhill ski competition—someone who had come up through the ranks—a complete beginner, an underdog. And the underdog knew that bike, knew how to ride it, sway it, milk it home. Every woman who rode held a banner for every woman who didn't. They crossed the finish line, they were the champions, and the crowd, literally, rose to its feet. Every person stood, clapping and screaming and begging for more, begging for that little bit of freedom, that short little chance.

After the bikes were over, there was a let-down, a deflated air in the room. Maybe we should have just had people ride the bikes throughout the show. That didn't occur to me at the time; I had been coordinating all the disparate elements of the performance—the backdrop, the singing, the scripts, the microphones.

The bicycles were magnificent and free. And what happened in that gym, on that day, brings back the wind spinning through the rider's hair, that myriad possibility dream-of-the-future wind. Now, when I see an old, funky bicycle, I can see one of the women, teetering impossibly large on that small seat, riding off into her future. I see her crossing the finish line, the crowd rising to its feet, her friends and family rushing to congratulate her; the smile on her face knowing that she rode the bike all by herself; how even though she had fallen off once and didn't know if she could get back up, she had. She had ridden and she had won.

This is the dream I had six years into the program I taught in the prison—the dream of every person successful, their families greeting them at the finish line. Later I learned that when I see a woman leave the compound, no one is there to meet them. They go to a halfway house and spend time getting a driver's license and figuring out how to use the bus system that has changed in the ten years they've been gone. They can't see their children who are in foster care, and they don't know how to apply for jobs. Many end up back on the streets, using. I see this over and over and over until I grow sick of my own dreams, of my hopes for them, and even, for myself.

I can still see them, though, the riders, with the bicycles gleaming in the hot stuffy gym. I can see them ride, can see the uncontrollable joy on their faces for having ridden, can see the audience rise to its feet, clapping and screaming. I think that moment is worth everything. It changes how you view what has happened and what will happen. It gives you a clear eye to view people who are always seen through a dirty lens. And for that moment, they are champions.

II. COMING HOME

"Hey. . . .do you guys do karate?" This was the first question the women asked the Japanese guests we had brought in to perform during our program at the prison. Their names were Itto and Mika and we were bringing them in to perform Butoh dance as part of our performing arts program. This was their first visit to the US, and their first time inside a prison. My co-worker, Saiko Kobayashi, always completely formal, bursts into uncontrollable laughter.

During the classes preceding the performance, Saiko had brought in a book of photographs detailing the work of Kazuo Ohno, one of the founders of Japanese Butoh dance. The book contained large, beautiful color photographs of Mr. Ohno performing various characters or states of being, as is common in the form of Butoh. In one photograph, Mr. Ohno is dressed as his mother. One woman raises her hand and says "Hey I know what this guy is—this guy's a drag queen. I know lots of drag queens." Saiko tried to explain that one of the ideas of Butoh was to 'embody' another thing, to literally 'become' it. So, in this photo, Mr. Ohno is 'becoming' his mother. After a lengthy explanation, the same woman says "yea, but I know a drag queen when I see one, and that guy's a drag queen."

During one of the classes, I start going into a description of what the performance might look like: "In Butoh dance someone might be lying on the floor, covered in white body makeup, contorted and moving slowly, to music that may or may not have any relationship to what they are doing. The person's costume might be a loincloth to give the audience a completely open sense of the body and how it moves." This draws snickers all around. "They also might look like a little bit like a corpse, i.e., they wear white body makeup. This is to give one the sense of the body as a canvas, clean and open." The more I talk about it, the weirder it seems. I keep getting looks like 'Why the fuck somebody do that?' I love Butoh. But I don't think I'm communicating that very well. I want to say *Butoh is weird—but weird is really really cool.*

When Itto and Mika arrived, they were taken into the prison for clearance. The prison publicity person was sick on that day; I knew things were looking up when she wasn't there. She didn't want them wearing 'costumes.' I'm not sure whether she would be able to tell if they were actually *wearing* costumes, but she was on the lookout. She was born-again and was sure that there would be some sort of inappropriate sexual conduct involved. She didn't know what Butoh dance was and didn't want to know. It was just too 'exposed' for her taste, and therefore, not appropriate for the women.

Itto and Mika walked with Saiko and me through security, wearing their costumes, which consisted of pants and shirts—no loincloths or painted white skin. I felt the pressure of making a good impression. But then I thought: *I'm worrying about making a good impression on someone who is coming inside a prison to perform a wildly arcane art form that no one will understand.*

Saiko and I take our Japanese guests through the three locking gates and into the gym where they'll be performing. Before Itto and Mika enter the room, I stand up and say "guys, guys, listen . . . this is going to be weird, ok? This might be one of the weirdest things you're ever going to see . . . but these people are our guests, and we need to be respectful. Please. . . .be respectful, ok?"

Saiko helps them set up for the performance as I scan around the room to see what people are doing. To my left there is a long bank of clear reinforced hip-to-ceiling glass windows, so inmates can be observed at all times. All along the windows people's faces are smashed in a mass of multicolored flesh that looks like toys or jellyfish. The security officer is pressed there too, slightly above the others. They all want to see what's going on—what weird stuff is going to happen with the two dancers.

Saiko introduces Itto and Mika and says they are from Japan. She says they will be performing a short dance piece in the Butoh form and that the performance will be followed by a discussion. We are all holding our breath. At this moment I'm thinking *why did I want to bring Butoh dance artists into the prison—what was the reasoning behind this . . . I know it's going to be a disaster—either everyone bursts out laughing and can't stop, or they get up and walk out of the room during the performance and slam the door as they leave.* This kind of behavior is normal for prison. People inside know that they may never see you again; they have a kind of honesty most performers find pretty refreshing. But no matter how steely your ego is, when people stand up, walk out the door and then let it slam behind them, it makes you feel bad—uncared for.

As my eyes rescan the smashed faces against the glass in my left field of vision, my gaze stops at Itto and Mika lying on the carpeted floor in the small room. They have started, slowly, to move. Mackie, an inmate sitting in front of me who's come to watch the performance, can barely contain herself—she keeps turning to the sea of faces against the glass and gives them a hysterical half-grin, like a shark. She's visibly shaking because she's trying so hard not to laugh—she can't take it in—can't put it anywhere identifiable. She catches my eye and says. . . . "Hey, I know what this is about . . . it's just like Michael Jackson in *Thriller.*" "Yea . . ." I say, "I can see that." *But of course, I can't. I feel wild and insane, as I think this comment is hysterical.*

After a short while in silence, the music comes on, and actually has a down-beat. I find this is either an amazing compromise made by the artists or else they have very bad taste in music. The beat swells and the dancers begin to get up from the floor. Itto gets up first and through an amazing kind of unwinding contortionist stance, slowly comes to standing. Mika joins him and they start doing dance partnering very slowly, gradually increasing their speed and daring. They swing, they fly; they are looking very dangerous in this suddenly small room. A held breath goes through the room, where suppressed laughter turns into something else. Quiet. And then awe.

Gradually, Itto, who has Mika coiled around this waist as he swings her out in space, slows down. He winds down like a maypole, with Mika trailing like a spent flag. During that final swing it was as if we were all taken into flight by Itto, made to be children. As Mika slides to the floor, the music ends and there is a stillness. It is over. It's not like before as if everyone is about to burst, but there's a quiet, like we're all outside together on a vast open plain. We've been somewhere and now we're here. We're home.

After taking several breaths, I look around the room at all the faces. Something has happened here, but I'm not sure what. I look to my right, to the young gang-banger girls, with their hats pulled down over their hair, just showing a little bit of face. I gather a breath and say: "So, do you guys have any questions?" One person raises her hand and says, "Are you two together?" Then Saiko translates, and Itto answers "No, we're just dance partners." I take another breath and Myra raises her hand and says, "I know what that was like—it was like the story of my life . . . you unwinding up to standing is like a big tree growing up, it was just like the story of my life." Itto begins to step forward, towards Myra, his eyes filling with tears. Then Tama-Lisa stands up and says, "it was beautiful—wow, it was really beautiful." Itto steps further towards them. It is a small space, so he doesn't have to walk very far. A bridge of connection comes out of his eyes, some kind of understanding where the two of them are crying. He is amazed by this; I can see it—and so are they. We are all very quiet.

After the performance and discussion are over, we gather our things and leave. It feels like we are walking into a small clanking town from the edge of a long clear desert.

The following week, as part of our regular program, we complete an exercise that is writing a letter to yourself as a young girl from the woman you are today. Some of the stories wrench me in such a deep way that tears begin filling my eyes and falling down my cheeks. I cannot stop this flow. I don't know why this particular story on this particular day elicits this response from me, but one of the women starts saying "hey, let's have a soul train line—come on, Pat, let's have a soul train line." The women don't want me to be sad—they want me to be above their pain like I usually am, cajoling them, making jokes to make everyone feel okay. Someone puts on music, and everyone starts dancing. We form two lines facing each other with a pathway in the middle and then the women, one by one, start 'goin' on down the line,' doing solos.

I am still crying, but I'm dancing anyway, joining in with everyone, and then I notice that one by one, each person is doing their own version of Itto and Mika's dance. As each person goes down to the floor and comes up again, I realize they're doing a condensed form of Itto's rise from the floor. They had noticed everything—every movement. And at each new contortion, the group claps louder and louder, until everyone in the room is doing wildly slow movements with a strong rhythmic beat—a Hip Hop version of Butoh.

Suddenly we're back again, back out on that wide, open plateau, breathing the same clean air, sharing the same experience.

I feel like I've finally come home.

Janus Head

BIRTH

I came into the world slow, my mother climbing up and down stairs, begging me to leave and start screaming. I clung to her, grew heavier, and grew a head of thick black hair. By the time the doctors ordered a C-section at 9 a.m. in late January, I was three weeks late coming into the world. I was born with teeth. I was born into winter. When the days are short. When the night sky is at its heaviest.

I was born with a Janus head. Two faces, simultaneously looking towards the future and the past. I was born on the threshold of the year, when people are readjusting. I've been caught like this for a long time.

I was born to two alcoholics, two wonderful parents who loved me very much. We lived on the mainland of a mile-long island called Solomons. My mother, a dark-skinned Italian woman, with eyes like espresso. My father, a blonde and blue-eyed American mutt, tall and skinny as a rail. Back then, everyone knew my father was a drunk and that my mother left him. They knew when my mother succumbed to addiction as well. An awareness of my family system, how they interacted with the community and my identity, bubbled up at early age. I learned to hide and run away as a result.

In a landscape abundant with trees and wildlife, dark murky river water, and fish skeletons, I thrived. I felt safer out there. I'd come home with it stuck under my nails and in my hair. The nights my parents fought, I'd come hurling out of the house like a shot. My feet would pound into moss and mud, I'd run through the woods, head reared back, mouth open and howling. I first learned to understand the world through disappearing into the dark.

At sixteen my mother ripped the braces from her teeth.

Flesh and blood splattered the sink. She looked to her reflection and smiled, pliers clinking against porcelain. Her bottom row of teeth is crooked now. The top is pearly white, almost translucent. "I have a fucking beautiful face," she would say, years later, drunk on wine. Her lips were cracked and almost black. She sat at the kitchen table. Her head seemed too heavy for her neck. She was bankrupt and alone, no husband, with two adult children. She was living in a house held together by plywood and exposed insulation. I took her by the hand and led her to bed. She was the most extraordinary creature, even as she dragged her feet and gurgled spit.

This is my mother.

Or a part of my mother. A part of me. In order for you to picture her, you'd have to picture someone just like me: big brown eyes, a mass of curly hair, chesty, dramatic eyebrows, and a laugh that's more like a cackle. People still ask us if we are sisters.

She moved from Solomons Island to Florida and quit drinking for a man, a man I barely knew. He seemed nice, took care of her. In time, they grey grew gardens under palm trees.

My mother tells me that he's the love of her life and I believe that. She sits in the sun, her skin naked and bright.

She is calm, if only for this moment, and then another.

My mother sent me into the woods.

By the time I received my MFA from Chatham University in Pittsburgh, my mother had moved to Florida and found sobriety. My father had disappeared. As my mother made her way back to me, her voice losing its grit, her soft eyes finding hope in things like lilies and fishing boats and new love, my father slipped off the edge and tumbled into obscurity. I still carried their story with me, from the mile-long island where I grew up. It was something I didn't talk about or admit to, until I became a teacher. Until I started to use the past in order to unveil a future that didn't mirror a life struggling in the clutches of addiction.

I knew about Chatham's social justice program when I applied, but I didn't see myself as a mentor. I also lacked the confidence to scrutinize and assess my own struggles with addiction. But I decided to shadow creative writing classes at a halfway house anyway, feeling comfortable on the margins, observing, helping when it made sense. In two years' time I had become a teacher. Twelve students, a full house.

The first time I buzzed myself in to face my own class, my first lesson plan tucked between the pages of Jan Beatty's *Boneshaker*, my whole body pulsed, blood pushed up against my skin. Surely someone could have seen my heart. A tall pinkish 19th Century Revival with beautiful arched windows and balconies, the center rests immaculate and inviting off a busy neighborhood street. Lady-Liberty-green doors open to a foyer that splits into two levels. Upstairs are offices and apartments for residents, up to fifteen at a time. They may keep their children with them—as many as four or five, infants, preteens—as they go through a six-month treatment program. I felt greedy for coming back again and again, but I needed these women. I knew that as soon as I crossed the threshold.

Downstairs are more offices for counselors and social workers. At the end of a well-lit hallway, decorated with finger paintings and watercolors, are two doors. One leads to the children's day care, the other to the classroom where I teach. It was during that first class that I wrote the words: *My mother sent me into the woods. Time had changed my father when I met him on the path.* I had started to travel back in time, revisiting that long, low house on the Patuxent's shore.

There's something about putting the words down on a page, articulating the inexplicable. Even if the metaphor is rooted in magic, even if the writing leans towards the strange, it allows you to step back and name your monster. To whisper the name, Janus. To hear the hiss of the *ssss*, and the echo behind your neck. To say, *look, this is how it feels, this is my truth.* It is naming the ether, drawing an outline out of the dark, discerning black from black. No longer out and swirling, you've pinned it down.

I've never told this to anybody.

Social justice programs are about giving marginal groups voice. However, I am not sure if these women would have become writers if they hadn't struggled with substance use first. Not always are women given the permission to write and be creative. Literacy is a privilege—metaphor, simile, poems, novels, imagery are gifts. Specifics are often nonexistent in my students' early writing. They don't believe their daughter's stuffed owl with the missing eye is an interesting artifact, a luminous detail. Why would anyone find them or such a memory interesting?

She doesn't have the words to articulate her situation fully, but her situation dictates whether she can access these words. Simone De Beauvoir describes this in *The Second Sex*, interviewing French prostitutes in the late 1940s who didn't have the language to describe what had happened to them. Between its pages I hear my students' voices describing ripped panties by the Allegheny River, drunken fathers coming home from the steel mills, their lips wet in the middle of the night . . . a mother describing the time she dropped her son on railroad tracks at a crossing in East McKeesport when she fell drunk against a signal gate assembly. "I've never told this to anybody," she said.

And I heard what I didn't hear: It isn't so much their poverty of language; it's lack of agency to interpret what has happened to them—what continues to happen to them—and to slash back against it as a birth right, first on the page of their own journals and then as reimagined women who are willing to slash back against it in their own lives.

How did I become this woman?

The very first class seemed to pass in slow motion. I studied their faces, trying to quickly memorize names, trying not to look at the track marks on their arms or the collections of recovery medallions and tokens, red, green, and blue key chains cluttering their desks to indicate one month, ninety days, or a year of sobriety.

We went around the room introducing ourselves. We played a game. Green light: share something people don't realize about you upon first meeting. Yellow light: share something that gives you pause. Red light: share something that only a few people know about you.

"I'm a heroin addict."

Leslie, a slender Italian woman who plopped down next to me said, "You have beautiful eyelashes!" Her pulled back black hair accentuated her high cheekbones. She fidgeted in her chair, tapped her pencil. Her Pittsburgh accent drew out her O's, so they sound liked A's: *Dahntahn* instead of *Downtown*. Like my mother's and grandmother's, her hands worked like a maestro's as she talked—her whole body wrapped up in her words, as if my mother were sitting next to me, and I wondered how differently my mother's life would have turned out had she not quit drinking. I imagined her, skinny and strung out, carrying bags through the front door of the center upstairs. What would she write in a workshop like this? Poems about her daughter, a dark-haired girl with her face, her boney knees? Would she write about herself, or her missed opportunities, her drunk ex-husband and how he left her with two babies. Would she describe wine as the color of black blood clotting in the hearts of her children?

The Hanged Man

When I say that all my students inspire me, I mean every single one of them. These mothers who fight addiction, who have used during pregnancy and lost their children to the state, who ask me questions about stanzas and line breaks, word choice and imagery, who ask me for more books, more copies of poems, who read words as if they are starving, have coaxed me forward, out of my own belly, through the cave of my heart and onto the page. When I brought out tarot cards, passing out one to each student—The Hermit, The Magician, The World, The Emperor—they pored over the intricate designs, listened patiently to my readings . . . *your past is influencing this current station. It's clouding your mind. Don't let it dictate what happens in the following months. You can always change your cards. The future card is a suggestion. The past card is here because it's important, permanent, and influential* . . . and then they reimagined the images and readings as stories and poems and essays.

I handed The Hanged Man to Leslie. The Hanged Man hangs upside down, tied at one foot, like a child suspended in the womb, waiting for his life to start. The card symbolizes self-sacrifice: the martyr is alive and well, though the ground has been swept from beneath him.

"It is both a card of contemplation and rebirth," I said. "A writer's card."

She writes that she is no longer faint of heart, her chest betraying her in a room full of people. Her hands still shake when she reads her words out loud, she says, but not as badly as they used to. She says she recognizes her face in the mirror again. She says that if she reaches behind, she can feel the other face, too, the nose and its whispering mouth, slowly disappearing into nothing. She says that no matter what she tried to write before—the drunken poems, love letters, dream journals—it was all a distraction. Any other subject and any other place were better than the place she came from. *But now,* she said, *my ribcage is cracked wide open.*

She writes about being hoisted up by the men who have hurt her. They tie her legs with a rope and pull her up until she is suspended above everyone and everything. The wood they tie her to is splintered and sunbleached. She finds peace hoisted above her assailants. Describes the air as clean and cool, says her face is closer to the sun.

Slice

It's always the mother, isn't it? Their wombs, your first home when you glimmer into consciousness, their arms and breasts the warmest and softest place when you are mute. They teach you language, they name you. Losing that home is our first pain. And later, to watch a mother destroy herself, like a hurricane ravaging the pines, leaves you stranded, helpless. All you can do is wait and pray the split wood left over can be salvaged.

I visited my mother in Florida nearly two years after she left Solomons Island. A semester away from obtaining a master's degree, I was about to turn twenty-five. When she picked me up from the airport, I realized I couldn't remember the last time we had been alone together.

"I don't drive a whole lot anymore," she said, peering over the steering wheel. She looked older. She was tan, but her fingers looked delicate. Her hands had started to wrinkle. But her skin looked good and clean. I could tell she hadn't been drinking like she used to. I watched her as she drove but avoided eye contact.

I tried to place the feeling. There was a new distance between us, almost as if she were an old lover. But I felt comfortable in the silence, mature in my lack of expectation. I knew her smell, her smile, the sound of her exhaling cigarette smoke, but they no longer drew my spine and jaw into tight lines. I could breathe.

Two days into my visit, I asked her to cut my hair. I'd grown too afraid to do it over the past few years, and I didn't trust hair salons or strangers. So it grew tangled and massed, hiding my face, covering all my back, trailing behind me like a weed. She said she would without hesitation. I walked out to the back yard of her little blue house. I stood barefoot in a patch of gray-white sand. She followed me with a pair of black-handled scissors.

I could feel her breath on my neck, could almost feel her pulse as the sun warmed my shoulders. I closed my eyes. I smelled salt and fryer grease. *She is leaning in to brush the hair from my neck. The metal legs slicing, my curls dropping to my feet.*

Catch & Release

I had a long lunch, sans agenda, last week with Ann Teplick, a treasured friend who has been with the Pongo Teen Writing Program, a nonprofit that helps young people leading difficult lives to express themselves through writing, for fifteen years. Ann is brilliantly skilled at many things but accepting compliments is not one of them, so I'm rather relieved she's not here chiding me, trying to deflect attention with, "Oh I'm just fortunate to be in a position to . . ." etc. While I appreciate her humility, even more admirable is her ready smile, keen intellect, heightened sense of awareness, and killer writing skills. Additionally, and perhaps most significant of all, Ann exudes a job qualification that is absolutely required on the resume of anyone who works for Pongo: empathy.

> Empathy: *The psychological identification with or vicarious experiencing of the feelings, thoughts, or attitudes of another.*

This word is often confused with "sympathy," which typically involves feeling pity or sorrow for another person. Empathy is much more than that. Empathy allows the quality of vulnerability needed to take on the trauma of the kid at the psychiatric ward or juvenile detention center and make that turmoil one's own. No one I've met in my 58 years on Mother Earth does empathy better than Pongoites, as founder Richard Gold refers to us. We seem to live for the comfort of being uncomfortable. Ann and I discussed this ambiguity the other day. Most people go out of their way to avoid conflict. Ann goes out of her way to find it. And when she does, she pulls up a chair and makes herself at home. Cognitive dissonance is more of a speed bump than a roadblock.

As Dr. Brené Brown says, "Empathy fuels connection. Sympathy drives disconnection." She maintains there are four parts to empathy: 1. Perspective taking; 2. Staying out of judgment; 3. Recognizing emotion in other people; 4. Communicating that emotion. Feeling what others feel is a conscious decision to make oneself vulnerable. Brown contends it is like saying, "I don't even know what to say, but I'm so glad you told me." And almost always, that's *exactly* what the kids in the psyche ward or juvie want to hear. But it's a slippery slope indeed. How does one insulate one's heart? How does one prevent this vicarious pain and suffering from seeping into one's soul?

People who work for Pongo have usually had trauma in their own lives, either personally or vis-à-vis a friend or family member. One doesn't just ponder one day: "Well, should I play golf, take up oil painting, or help a kid sinking into the abyss to write poetry?" It helps to have some demonstrative tragedy in one's own past to stay motivated, to keep the fires burning.

To paraphrase Richard's book "Writing with At-Risk Youth: The Pongo Teen Writing Method," the residual effect of emotional trauma that goes unarticulated often ends in depression, addiction, recklessness, lawlessness, and, worst of all, hopelessness. The kids feel guilt, but while guilt is like the surface of the Earth, they also feel shame, which is the core. Shame isn't saying *I did something wrong;* it's saying, *I am something wrong.*

Today, finding young people who've endured domestic violence, sexual assault, and abject neglect is about as easy as hooking a fish at one of those catch-and-release trout farms where parents take their kids. Toss your line in the water and within minutes, you're bound to get a bite. But like watching the little fish with gills struggling to survive, Pongoites must catch the distress, metabolize it, and learn to release it. One must attempt to genuinely feel what the kid is feeling, to hold it inside in an authentic way and use it to elicit a poem, then let it go. And it's not always easy to let go.

For the first three months I volunteered for Pongo at King County Youth Detention, I'd drive home in tears from the depravity and brutality these kids had been forced to endure. I once worked with a girl who was thirteen years old and had already become a prostitute, got addicted to heroin, was impregnated, and had hundreds of razor blade cuts up and down her arms. I wasn't going to let her see me cry, but in the car as I drove home, I cranked up the old Pat Benatar tune "Hell is for Children" so loud that the dashboard vibrated, the sound drowning out what I had seen and heard. Ann told me that in the early days, she'd occasionally go into the bathroom and cry.

I once asked Adrienne Bentsen, an esteemed former Pongoite and licensed therapist, how she did it. "If you really want to help the next person the next day," she replied, "you have to be able to let it go." Again, easier said than done, but in time I learned to do it. I'd usually go to the steam room at my athletic club until I almost passed out, where no one could see the tears. Then I'd go home and write two pages as fast as I could and forget about it for a few days.

Catch and release. That's the trick. Being comfortable with discomfort is all about catch and release. (Right, Ann?) Because at the end of the day, to keep it, you must give it away. There's just no other way.

Helen Elaine Lee

ALPHABET

"Tomás," my mother used to tell me, "Tu tienes que hablar por mi."

So I would go with her down to the welfare or some other place, the post office, the bank, the school, and I would be her voice.

I could always talk real good, and come to think of it, I could conversate with just about anybody. I knew how to break the ice, knew what to say. Knew how to stir things up, too, how to get at someone right where they lived, like a stun gun. I was always good with words.

At my trials I didn't get to use no words at all, seeing as my lawyers thought it best I decline to testify. I wanted to talk for myself, to say what I was thinking, or to be more accurate, how I was too doped up and twisted around and clouded to do much thinking at all, just too caught up in the wanting and needing that was my whole life from waking to sleeping, to do anything but beg and con and sell and steal my way there. At the sentencing I got to say sorry, but who believes you then?

Sí, I always was good with words. *Palabras* that you say out loud, that is. Who had time for school? There was too much other stuff to do. Watching *los niños,* making rice and *gándules,* and *perníl* on special occasions, hustling up the money for the rent, fakin' all the things I missed by being gone. Slippin' out to see what was shakin' on the street. I dodged detention, and the corner was my school; that's just where I wanted to be, and I got to tell you, I had the finest teachers and I got straight A's.

But now I can do more than talk out loud, and this pen feels good in my hands, almost like a weapon, which it can become, easy, with some masking tape and some concrete, and there's plenty of that to sharpen it on in here. They give us these little limp ones, thinking we can't hurt nobody with these, but everyone should know that anything, anything at all can be turned to hurting.

You can barely use these floppy pens, though, which is purely a new issue of mine's, since it's been *mi secreto,* for every day of mi thirty-eight-year *vida,* 'til three years ago last April, that I never learned to read or write.

I know how to put my words down now. I know how to spell them and I study where they come from, how they're put together, how they came to be. And I love me some words. I survived the shame, Mama's and my own, for not knowing what even little *niños* know. I was second generation what you call illiterate, 'til I owned that fact, and mostly I didn't get no grief.

They know who I am in here, and that's not the kind of thing that makes a punk. That's way too close to home.

I know words are not the same as *la vida*, even the wrote-down kind. They give you somewhere to lean, though, and something to choose. They give a way to name it all.

One day I'ma write a letter to m'hija. She's a woman now, I'll have to find her first.

I can't get enough of reading and writing down what I could only talk before, and no one has to do it for me, pa'yo. I'ma stay with this book until the lights go out and start again at six when they come on again. And soon I'ma start working on my GED. *Las letras, las palabras*, they're all the way mine.

My first sentence? "I am Tomás." That's it. I exist. This is my own name. Tomás, or Boo to you.

And now that it really belongs to me, I'm redoing the alphabet. This here's my own version, and I fought hard for each letter, so we not having no "A is for Apple, B is for Ball . . ." I'll be deciding on what stands for what. I'ma tell you in a minute how it goes, and it won't begin at the beginning, 'cause what does? It'll begin in the middle, it'll begin anywhere, it'll begin at the end. And that seems just about right, since everything inside here is turned around, pushed inside out, backward, and jumbled up.

You're a child instead of a man.
Wrong before you open your mouth.
Sickened before you're hungry.
Finished before you begin.

You live your life on rewind here, and the bottom's where you start.

That's why I'm starting with Z. Z is for catching some Zs, zzzzzzz, and that's one way to go, 'cause you can sleep away your time, and still never get rested. Sweet, unbothered sleep? Damn near impossible in here.

In the learn-to-read books, Z is always for Zebra, and as a matter of fact, that works for me, too, 'cause the light coming in the cell at just about 2:00 stripes me, with the bars. White on black? Black on white? Who knows, I'm a zebra, caged.

What's next? Y is for Yes and N is for No. Yes, No. Yes, No. Can I change? Do I want to? Will it last? Can I change? Will life let me? Can I change? What for? Yes, No, Maybe So. Yes, No, Maybe So. Yes.

W? W is for Wanting, or you can change one letter and it's for Waiting. They're part of the same damn thing. They're the way we live now.

V is for Vergüenza. *La vergüenza de mi madre*, her own junkie shame. Then mine. My own inheritance.

U. Under. Underground. Understand. Undermine. Underestimate.

And that brings me to T, which is for *Tiempo*, Time. "Don't let time do you. Do time," they say, like a broken record. Yeah? Fuck you. Which, as you'll see, is mostly what F is for.

S is most definitely for Stank, or Stench, a word I just got. The three smells in here being the smells of shit, which is out in the open and everywhere, of food you would only eat if you had to, which is mostly the case, except for the canteen ramen noodles and flip-top tuna, crackers with peanut butter and Velveeta cheese . . . and body funk. Sweat. Fear. Sex. Anger. And when those smells all happen together, which is every day, watch out. Stench.

R is for two things, and don't tell me I can only have one thing for every letter. I'll have as many as I damn well please. R is for Respect, *Respeto*, which is all any man wants and the thing none of us can do without.

And it's for Remorse, *arrrrrrrrrepentimiento*, which is what you're supposed to show the Review Board, even if you didn't do the crime. I got remorse, all right. For damn near everything about the way I lived. For leaving out of school and making my way through without knowing a goddam thing before I did drop out. For the stick-ups and the let-downs and the dope I put inside my veins. For Layla Johnson, and the way I smiled when she peed her pants in fear.

For keeping in motion, motion, motion, so I wouldn't have to stop and see what all I was doing, what all I was. I got remorse for all the things I missed, for not living the life I had, letting good dreams and daylilies and being a father pass me by. For being a no-show. For not just going back to the island, where I could make a different start, and for never saying *"Te quiero. Bendición,"* to *mi abuelita* and meaning it, before she died. For leaving *mi Mamita* without no one to speak for her, even if she couldn't mostly speak for nobody except herself, and for nothing besides her dope. Those are my remorses, and those are my R's.

Q. *Qué, qué, q'onda?* Q words are harder in English. Quilt. Q is for a Quilt *mi abuelita* made me, from all our faded and secondhand but washed-clean clothes. And I wonder where that quilt is. When did I see it last? Quarrel. Qualm. Quandary. Question. Quest.

P is for Pen or Pencil. And it's always been for Pussy, too, though I try not to use that word no more, and I try my best not to dwell on what I've not got.

O is for OG, which is what I wanted to be when I grew up. Far back as I can remember, which ain't too far, Big Cruz, *The* Original Gangster, and Mack, too, would come riding down the block in his Beamer with the strobe lights to fuck up anyone fool enough to chase him, handing out tube socks and jerseys and scattering Jolly Ranchers like parade confetti, rolling instead of walking, Big Cruz, who was crazy as hell, and sure, and brave, who had no slave past, no past at all, but was pure present, every-thing ripe and sweet and waiting to be plucked. And we'd all flock to the car and wonder, while we peeked inside and talked to him, and were proud that he remembered our names, whether the stories we heard about his trigger-happy, ruthless acts were true, whether we could make the shiny, candy ladies in there look our way some day and become Big Tomás, Big Boo, Big Whoever, whether we might be legends and roll instead of walk-ing one day.

We already been through N along with Y, so that's all taken care of. N for No. Two letters. The shortest word with the longest meaning of all.

M is for Man, which I am trying hard to be in this here zoo.

And oh, I know a world of L's. L has always been for Love. Too easy to say and too hard to do. Love, the contraband word. The reason for *la vida* for some folks, and a prison for others. Some get they ass kicked in the name of love. Some, they try to have it, do it, but they just can't get it right. And L is for Laughing, 'cause if you stop doing that, you die. And it's for Leaving, the art I mastered but can't no longer practice, except inside my head. In any case, I'm trying to stick around this time, see what I can find out, seeing as I'm locked inside this muthafucka for five years. And now L is also for Loud, which it always is in here, voices raised, bars and doors buzzing and slamming shut, music and TVs playing, hacks shouting, COUNT, COUNT, COUNT.

And L is for LIFE. Life Sentence. Life Without. Life story. What hap-pened to my Life?

K. Mmn mmm. I don't talk about it, and I try not to think about it, but this one's my daughter's name. Before, before I had *el alfabeto*, and *las pal-abras*, I couldn't have wrote her a letter, even if I hadda wanted to. She was nine when I started my bid here, and I haven't seen her in near eleven years.

And J. J is for *Jamás*. How can I ever add up all the nevers? I'll just use this single word.

I is just for I, me, I am. That's all.

We can take G and H together. They stand for Ghost, because that's what we are here, mostly, especially those who's doing letters 'stead of numbers. And that's who we talk to in the nighttime, who be visiting from the past. All the men who been through here, and some who never made it out. We can hear their voices sometimes, singin' *O Lordy,* or about *workin' from can to can't,* singin' about home or *Rosie* this or *Rosie* that, about some woman or other, someone who stood by you, someone who done you wrong. G, for Ghosts, living and dead.

And G is also for tell me something Good. Anything. Anything Good At All.

In here it's always loud, and then there's the empty quiet inside the loud. And it's tight, with what all might jump off, and no space at all for any single one of us. There's nowhere to lean and we are starved for good.

I focus on something good to eat, something that you can really taste in your mouth. Caramels. Red and white peppermint wheels. Something from the commissary. Some of that Neapolitan ice cream, looking like a pastel flag from some kiddie country. I go for that. Or I focus on that thin slice of sky I can see from my window if I lie down at the bottom edge of my bunk, or those geese you can see if you strain, in the distance, just past the razor wire. Try to see them and ignore the trail of green shit they leave behind. Do they live here or visit? Can they? Live here? Can't choose a letter or a visit, so I focus on a magazine or a book, a message from the free world.

Some days I try to make a list of whatall I got. I used to call it off inside my head, but now I write it down. I got new words. And I got what might could happen in the future, what might be partway good. I got what I remember, but the bad memories, they're no kind of gift, and the good ones hurt too much sometimes. Knowing and remembering, those are mixed.

I got what I avoided and walked away from: a fight or diss, a trip into smoking, red-ash anger, a hack's hateful tone. I got a day without trouble. And then I put on my list the little things that eased the tightness up. Wind. Dominoes. Good dreams. A new word I learnt and could write with my flaccid pen. Flaccid, that's a F word I just now claimed.

So F is for Flaccid and it's for Fuck You, most of the time, and when it's not, it's for Forgetting. And like I said, since my list of what I got is made of the bad I dodged, that means keeping to yourself, and that also means the Fuck You's mostly got to be silent, between you and you.

E is for Elmwood Street, and sometimes we are back there, Mama out there leaving and leaving again to get her high on, leaving me behind. And me running for Big Cruz and then slangin' for myself. I am six and Mama's disappearing. I go back. I go back. I am six and seventeen and now. Back on Elmwood Street, all over again.

D is for Denied. That's what the Parole Board says, and no doubt will again. Denied. It's for Determination, too.

And D is for those Daylilies I've always loved. Tia Clara grew a patch beside that house of hers that seemed to shrug and say, "Whatever." And I'll never forget their bright orange up against the brown, asphalt shingles of that tired, shrugging house. I would look down into those daylilies from the kitchen window, leaning, like this, on the sill. Down into their sword leaves, waiting for one to open and make a flower that would only live one day. "Qué es lo que tanto miras? Vente p'aca, niño!" Tia Clara would say, nudging my arm, "come away from that window and wash your hands or set the table or do your lessons or brush your teeth." But I'd sneak back to that ventana, afraid I'd miss that flower's quick, starburst life.

C. C is for *coquí*, the sound from home I can't forget, though I barely remember except for the telling, especially with winter right around the bend. *Coqui . . . coqui . . .* I try to hear it in the night, that frog making its Puerto Rico sound. And C is for Clean. I got three clean years next month.

B is for Boo, and that's how most folks know me, even though mi madre named me Tomás. Boo! For the scaredy cat they said I was, crying in the dark, and if they teased me, and crying whenever she left. Boo Boo for Yogi Bear's sidekick, I used to say. Boo boo, I suspected, for mi madre's mistake.

And here we are, back at the beginning, here in Oak Ridge, Cellblock A. A? A is for Absence. *Ausencia.* Mine and yours, and all I might've had. And now that words are mine, I can name what all is missing. I can name everything I've lost.

Tiger Lily Wants to Know About Freedom

Thursday evening, I trash my 6:30 p.m. half-full cup of coffee before going through the metal detectors. Unless it's an unopened bottle of water or a clear container to be filled at the fountain, it's a goner. Lately at the women's prison where I teach, after removing shoes to pass through scanning, clearance check, ID pick up, and sign in, I've had to wait in an empty classroom for up to forty minutes—no phone, no book, no caffeine. Just me and my lesson plans. The women cannot walk freely between activities on the prison grounds; everyone moves at once to their next destination. Movement is late, again. I look out the window where a skunk and her babies amble along the patch of lawn in the small courtyard. The cut grass smells like summer. It is impossibly quiet. Minutes later the buzz of radios grumbles out fuzzy voices that echo through the hall and the air stirs. On the first floor I watch a door open, and strollers parade out. The mothers, all in state-issued green uniforms, push their babies round and round in a small circle while chatting. This signals class will begin soon.

When the first writer rushes forward to greet with an embrace, the passing officer grumbles *hug her in your mind, ladies,* and we shake hands instead. It is our poetry class's second year together and the exercises have gotten meatier. I try to outdo myself each week because I know the group is poking at me for a challenge. It also makes me feel good to deliver a prompt that is multi-layered with lots of ports to pull the ship up to. I want each session to be better than the previous. We've been exploring the gray area between various dichotomies: Masculine vs. Feminine, Standing Out vs. Fitting In, Good vs. Evil. Because of the particular slant towards socioemotional-oriented writing, in this class we hover between support group and open mic night, and the ritual has been to place a roll of toilet paper in the circle's center. Without fail, someone will cry. It is the marker of the trust in the room, and it is a trust we've worked to earn.

Because everyone wants to know details when they find out I teach in prisons, I try to sweep the conversation out of the way quickly: The women sign up for class, must commit to each of the semester's sessions, and participate in a yearly three-evening orientation for the arts organization I teach for. In other words, they want to be in the room. If they don't enjoy it, they'll drop the class quickly, anyway. I am lucky for the self-selection. It makes for the most electric classroom to engage—hyper-present, hungry, and committed. I've found myself slow at turning the phrasing from *my women* to *the women*, because the women are distinctly their own bright, autonomous beings, representing a diversity of backgrounds, life experiences and stories. What they have in common, among other things, is prison. What we have in common, among other things, is writing. Any language of ownership, even the standard teacher's classic tune of *my students* feels excessively wrong in this space.

Oh, and the other thing people always ask: *What did they do?* The question used to annoy my self-righteousness, but now I soften to the reality of why it arrives, recognizing the same inquiry in myself. I won't know unless it comes out in the writing, revealed in a step towards healing, reclamation, or responsibility. And it truly doesn't matter, I will say—the same mantra I told myself in the beginning. Except of course, it does matter. Our actions matter. Our stories matter. Our humanity matters. Our histories matter, individual and collective. And still, everyone deserves to be someone whole, to identify beyond their crime, at the very least for the time spent in our room. That is truth they are working towards each week: That you must hold multiple truths.

Tonight, we are revealing the poems written under the umbrella of Silence vs. Noise. A golden lab from the puppy program lolls on the floor at the foot of the writer who trains her, tongue floppy in the heat. Soon she will leave the prison and venture out into the larger world to support a veteran, but tonight she plays the role of disinterested audience. Our classroom is a typical teaching space, the cinder block walls are painted white, a chalkboard positioned at the front of the room, the desks are pushed aside to create our circle, windows cracked as far as they will go because there is no A/C and we are all visibly dripping. It takes a moment for us to settle into the opening ritual, there is always excess energy kicking in the air for the camaraderie that class offers. This evening the meditation is freestyled with sincerity—the assigned poet forgot to bring a reading, and she chooses to drop us onto a beach where the sun's heat, cleaner when magnified by sand, soaks into our skin and dolphins leap mystically from water. It's so sweet; I can feel everyone in the circle grinning wide with their eyes closed.

There is never a shortage of volunteers to read first. Tonight, our opening poem quickly yanks us from the momentary vacation and nosedives straight into emotional terrain. The piece is about the journey of learning to be alone in prison and describes the move between two extremes: A dorm setup, where privacy is nonexistent, to a single cell lock-in, where being alone equates to a strong contending with self. As poems often do, this shakes loose a charged conversation, stories traded across the room like an invisible ball. Everyone is on the same team, and shares their experiences with vigorous head nodding, deep recognition. I learn about what it means to cry at night on the top bunk, visible to seventy other women witnessing your outpour. Private pain or pleasure is no longer. It is inferred what other kinds of expression feel too vulnerable to express in this context.

Though distinctly alone, I am told, it can be easier to choose this forced community. There is the rhythm of human breathing, the warmth of other bodies, a form of distraction helping to fake the feeling of emotional proximity. For many, if they ever choose—or are forced into—the other option, it takes time to cultivate a relationship with the stark alone one faces in their own cell. Meditation can help lean into that stillness and expand the tight space until it becomes comfortable, elastic. But at first the thought is frightening, often debilitating. Will I go crazy with this much time to think about what I've done, what I've lost, the reality I live in now?

After describing county jail, where she was locked for 30 days straight, illegally, without leaving her cell once, another poet shares a letter written to the parole board that will never be sent. When the full-bodied sobs cease to small waves and breath returns, she reads aloud: *Who are you to judge me? What have you done in your life? Am I not paying for my crime? Can I ever also be someone else, someone of value?* She asks, *Was I an animal when I came here, or did this place make me an animal?* This set of questions will become the revolving door in our room, we will cycle through them constantly. They shape into the anchor that all of life is tethered to behind these walls. Our warmth allows tears to arrive sure as the weather. They come in the telling or in the listening, alike. But at the end of the day, the only way we can come into this room each week is by knowing we will laugh tonight, too. It is the only way to feel fully human, to slide down that full and vibrant spectrum. If you open up that tender space, I've learned, you better know to wrap it back up responsibly.

Little do I know, tonight I'm the one who is unwittingly about to bring the laughter. It is halfway through class when I discover that the red spot in my underwear is the reason for my dragging. We pause conversation in service of my need, though most often we plow through the two and a half hours foregoing break. I don't ever bother going downstairs to use the officer's bathroom; it's too inconvenient. I shrug and shake my head with a wimpy smile while walking out of the classroom bathroom, glad we're all women. My purse is locked all the way through a series of buildings outside, through security. One woman disappears and returns with a flimsy menstrual pad that I stick on in the bathroom with no locks. She jokes that the male officer in the law library next door misinterpreted the request and offered up a yellow legal pad. The maxis are notoriously thin. On a heavy flow, I'm told, one might stack them four thick to keep private blood private. There is a shortage of pads because they are used for many tasks:

cleaning the shared bathrooms, as a cooling device when soaked in cold water and placed on the neck. I hear the women chatting through the door and feel exposed and vulnerable, which I say aloud.

The women all—well, the word sounds off, but they do—*giggle* as they chorus out. "Welcome to prison!"

I feel like I belong.

Each Thursday when Veronica walks through the classroom's threshold, she sizes me up, head nods, grinning, nose scrunched up in a *hell yes* expression. I've arranged the plastic chairs into our customary circle and written the theme of the night and a loose agenda on the board: Opening meditation, sharing work, discussing the sample poems, walking through the takeaway writing exercise. Most nights I am already sitting in a chair, but sometimes I remember the power of greeting everyone at the door with a handshake, which I used to do religiously before I got too comfy. Veronica's refrain changes each time to match my presentation, but the basic sentiment remains steady.

"I love your boots. Oh, and your jacket, earrings, yuuuup, actually I love your whole outfit!" Then she turns to a friend: "She's the best dresser, I swear."

I laugh and roll my eyes but make little effort to hide the fact that I eat it up. It's become a bit of a sweet routine, the weekly outfit reveal. Veronica often shares her own outfit choices before coming to prison, or what she's inspired to buy when she gets out. Admittedly, I dress up a bit for The Veronica Show.

But today nothing in the closet suits me. I hate everything I own. I fantasize that my taste is bad enough for someone to elect me onto a makeover show where I'll emerge with a flattering new wardrobe. When that fails to satisfy, I'll ditch it all and buy seven pairs of black jeans and black tees. My hair is ever-evolving, and currently frames my face asymmetrically, shaved over one ear, otherwise long platinum blonde with dark roots. This cut limits my options for what is passable in clothing and adornment, making each morning a tricky set of aesthetic choices. I eventually decide on my husband's oversized gray dress shirt, blue jeans, the uniform of my worndown Doc Martins. Earrings that chime when I walk. I lost my favorite lipstick in a Chicago bar a few weeks ago, so go heavy with liner on the eyes.

I have never fully counted the number of choices I make in a day, though I have considered keeping a record, just to see where the number lands. Wake or snooze? Email check or brief meditation? Shower then breakfast, or oatmeal before scrubbing off sleep? Or smoothie? Is there time for eggs? Do the dishes in the sink really need washing? Nah, leave them for later (which inevitably becomes tomorrow, prompting a new series of choices). Should I act like a responsible adult and replace the toilet paper roll, toss the cardboard skeleton, or just teeter a new one lazily on the bathtub edge? Umbrella just in case or risk it? Bus or subway? Faithful Bustelo or grab a cup on the go? Bodega-cheap or coffee-shop-good? Music or podcast or which book of the three in current rotation or start the workday early by grading on the ride? Get off at 145th for the extra walk or closer to campus? Which hill is the shortest hike? I get as far as bring bag to classroom or dump in office first and then I give up.

Our last Thursday session before the final reading, I am sweating on the palms, nerves humming. Last week our final prompt of the semester stated *what is freedom,* and I knew it was toeing the line. Who am I to pose this question so boldly? I questioned myself up until the last minute, but decided to go for it, scratching its sharp faced letters on the board. I shook off my usual confidence saying the word *freedom* out loud in the room. It felt like a cuss word coming out of my mouth.

It is our final reading, which we stage low key in the classroom by arranging the chairs into a small audience, a list of readers chalked on the board. Each participant is welcomed to invite two friends to fill the seats: Some look bored at the prospect of poems, others curious or proud. I introduce the group and allow each reader to fall into place behind the next, allowing me the pleasure of becoming a full audience member, hearing familiar poems that jingle in memory, some that are new packages opening onto the air. Everyone chooses two pieces to read, and if we have time, a third.

One of my most connected students, whom I call the second facilitator in the room because she is emotionally sharp, supportive, and self-aware, steps up and speaks with a strong voice. She is revealing a poem addressing me. In the piece's opening lines Sammie thinly disguises my name, pointing out my bright clothing, my noisy earrings, my nasty sneakers. My new moniker, Tiger Lily, the name of a flower, is a direct reference to my newly-dyed-orange hair. Of course everyone knows who is who in a room of otherwise matching greens. She mocks my own question back to me: *What Is Freedom?* And then she gives it to me like it is.

In the poem my words lob back into the air, throbbing with a palpable ache, unpalatable, spitting off the tongue. *Freedom,* Sammie tells me sharply, is that I can wear piercings and jewelry of my choosing and no guard points a finger. Freedom is interracial, intercultural marriage (don't forget it was once illegal), is access to a passport with the kind of photo we might joke *looks like a mugshot* on the outside. Hell, think of it. Freedom is access to the Internet and the ability to utilize this tool to write of and share my travels, of being able to travel on two good legs in the first place. Freedom—*ha, ha*—our group recalls my mishap—is tampons. As many as I need.

I add a few of my own to the list as I listen, swallowing often to move the ball in my throat down to my stomach, biting back forming tears. Freedom is complaining about a too-hot apartment in blistering winter, or being too lazy to cook dinner and ordering in. Freedom is *where do you want to eat tonight? No, where do you want to eat tonight? God, can't you decide on anything for once, I always have to choose!* Freedom is a glass of wine after a long week, a table decorated with a candle and open flame. Freedom is being bored by a closet full of perfectly fine clothes. Freedom is wondering where you fit in a world wide open to you, the luxury of playing the part of outsider when there is nothing but your own psyche fencing you in.

The poem stings, nearly physically. I am not used to critique being turned on me in this room. I am humbled. The question is now a giant neon sign in the shape of a finger pointing back at me. The poet is kind enough to know it will hurt to hear and continues to also name my class as a space of freedom. I am embarrassed. I am also grateful for the message to arrive in gentle packaging—it is strong medicine. Her poem illustrates the experience of our room where there are no rules on the page, where we spill out our internal dark sky, where our pain is lit under the warm hand of sun. Perhaps most importantly, where the noise of officers and loud voices and fights and doors slamming and crying and reprimands and threats and guilt turns all the way down to the hum of white noise for our brief time together.

The poem reopens an awareness in me that had faded with time. As comfortable as we become with each other, as much like family we exaggeratedly proclaim in our best moments, in the room I am not wearing a shapeless green uniform. In the room I am, indeed, allowed my funky earrings. In the room I choose the topic, I carefully nudge us in the direction of my own curiosity, and hope it leads us down the right path. Most importantly, when the day is done, the writers walk up the hill to dorms and cells to lock in. I stop for pizza before boarding the train. Freedom is feeling like you belong in a classroom in prison when you get to go home to your partner, to your own bed. While this knowledge should never dictate the classroom, it should not be forgotten, either.

This is how it's explained to me, the reason why the hunger for creativity, connection and truth-telling is so palpable in our room. Here is the question everyone who passes those gates must ask themselves: How is it that I am going to face the endless hours that stretch ahead? How am I going to walk through the experience of being surrounded by nearly one thousand women but, most essentially, alone? Alone with a depth I've never experienced before. How am I going to wake up every day and face this, face myself? Sure, the daily choices are missed, but the biggest choice, the choice with the most weight and consequence is *who am I going to be during my sentence*? The last charge on the list is an arrow aimed at all who enter our room, regardless of what we wear on our bodies or the paths that have led us to this table or if we get to leave at the end of the evening: Am I going to choose to become better?

Kathy Park

Four Vignettes from a Prison Volunteer

I. *VOLUNTEER ORIENTATION*

I am sitting in my first volunteer orientation in one of the prison's staff conference rooms. It is the first night of bombing Baghdad in the Persian Gulf War. The man giving the orientation is dressed in his guard uniform. He is nervous. He's pacing back and forth, jumping around from topic to topic. I can see President Bush and maps of Iraq on a TV screen, but the sound has been turned off. The guard is rattling off facts and figures:

"Inmates are staying longer in prison because of longer sentences and mandatory minimums, and that's why there's a population crunch.

"The average stay is seven years.

"Currently there are 887 women. Roughly a third are black, a third white and a third Hispanic.

"This is an administrative prison, accommodating all levels of security.

"There's a medicine man for the American Indians.

"Women are more docile and more easily managed than men, who are more aggressive.

"Information is strictly on a 'need to know' basis. No one can give out official information or else we'd be liable for suit.

"You're not allowed to accept any gifts or favors. If you are arrested for any offense, you must report to your sponsors . . ."

I look around the room. Most people here at the orientation seem to be connected to the prison ministry. I am younger than most. I feel lonely.

"Keep it professional," the guard is saying. "Keep your personal life separate, private. Keep your boundaries distinct. Be willing to say NO. Put limits on your responsibility. Avoid grandiosity. Don't discuss your personal affairs. Read body language. The staff takes care of censorship of mail. There's lots of pressure on the inside—frustration, anger, and pain."

He is pacing like a caged lion, coffee cup glued to his hand. His voice, his diatribe, are a dull drone.

"Avoid any physical contact with inmates. We recommend you keep a distance of four feet. This is for your own safety . . ."

The doodle I'm drawing has started to tear through the paper to the desk.

"The prison was made for 300," he drones on. "There are regular counts in the rooms, several each day and night, plus census counts.

"Here's what to dial in case of emergency. Please understand that we have a policy of not dealing with hostages, period, in the federal system. If you're in trouble, take the phone off the hook, or dial 222. Inmates are aware of this . . ."

He opens a box full of contraband that has been confiscated in the prison, shows and explains each item to us: A ballpoint pen that has been rigged up to be a tattooing pen; a piece of wood with several rows of thumbtacks carefully taped on, business side out. He explains that women like to scar each other's faces. He holds up a garrote and a homemade shiv or knife made from a file. He shows us handkerchiefs and T-shirts with elaborate designs drawn with a pen, supposedly evidence of gangs. After each item, the guard leans towards us and confides: "And a WOMAN made this."

He passes the items among us for our examination. I am struck by the ingenuity, cleverness, and patient artistry of each creation. If only this creativity could be redirected. *And a woman made this*, indeed.

It is time for a break. Most folks head up to the coffee, donuts, and TV to watch the war. I step outside on the porch for some air and to let some steam come out my ears. I try to sort the information and recommendations I've heard into two piles: Those that seem valid and useful, and those by which I cannot abide, like the rule of not touching. My work is *based* on touching. I am ranting to myself when I overhear two ministry volunteers also on the porch; one says to the other: "I always hug them, too."

I smile. Maybe I'm not so alone.

II. *WRAPPING A BLACK BELT AROUND YOUR ENEMY*

Sadie was what the prisoners termed "short and shitty," meaning her time was getting short and her anxiety about being released into the "free world" was making her feel and act shitty. It's a time when the pressure is too much to bear, when something cracks and breaks, when self-sabotage kicks in. A woman may find herself with a major offense, secluded in the SHU (Segregated Housing Unit), having blown her chance to get out. Sadie was so tight I was afraid she would grind her molars down to the gum.

Sadie hid herself behind a layer of toughness and black shades. Her hair had a partial buzz cut with shaved geometric designs. Her "don't-mess-with-me" attitude extended twenty feet in all directions.

She showed up one day to Stress Group—a day I had a guest instructor—and signaled that she needed to talk. We sat in the stairwell within hearing range of the workshop. She was shaking and very pale.

"Kathy," she confided, looking down at her hands, "I came within a heartbeat of blowing it big time, and if it hadn't been for my roomy, I'd be in the SHU right now."

When she said she was sure her father would have killed her too, I guessed how she had almost blown it.

Sadie and I both studied the martial arts. While I was familiar with Karate and the non-fighting art of Aikido, Sadie had learned a form of Thai kick boxing from her father, himself a well-known martial artist in his prime. We had talked previously about our backgrounds and the martial art code.

Most martial arts, whether they are fighting or non-fighting forms, have at their core strict ethical rules and constraints, passed down from teacher to student, that spell out when and where you may use your skill. Sadie had almost crossed the line. Far worse than the reaction of the prison authorities was the possibility of her father's disappointment in her loss of self-control, in her transgression of the code, in HER.

"What happened, exactly?" I asked.

"Me and my roomy were waiting in line for food services to open," she replied.

(Waiting in lines for food services, for the laundry, the phone, the shower, the commissary, the clinic, for EVERYTHING, was a very sore point for most of the women in prison, especially given the overcrowded conditions. This was further exacerbated by the common practice of butting in line, an irritation that had ignited many fights, grudges, feuds, name-callings and racial slurs.)

"Someone butted in front of us," Sadie continued. "She was real rude. I tried to ask her nice and calm not to do that, but she said something ugly and nasty.

"Right then and there," Sadie said, her eyes darting left and right, "I could almost feel the impact of my fist on her face. In my mind it was already done. But just as fast, I realized I'd already crossed the line. I'd broken the code. I'd lost my cool. Worst of all, my father had already turned his back."

She looked at me with utter anguish.

"If it hadn't been for my roomy stepping in, I would have hit her. How can I possibly trust myself now?"

I sat and thought for a while. Then I chuckled.

"Sadie," I said. "You'll probably think I'm crazy to tell you this. But in your mind you need to wrap a black belt around the woman who butted in front of you. You need to bow to her like you would another black belt and thank her for what she is teaching you."

Sadie drew back and looked at met with wide eyes. I could see her struggling with a thousand *But, but, buts* . . .

I took advantage of her confusion and added, "And it would probably be a good idea for you to, at least in your mind, thank everyone who butts in line or irritates you in any way from now on until you get out of here, and maybe even after that as well. Because they are teaching you about discipline, composure, the ability to pick your battles and not sweat the small stuff."

Slowly she began to nod and smile. Then, looking at me with that familiar glint of defiance in her eyes, Sadie said, "That would turn it on its head, wouldn't it?"

III. SOMEBODY TO LOVE

During the four years I volunteered in prison, the compound was frequented by a number of feral cats. Apparently they had no trouble getting through the razor fence. These motley, feisty felines provoked mixed feelings among the women and especially the staff. But for those women who took the trouble to befriend them, the cats were a source of warm and furry comfort, affection, and love.

The need to love and be loved cannot be overstated. In prison this need is denied, thwarted, and beset with bureaucratic hoops and regulations. One has only to observe the visitor's room to see how painful it is to be in the company of loved ones without the freedom to touch, relax, or be intimate. It is well documented that most incarcerated women are also mothers. They are lucky if their families take up the slack and care for their children. Luckier still if their families live nearby and have the wherewithal and patience to go through the ordeal of visiting. They are unlucky if they have to give their children over to the authorities. In the stress groups I ran, the most common feelings or stories concerned children.

Such a flood of pent-up, dammed-up, sublimated love naturally sought an outlet. Those lucky cats.

Those wild, wary cats were tamed in a hurry, especially the kittens. They learned to come to soft calls and softer caresses and offers of carefully saved scraps of food. They learned to run when they heard the jingle of key chains and the tread of heavy shoes.

For many years the cats were unofficially tolerated by the staff, but only barely. The standoff changed with a skillful memo to the administration. Citing the many scientific studies which show the increased health benefits resulting from physical contact with animals, it advocated convincingly that the prison adopt a compromise solution for a limited, neutered, vaccinated, and regulated cat population. For a brief period, the cats were officially sanctioned, complete with "kitty condos" and feeding stations, until one of the women brought a cat into her room for the night. The cat sprayed, the Warden freaked out, and all the cats were rounded up and shipped out.

It was not only cats that were loved. Special flowerbeds were babied and coddled. Love was sent to certain trees and hills on the other side of the razor wire fence. The sun and moon were worshipped. Certain women carried special pebbles, touchstones they loved and cherished. Other women had secret crushes on staff and volunteers. Flirting and full-on love affairs were shouted across the field to the men in the basketball courts of the detention center next door. And there were deep loves among the women themselves—loves that had to be doubly hidden.

But the strangest love I heard about was Jazmin and her pet spider. A little spider had spun her web in a windowsill near Jaz's bunk. Every day she checked to see what was in the spider's web, and whether she was resting or hiding or spinning. She made sure that her two roommates knew not to disturb the web. Every time the guards shook down the units looking for contraband, she worried that they would destroy the spider and her web. She spoke to it after the day was done and told it her troubles, and she greeted it each morning.

The day Jazmin told the stress group about her spider, the other women nodded matter-of-factly, telling stories of mice or birds or bugs they had befriended while in various jails or prisons, as if it were the most natural thing in the world to do.

I came to see that this need to love, to be loved and to spread love was, like the spider's web, a web the women were spinning, weaving and constantly repairing. The blessings of this love were not just for themselves or their families; in their prayers, thoughts and meditations, many of the women quite consciously sent their love out in a much wider circle to include their fellow sisters, the prison staff and the volunteers, and home to their communities, their friends and comrades, their nations.

The power of this love came home to me when I learned that on the day the women heard that my mother had had a massive stroke, they spontaneously formed a prayer circle. In the middle of the compound, in full sight and total defiance, they held hands and sent their love to my mother.

A number of rules with grave consequences were broken by this simple act, and yet the women never hesitated. Later, when I asked them why they chanced it, one of them wryly quipped, "What could they do to us? Throw us in jail?"

I was stunned by the gesture of this prayer circle. Most of the women had never even met my mother. Only a few had been briefly introduced when she came out to the prison for a special volunteer appreciation event. Why, then, did the women take such a big risk for my mother, for me? What was it really about?

I looked for answers. I was compelled to make a painting about it but felt it wouldn't be enough. So I made a large quilt with multi-colored appliquéd figures holding hands in a circle, and embroidered around the edges (photo appears after essay):

Forbidden prayer circle
an unbreakable hoop
of incarcerated women
who defy the rules
to stand in silent vigil
saying a prayer for my mother
for their mothers
melding hands, hearts and spirits
radiating power
banishing impotence
wrenching themselves
from bone marrow grief
to broadcast a blessing
to all who would be healed

IV. *A PRISON OF MY OWN MAKING*

I looked around the circle of women sitting on the floor, felt my weariness and then tried to rally and focus my energy to facilitate this group. Slowly we went around the circle, each woman giving her *weather report*. For some women, articulating these inner "weather conditions" came naturally. Others were consistently quiet, reticent, perhaps unwilling to crack the lid open and peer inside.

I considered one woman in particular a "sleeper." While it was difficult to get her to talk and open up, when she did whatever came out of her mouth was worth listening to. She was a young woman, slight in build with a gap-toothed smile and long straight brown hair. She spoke with a slight lisp. She worked as an administrative clerk in the Warden's office. When it came time for her weather report, she chose instead to look across the circle and report on what she saw and felt in me.

"Kathy," she began. "For a year now, you seem to be caught in a prison of your own making. The task of directing the holistic health program has become for you an invisible emotional prison. You seem burdened with not being funded and frustrated with grant-writing and collecting foundation rejection notices."

Before I could protest, she took a breath and continued. "Kathy, you're tired, dragged down, depressed. You say you never sleep well the night before you come into prison. You say the two-hour drive to get here by 7:30 AM is getting to you. You say you're throwing bones at your art. I think you're burning out. In comparison, we are enduring our imprisonment with more ease than you are."

Although her words struck a chord, I couldn't get over their irony. Here was a woman who had served thirteen years and was looking at the probability of many more. Here was a young vital woman who was saying that she and her incarcerated sisters had learned to carry the forced burden of imprisonment with more ease than a free person was able to carry the chosen burden of running a volunteer program.

"Kathy," she continued. "You need to get out of here. You're no good to yourself or us if you're burnt out. Go. Make your art. Follow your dreams. That's what you're always telling us, right?"

I felt a strange vertigo—the kind you feel when the world gets turned on its head. I knew Serafina was right. I remember shaking myself out of my reverie, looking at the women in the circle and feeling each one's kind regard. I looked across to the woman who had just put the mirror in front of me, feeling very "seen" by her. I was curious how she knew what she knew.

How is it that, even though we may live as free people in a free country, we can still be imprisoned within our lives, our bodies, mind and soul? What is freedom, really? How can it be that someone locked up in a high security prison can feel free? What is the secret she knows?

The questions generated that day and every day I went into prison still live in me. They have helped to create many works of art and these prison stories: Stories of courage, creativity, and determination; stories I hope will encourage us "free" people to take a good look at our tendency toward self-incarceration; stories that might make us ask why we as a nation build so many prisons; stories that have soared over the walls and sing a song of freedom.

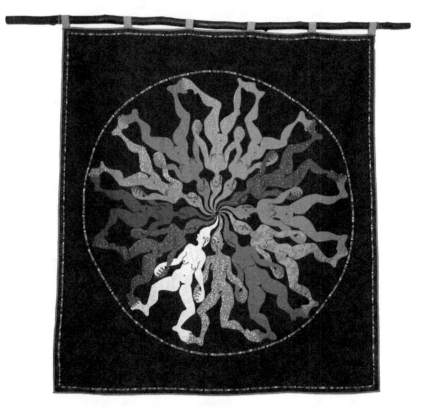

Photo of a quilt made of appliqued, embroidered, and quilted cotton, 77×70". The original colors feature a dark blue background with multi-colored figures in blue, red, orange, pink, and purple, arranged in a thin rainbow circle. A rainbow rectangle borders the quilt's edges.

Created and photographed by Kathy Park, 1997.

Janie Paul

_____

Jeff's House

In the summer of 1997, my husband Buzz Alexander and I rented and lived in an eccentrically reconditioned old farmhouse in upstate New York. Finding this house was an adventure. From Michigan, I'd put ads in local papers in the areas we were interested in and had people we knew put up signs in stores. I got three responses that sounded promising. On a day in June, we packed up our two cars with all our stuff and took off across Canada, landing on the second day near the Susquehanna River in the northern Catskills. We stopped at the first place, and it wasn't quite right, so we went on to the second place, which didn't feel quite right either. The afternoon was wearing on and the sun slanted on the fields as we neared our last possible home for the summer, with all our stuff—like turtles in our two cars. We were climbing in altitude; the vegetation got lower, and the road had a smooth, almost velvety feel as it snaked through pastures with old farms every five miles or so, the landscape seeming to quiet down into a calm.

Coming down a hill and turning to the right we came up the house: An old farmhouse with columns, a pond off to the side, a lawn in front, and across a vast field, with a crossroad going off into the distance. Jeff, the energetic owner, came out to meet us and show us around. A carpenter and all-around inventive person, Jeff had gotten rid of the ceiling in part of the house so it had a great hall effect, and the house was filled with nooks and crannies and eccentric and fascinating objects like stuffed birds and an old-fashioned organ. We immediately felt at home. Since Jeff's job was making painting supports for artists, he knew what kind of a space I would need and had fixed up the garage as a studio. This was definitely it. We made our arrangements and Jeff went off to his other home in Cooperstown. Buzz and I began to settle into our fascinating new environment.

By that summer we had curated two of the Annual Exhibitions of Art by Michigan Prisoners, a project of the Prison Creative Arts Project, which Buzz had founded in 1990, working mostly by ourselves with a few friends and student volunteers. It was a lot of work and though incredibly gratifying, the exhaustion we felt at the close of the show led us to seek a quiet refuge during the summers where we could gather ourselves. *How*, I wondered, *did the prisoners do that?* In some sense during those years we were looking for a place to be at home in. I had moved into Buzz's house near central campus. His house held the history of a previous marriage and family and though a wonderful house, it wasn't quite ours. In our adventure to the Catskills, we were looking for something new and something familiar, someplace to settle. (Several years later, we moved into a house near the Huron River, a bit out of town but still in Ann Arbor, and that became our home.) Those days at Jeff's house, sitting in my garage studio looking out over the fields or now, sitting comfortably in my rocking chair, I wondered how prisoners find any sense of settling.

This is one of the most terrible things about being in prison - the constant noise and artificial light, the constant activity or the constant solitude if one is in solitary confinement, the lack of any meaningful objects or clothing or attachment to animals or nature, the things we hold onto that let us settle into ourselves that made us feel at home. Prisoners often say, *You must never call prison home.* And yet, there are many lifers living in prison who will never get out; who, while never calling prison home, must find a way to feel at home in themselves because this is a basic human need. I watch my cat in the sunlight on the rug, circling after she chooses her spot and sits or lies down in it, and wonder if this is more than a human need.

How do people create a sense of being at home without making prison a home? Meditation, yoga, religious practice, and art. I have known two women who maintained a rigorous yoga practice by rising at 3 or 4 in the morning to do asanas in their cell or cube quietly before others were awake. A man I know connected with the National Buddhist Sanga and got an advisor who said, *Look to your sensitive side, your feelings, what you understand.* He maintained a regular meditation practice while inside. Many people find faith or continue their religious practice, often with the help of religious volunteers who go into prisons. Artists or writers find a sense of settling, or peace, of being at home with themselves through the practice that they carve out of daily life in prison.

For a visual artist, the physicality of the materials and the processes are an asset. Even if you sit at a table in a crowded recreation room with a bunch of other people sitting at the same table, you can carve out your physical and your psychic space by placing your paper in front of you, by the arrangement of your pencils or charcoal or paints by your side, with the processes that you learn or invent to make your images. The processes that artists develop, incarcerated or not, become rituals. The repeated ordering and organizing of experiences into familiar patterns is a way of confronting the chaos and the uncertainty of the creative process.

These rituals and processes become even more important in prison where the need for one's own territory is so urgent. You enter your territory of art with the tools and processes as you have organized them; the signposts are familiar and you begin down the path of discovery. The surface becomes a portal for your journey as soon as you begin making marks on it. You use what you know, what you have learned, to transcend the prison you are in but at the same time to join with the world in all its intensity.

You make the jump into it in order to not let your soul die. Because you need to be of the world, to love something or to explain something or to rail against something or to cherish something, to explore or reveal something, to be the creator of something that no one has seen, or to be in a place that you remember and cherish or invent a place that you haven't been to.

Showing Up

It is ten minutes by car from Karen's Bakery to the prison across the river, through the false-front row of Wild West Trinketeers, antique dealers, and upscale coffee houses. Past the park, senior center, and City Hall, left onto Prison Road with signs every 50 feet: "NO STOPPING OR TURNING." Old oaks stand mighty and quiet. Golden leaves loosened by the breeze spin in the air and take their time falling. The roll of the hill hides what lies on the other side; for about half a mile I can pretend I am in a skatepark or animal sanctuary. The deer step carefully to the main gate where the green grass grows thick around a steam vent. A first-rate prison requires acres of undeveloped space, and this land was purchased cheap, long before suburbanites decided to live in the area. Represa, California, land once belonging to the Maidu, now houses over 5,000 incarcerated people, none of whom are allowed to vote.

It's smiles and small talk while I wait for my gate pass. The Boys from Minimum"—grown men with beards and aging mothers—keep their eyes down as they meticulously shape shrubs and water marigolds. Once inside, it's a quarter-mile walk to the A/B gate metal detector and two flimsy guardhouses that remind me of the leaky portable classrooms of my high school. A river rock weighs down the pages of the sign-in book. I move it slightly to add my name, then hold up the back of my hand for the rubber stamp and watch as the ink runs through the fissures on dry skin. "Remember, California does not honor hostage negotiations," says the guard as he hands back my ID. I laugh, follow the script. The tower guard releases the lock. I close the heavy door behind me.

There are no more marigolds. Lines of dark moss and piles of bird poop sparingly break up the gray of the concrete. A clinician, dressed for business, pushes in behind me, scurrying toward the flat face of A Facility with a manila folder held over her head. "Damn seagulls," she grunts, chopping her sensible heels against the uneven concrete, a crate of files bumping beside her on small plastic wheels. I hadn't noticed the gulls dipping behind the wall, circling, their short cries muffled by the echo and din around me: metal scraping metal, human voices, keys, leather, fans and hissing steam. I imagine the ocean. It is far away. Here, seagulls are a sign of garbage, crowding. The drop gooey turds on hot pavement—reminders that no one here is on vacation.

It is a five-minute walk to C Facility. The road is straight. I think about class. To my right is the exterior wall of a housing block—a squat, scarred giant with rusty tears seeping from eight-inch slits of dark glass, one eye for each cell. The giant looks out, without interest, over a twenty-foot, two-ply electric fence, whipstitched with concertina. The hand with my gate pass and ID is cold in my pocket. On the fence, at eye level, a black-and-white sign shows a falling stick figure, lightning bolts at his feet: *"PELIGRO."*

I enter C Facility behind four officers and their cuffed charges. As my eyes adjust to the dark, I show my ID for a third time. The floor of the guardroom is raised, so I stare at the guard's belt-buckle while she looks at my license. On the way out, her replacement will ask me why the hell someone from Washington would want to come all this way. I will imagine acting surprised and saying something clever about already having been to Pier 39, but instead I will say nothing.

The fluorescent hallway between the guardroom and the sallyport is lined with medical cubicles—large windows, small examining rooms. I avert my eyes in a reflexive act of privacy as I pass the cells reserved for inmates on suicide watch. A guy who came to class once mops the floor. We say hello without shaking hands.

Spoon is sitting on an upturned milk crate outside the Arts-In-Corrections (AIC) classroom, face turned toward the small side yard and the pigeons who wait for him, stretching their necks through the chain link, blinking down the bread crumbs he spreads for them. Spoon is from the Mojave and feels a deep need for open space. Come November, the Blacks and Northern Mexicans will be locked down for one full calendar year, only leaving their cells for twice-weekly showers. The pigeons will continue to come the first two months. Everyone will be hungry.

I set down my bag. I am the guest teacher for the Tuesday poetry class that Spoon teaches. We choose a topic and begin to brain- storm. I shake a stub of chalk between my cupped hands as I wait for the thawing of defenses and the warming of the words that will fill the chalkboard. My fidgeting reminds me of the song I learned in Brownies that makes no sense and strikes me now as part of the landscape of unexamined White privilege that was my childhood: *I'm shaking up my baby bumblebee/Won't my mommy be so proud of me.* One of the new writers points out the line of chalk dust on my slacks. After three hours I will go out the way I came in, but while I am here, we will write from deep wells, some recently discovered under the concrete strewn with broken glass and bits of bone.

Years will pass while I try to write about why incarcerated people need to have significant say in how they use the writing classroom space. While

I grapple with the lingering colonial sensibility of a profession that hungers for narratives of transformation, the AIC program will be defunded and the incarcerated teachers will be transferred to other institutions; new classes with new writers will begin, and we will all hold our breath for a moment before meeting to show our respect for the ghosts of those who have moved on, whether by force or choice, from this place where we write with terrifying honesty stories both real and imagined.

In those same two years, a community of writers will form in A Facility. They will begin working on a book. A man who was pad-locked into a padded suit the first time I met him will write his way out of solitary and into a class where he can sit in a chair instead of a cage. Men will come and go. For some, writing will be life-saving. For others it will be a diversion. For most, the experience of writing in community will fall somewhere between fully transformative and merely entertaining. And because I, like all the other writing teachers taking their satchels into the prison, will have little real power to determine the direction of each writer's experience my focus will not be on justifying my place as teacher/transformer but on doing my part to make the classroom generative, safe. I will come with paperback books to leave and reams of photocopied passages that I think may speak to the writers. Sometimes I will stand at the chalkboard and sometimes I will sit quietly while writers stand to embrace one another or speak encouragement into the raw silence that follows a reading. But whether I play the role of chalkboard scribbler or silent witness, I will only ever be a guest—invited to listen, not to fix or save.

As I walk both from the front gate to the classroom at New Folsom Prison and from my house to the college campus where I teach, I will think about the prison. And how it is a nearly totalizing place. And how sometimes incarcerated writers add their CDCR numbers to the top right-hand corner of the page, either before or after their names. As I walk and as I read the work of other prison scholars, I will attempt to separate the value of the prison classroom from a practice of trafficking in transformational narratives—not because they are missing, but because they are so powerfully tempting to we teachers who want to know that what we are doing is doing something.

Rowan Renee

Letter Pictures

The envelope is rectangular and white, about the size and shape of a greeting card, which I know it contains. Despite being unopened, the letter is very well worn, showing signs of being held and shuttled from place to place for quite some time. From the bottom right corner there is a watery yellow stain creeping upward. Across the center are a series of diagonal creases, black ink smudges, and a gouge that nearly erases the first letter of my name. At the top left, written so close to the edge it appears to be testing the limits of the envelope itself, is the name of the sender, scuffed almost into oblivion. If you look closely, you can almost read the series of numbers immediately following it—K74296. At the top right, in much better condition, are two stamps—one 42 cent American Flag stamp and one 2 cent Navajo Jewelry stamp—which have been canceled with a big red and white square. Next to it, in tiny, machine-printed letters, are the words "from a State Correction Inst."

My first prison pen pal was my father. It was 2008, and he had been moved from the county jail in St. Lucie to the prison in Central Florida after taking a plea deal that was essentially a life sentence. He was 78 years old. Over the four years he lived in confinement, letters were our main mode of connection. I had been living in Brooklyn since graduating high-school, and it was difficult for me to make the trip across the country to visit him. But through his letters, I got a glimpse behind the screen of upbeat words he used to describe, and normalize, the mundane details of his day. I remember my unease as I noticed his handwriting transforming. A couple years into his sentence, the once precise, architectural script grew shaky and uneven. A few months later, he no longer made an effort to fill the page. Through these subtle visual cues, the letters tracked the decline of his health in a format perhaps more intimate, and harder to ignore, than it may have been if I could have seen him.

Prison is a place where cameras have been effectively forbidden[23]. Yet this dearth of documentation has not prevented the widespread consumption of prison imagery. Filtered through the imaginations of screenwriters, novelists, and filmmakers, we are bombarded with fantasies of prison breaks and uprisings, of court procedurals that create tidy tales of good vs. evil, of true crime stories that turn everyone into armchair detectives. Despite

---

23. Editors. "Prison Nation" *Aperture Magazine* 230, Prison Nation (2018), 19.

this over-saturation of prison imagery created either to entertain us, or moralize to us, actual images of prison life do leak out. Sometimes a person inside leaks photos, often through a contraband cell phone, at great personal risk, of the humanitarian crises unfolding within[24]. Or, in the case of the Covid-era media attention on the crisis on Rikers Island, the jail's own surveillance footage is released to the public as a result of lawsuits or litigation.[25] Or, as the scholar and curator Nicole Fleetwood writes, the families and the communities most affected by mass incarceration become the unwitting record-keepers of lives interrupted by confinement. Vernacular images, usually taken by prisoners themselves inside prison visiting rooms, are stored in shoeboxes, or held to refrigerator doors with magnets, depicting the brief moments of connection, human touch, and intimacy that are permitted under the careful watch of guards.[26]

But, save for these few exceptions, prisons remain a kind of black box where people go in, and the reality of what happens inside remains largely invisible to us. My thoughts circle back to my dad's letter, to the subtle messages carried across its surface. Learning to read these material traces is one way these letters taught me how to see. Feeling the weight of the letter in my hands, its undeniable presence, turns my thoughts to the way the letter physically enters and leaves the prison, literally slipping between the bars. I think of the mailroom staff, charged with monitoring prison security, who press each envelope between their hands, feeling for contraband. Once approved to leave, the letter is tossed onto a mound of other letters waiting to reach their destinations: family members, legal aid organizations, magazine subscriptions, ministries, pen pals. Then I imagine the locks buzzing and doors clanging as these letters exit the prison, navigating the maze of security that surely defines their journey until they enter the free world.

Could it be that these letters are a kind of portrait? That they offer the possibility of picturing the prison landscape that remains inaccessible from the outside? That, critically, expanding the definition of "picturing" makes it more possible for people on the inside to picture themselves, and claim agency over their own image and stories?

------

24. Keri Blakinger. "Prisoners Are Setting Fires to Protest Pandemic Conditions." The Marshall Project, Dec. 13, 2020. https://www.themarshallproject.org/

25. Jan Ransom. "A Look inside Rikers: 'Fight Night' and Gang Rule, Captured on Video." The New York Times, Jan. 13 2022.

26. Nicole R. Fleetwood. *Marking Time: Art in the Age of Mass Incarceration.* (Cambridge: Harvard University Press, 2020), 231–233.

Two years ago, largely as a result of the unexpected pathways of my own research, my focus shifted beyond my own family narrative to the much vaster landscape of confinement. I began a project called *Between the Lines*, a series of collaborative art workshops by correspondence with people currently incarcerated in Florida. Although my father had passed away ten years ago, I defined the project parameters largely in terms of what was familiar to me. I wanted to work with people in Florida, because that was where I grew up and where my narrative collided with the carceral system. I had a picture, another way of saying a *memory*, of what prison looked like. I remembered the landscape of slash pines and palmetto scrubs as we turned off the highway, drove past the nuclear power plant, ominously circled by buzzards, into the tightly fenced prison parking lot. I have an image of my father being wheeled into the visiting room by another inmate, whom he had paid in orange juice and peanut butter sandwiches because the guards *do not* wheel disabled prisoners. The room is basically an enclosed gazebo, like something you would see at a 1950s summer camp. There were no windows and no air-conditioning, just screens over rectangular holes in the cinderblock wall. We sat at wooden picnic tables. I assume they were bolted to the ground but I cannot remember checking.

Memory carried me forward, to the present, and back to the letter as a medium for connection. In that movement, I saw the possibility to redefine the relationship I once had to prison correspondence, removing it from the context of family trauma and into the same toolbox I called upon through art-making. I began to think of it as a visioning practice.

I was surprised at how quickly the first responses to my invitation and introductory letter for *Between the Lines* arrived. Nine people responded, out of the original fifteen on my mailing list, within just a few weeks. As each letter arrived, I spent time with not only the words they contained, but also the details of the letters themselves.

Leon's first letter arrives in a plain white business envelope. Enclosed with his letter is a slip of folded white paper. In careful, round, print, he writes: *Mail Room Rules. All incoming general correspondence must be white in color. If an incoming general correspondence to an inmate is in an envelope other than white, is written on paper other than white, is made from card stock, and/ or contains drawings, writings etc. made in crayon or marker, the correspondence will be rejected.*

I noticed Scott's handwriting first. He has a distinctive style, with oversized, flowing capital letters that recall script, although his writing is technically print. Unlike my father's machine processed letter, Scott's appears to be hand stamped with black ink, "mailed from a state correctional institution." His American Flag Forever stamp is placed askew, which I imagine is a deliberate gesture. In this letter, and others that come later, he carefully clips newspaper comic strips to share with me. He says he has a demented sense of humor. I am impressed that he has any sense of humor left at all, and I am grateful for this small lesson. How would anyone survive years of confinement without the ability to laugh?

My first letter to Maurice comes back Return to Sender, scrawled across the front with a thick, black sharpie marker. Looking closer, I realize I have left the first digit, a zero, off his registration number. In this moment, I quickly learn how power is wielded, with pointless cruelty, over the most miniscule procedural details. I imagine it took more time and resources to send the letter back than it would have to correct the error and deliver it.

Gerald's first letter is a greeting card, in a powder blue envelope. His introduction is short and effusive. Without even knowing me, or really much at all about what I plan to do, he thanks me for doing this project, for offering an opportunity for incarcerated voices to be heard.

Over the next year and a half, my connection develops with the nine *Between the Lines* collaborators. We share stories of family, childhood memories, books and poetry, identity, politics, legal issues and, of course, the many intricacies of sending and receiving mail. I've become accustomed to starting every letter I write with a summary of which letters I am responding to, along with their dates and contents. *This letter contains one workshop packet, 5 pieces of blank paper and one book of stamps. I am responding to two letters, dated 2/9 and 2/22.* This necessary vigilance towards the act of letter writing underscores the fact that each letter writer must navigate multiple levels of surveillance and censorship to maintain their correspondence. In the age of digital media, there is something comforting, even nostalgic about handwritten correspondence. But these are not everyday letters. They are marked, each one individually stamped "mailed from a State Correctional institution." Despite these obstacles that complicate and constrict their movement, the letters that make it through carry a sense of optimism. They enter and exit the prison, winding their way down the small, rural roadways where most prisons are situated, onto larger interstates, across state lines, into distribution hubs, spreading like fractals across a map, to be sorted and delivered to their recipients. This way of seeing the landscape, through the networks of written correspondence that connect people in prison to the people on the outside who care for them, is one way of reorienting ourselves. They help us see the impact of our everyday gestures of resistance.

A few months ago, Brother Truth, a comic and spoken word artist who I have been writing with through *Between the Lines,* sent me a copy of a drawing he created in response to a prompt from a call-for-art, which asked: *What does prison abolition look like?* Across the top left, Bro. Truth depicts the seemingly impenetrable structure of the prison's metal gate, topped with coils of barbed wire, and flanked by the shadowy structure of the prison's surveillance tower. However, in his rendering, these structures appear almost as relics of their former power. Across the front of the gate are the words "Prisoners Lives Matter." At the center of the drawing is a set of blue doors, flung wide open. A multi-racial group of men and women stand just beyond the opening, wearing orange jumpsuits and broad smiles. In the foreground, a group of protesters hold banners "Real Freedom Now," "Abolish Prison Now,"—while a crowd of people, including Bro. Truth, joyously embrace. This vision of freedom is unambiguous.

I know some of us on the outside, whether we can immediately see the impact the prison system has on our lives or not, have been asking ourselves a version of the question depicted by Bro. Truth: *What does the world look like without prisons?* Or, perhaps, *How can we imagine a world without prisons, when they have been so effectively concealed from us, and we struggle to see their impact?* Spending time with Brother Truth's drawing, I have wondered if the simplicity of his vision comes from his embeddedness in the prison's oppressive landscape. Perhaps, he can see with a clarity we cannot access from the outside.

Dear Reader, perhaps you struggle as I do with one's own capacity for visioning radical change. Perhaps you get stuck, as I have, on the most troubling cases or in our own deepest fears. Set against the wide-open blue doors of Brother Truth's vision, these feelings of hesitation and moderation contrast sharply. It's clear that what any envisioning process asks of us is a kind of radical openness and vulnerability to ideas and actions that stretch us outside the well-worn path. Rather than a picture of that pathway, perhaps what I can offer you is a gesture towards something that has helped me. I rekindled correspondence with people in prison because of a sense of longing that there could have been a different sort of response to the harm my father caused. Although I did not have a clear vision of what that something else looked like, I felt a readiness to open myself up. Not just to ideas, but to people who might help me imagine other ways of being and responding to violence. Building those connections across a landscape that holds so much traumatic memory, individually and collectively, feels like drawing a new horizon in the distance. For me, writing became a way to map this alternative landscape, a route that may help us see a path to healing our wounds.

Photo of a stained and slightly tattered envelope.

Photographed by Rowan Renee, 2021.

Pencil (originally color) and paper. In the center right there are bubble letters reading "PRISON HAS BEEN ABOLISHED." Fireworks illuminate the sky. The depicted scene is an imagined moment of what abolition might look like. Seven figures of different races and genders in jumpsuits, suggesting they were incarcerated, stand in front of a brick wall and metal fence with razor wire. One of them shouts "YES" with celebratory raised fists. Two of them are interacting with people not in jumpsuits. A small crowd of people are gathered in the bottom left corner holding signs that read: "ABOLISH PRISON NOW!" "REAL FREEDOM NOW" and "BE A PART OF THE SOLUTION NOT THE PROBLEM." "PRISONER'S LIVES MATTER" is printed on a sign above the prison.

Created by Bro. Truth, aka Bro. Hernandez Wiley, for Between the Lines *correspondence project (see Rowan Renee), 2021.*

Judith Tannenbaum

from In the Very Essence of Poetry
There is Something Indecent

Editor's Note:

The following excerpt is from a chapter in *Disguised as a Poem*, the late Judith Tannenbaum's memoir of her four years teaching poetry as poet-in-residence at San Quentin prison in the 1980s. I was lucky enough to speak with Judith and receive her blessing to include her work in this anthology before her death in 2020. Because this section is taken from the middle of her memoir, some background information is necessary: Tannenbaum taught through a (still active) program called California Arts-in-Corrections (AIC), which pays its teaching artists through grants. AIC places a professional artist at each California state prison to organize and coordinate an arts program at their respective institution; at the time Tannenbaum worked at San Quentin, Jim Carlson, who is mentioned several times in this chapter, served this coordinator's role. Other characters who appear in her story include Lynelle, who formerly taught art classes at San Quentin and, by the time Tannenbaum arrived, worked with men on Death Row; Luis, San Quentin's community resource manager; Phavia Kujichagulia, a Bay area poet who accompanied Tannenbaum to a class; and Sara, Tannenbaum's then-teenaged daughter. Also, Tannenbaum mentions her experience on the "Row," a euphemism for her time teaching cell-to-cell on Death Row with Lynelle. Finally, it is worth noting that Nobel Prize-winning poet Czeslaw Milosz—whose work appears in this excerpt—visited Tannenbaum's poetry class at San Quentin in 1986.

San Quentin's schooling was harsher than I'd reckoned upon. But once I stopped crying, I realized I still appreciated the prison's daily challenge that I notice my own assumptions and then move beyond them.

For I had certainly walked into San Quentin in August 1985 with assumptions. My automatic sympathies went to the powerless who, in this situation, I perceived to be the men behind bars. I was still singing "Which Side Are You On?" and still replying, "on the side of those without power."

The first year of once-a-week teaching intensified my innate reaction. For in those months, except for the information and advice given by Jim, what I knew about San Quentin was held within the three solid walls, and the one wall of half-glass, that shaped our buried classroom: What I knew about this foreign world I had entered came from my students. I very much liked each one of the men who made up our core group—Angel, Coties,

Elmo, Gabriel, Glenn, Richard, and Spoon—in alphabetical order. And, besides, they were my *students*. Support for the underdog, friendly feelings, and honoring what I felt to be the holiness of the student-teacher relationship conspired to make me a partisan.

In addition, I had walked into San Quentin full of assumptions about guards. During that first year I spent very little time with staff or administration and a great deal of time focused on my students, so my prejudice continued unchecked. This prejudice was born from my natural antiauthoritarianism, from the 1960s rhetoric I'd come of age hearing, and from what I'd seen with my own eyes.

During one antiwar demonstration in Berkeley, for example, I was with a group chased into an underground garage by two policemen. Most of us backed ourselves up against the structure's concrete walls, but one man climbed onto a car and attempted escape through a high window. A policeman grabbed him, dragged him down from the car, and repeatedly beat him. When I thought of "police," when I thought of "prison guard," when I thought of "criminal justice," it was that cop's nightstick raised for a blow that I saw; it was the whack of the baton on the protester's body that I heard.

The dehumanizing sentiments I heard staff express when I first entered the prison—all those "bozo/yo-yo/asshole" characterizations—reinforced my prejudices. Instances where I observed one guard or another flaunt some petty power confirmed my beliefs.

But, now, working under [a] grant took me beyond the walls of our classroom, into cell blocks and offices. In these situations, I experienced moments that ran counter to the anticop assumptions I carried. At such moments, I had to acknowledge that those representing the badge were, in addition to being agents of authority, also individual human beings with a wide range of personal traits.

Moment: When Phavia had visited the previous year, Luis spoke like a poet: "Gemini," he said of his sons. "The sign of split birth."

"Mexicans always have boys," Luis intoned.

That same evening Luis told Phavia and me about his college days in the Chicano movement. He asked if we'd read Corky Gonzales, a Chicano hero-poet from that era. "A revolutionary," Luis said. "Poets are *always* revolutionaries." Luis delivered this judgement not as a warning, but nearly as praise.

Moment: I'd walked into Luis's office to have him sign some proposal for our class, then sat there and listened. "I'm in a position of authority over people who grew up the same way I did," Luis said. "Mostly, your blue-collar criminal is watched by your blue-collar worker. One time there was a problem with Mexicans on the yard, and I called down to the officers,

'What are you guys doin' to my people?' The sergeant called back, 'Those aren't your people.' But, you know? He wasn't even close."

Moment: One afternoon I walked through Education with Officer DeSantis. We passed a desk and DeSantis picked up a drawing I would have passed right by. Staff, like convicts, tended to be alert to the periphery for anything might be a sign of trouble.

"Hey, look at this," Officer DeSantis said.

He pointed to the pentacle at the center of the page. "That's a sign of the devil. And these," his fingers brushed the shapes that fanned from the five-pointed star, "these are demons. There's no way to erase these," DeSantis continued. "You can only burn the paper itself."

I listened, confused.

"I read about Satanism and try to imagine why anyone would spend so much time drawing an image of the devil. There's only one answer: He must be possessed."

I guess I looked stunned, for DeSantis raised his hand. "Listen, don't get me wrong; I'm no Bible-belter. But to me, an image is real. I'm part Indian, must be from that. I believe in the power of image."

I started to say, "Well, I'm an artist, and I believe in the power of image myself," but prisoners were now walking into the building for afternoon outcount, DeSantis got busy taking their IDs, and we had no time for further discussion.

Moment: Every day Felix, the second-watch officer at Scope Gate, handed out candy, bought with his own money, to everyone passing through the checkpoint during his eight-hour shift. Candy and kind words to staff; candy and kind words to family and friends coming in to visit prisoners.

Moment: One night, while I was teaching a class at the medium security H-Unit outside the prison's walls, the lieutenant on duty stopped by. The men and I all looked up, expecting some kind of problem. Instead, the lieutenant launched into a by-heart rendition of "The Cremation of Sam McGee," his favorite poem.

Moment: I sat in our office and watched prisoners drop by across the hall to see Associate Warden Tabash. "You don't agree with their crime by treating inmates fairly and equitably," Henry often said. "They were sent here *as* punishment, not to *be* punished."

As I acknowledged that, like any group, the staff was composed of unique individuals, I became more curious about the nuanced ways in which these men and women looked at the world. I wondered who I might be if I found myself in a guard's situation.

My first chance to put myself in something like a guard's shoes came in early February, just before my trip up coast to Point Arena. The filmmaker Les blank had given Arts-in-Corrections copies of his music and culture videos. We had Lydia Mendoza, Lightning Hopkins, Clifton Chenier, the Balfa Brothers, Flaco Jimenez, and others to show in classes and on SQTV. We arranged a screening schedule with folks at the internal television station, and I made a poster to let prisoners know.

It was easy to get copies of this poster to those on main line, but I was stymied for a while about how to get the word to men in lock-up. I decided to ask permission to go into the blocks myself to deliver the schedule to these one thousand men.

Even with my experience on the Row with Lynnelle and my own cell-to-cell teaching—which should have provided ample warning—I entered the units with every intention of looking each man in the face. I assumed we'd exchange a few friendly words, and then I'd slide the poster into his cell. In my enthusiastic go-for-it mode I thought, hey, I have all afternoon. I can smile for four hours, no problem.

I managed such smiles for, maybe, one hour. After that, the usual cell block oppression—the heat, the smells, the noise, the sight of five tiers with their opposing gun rails, the fact that each lonely man was capable of talking to a sympathetic soul for hours, the sheer number of men who told me they couldn't *get* TV reception in their block and asked if I'd do something about it—wore me down. At the end of the four hours, I could barely speak or look at the man on the other side of the bars, let alone smile. At the end of four hours, I'd nearly stopped caring.

So, what about guards? I wondered. What about those men and women who spent eight hours each day in these units, taking up meals, delivering mail, escorting men to the showers? Even if an officer had the best heart in the world, how would he or she ever be able to manage being decent eight hours a day, five days a week, under these conditions? Was there a Berkeley revolutionary who could manage that?

When I was ten, there was a book in my mother's bookcase that told of a marriage and its dissolution. You first opened the pages to read the husband's story. Then you turned the book over and upside down and the story began anew, told this time by the wife.

Trying to find "truth" in prison was like reading this book about marriage. For example, in the long lockdown we'd just come through, I'd go from the Operations Building, where I'd hear staff talk about shanks being found, about missing metal, and rumors of stabbings, to the cell blocks, where some of the men regarded the lockdown as a way for the administration to prove that prison was a dangerous place so that it could ask the legislature for increased funding.

Elmo, my tour guide, said that prison by its very nature was adversarial: There were two sides, convicts and cops, and a prisoner had to draw lines to protect his basic human dignity. I knew that if I wanted to glimpse the whole these adversaries were each part of—as Bresson had urged me to do—I must first pay attention to each individual position.

I'd always been interested in point of view, as a literary tool and as a detail of consciousness. The first experience of shifting perspective I noted occurred when I was five, standing at the ocean's edge with my father. He wanted me to join him in the water, but I stood on shore, very afraid. He tried to convince me that those waves causing me terror were, in fact, harmless and small. Finally he stopped talking and bent down until his head was level with my own. "Goodness," he said. "Those waves sure are big from down here!"

I was accustomed to lending my eyes to my father's sight, but that August afternoon at the beach he'd brought himself in line with *my* vision. He had acknowledged my perception.

Despite this early gift, I often had trouble holding onto my vision; I spent much of my life assuming that if someone else's point of view made sense, my own must be wrong. In many ways, this self-doubt gave birth to me as a writer. For in writing words down on paper, or making up stories in my head, I could see what I saw without also considering someone else's viewpoint or having to explain myself clearly in my father's language. In my imagination, I was free from interference.

Not that either of my parents intended to interfere. Both of them loved and supported me; each valued language. My mother spent much of her time in an armchair reading a novel; one of her daily joys was completing the newspaper's crossword puzzle. My father made up the bedtime stories he told my sister and me, encouraged us to find words to express our feelings, and loved puns. (My father often repeated the first poem he had composed when he was a small boy: "There is no peace/ in the pen with the geese." Rhymed couplets were his form of choice. Once, when a high school English teacher asked me to bring in a permission note before he'd let me read a Tennessee Williams play, my father wrote a poem that included this couplet: "Why then wait for the mañana/ to read 'The Night of the Iguana'?")

My father certainly had a playful imagination and enjoyed joking with words, but primarily, he believed in meaning, in the literal. When I was three, sleeping alone in the room where one year before my father had told me of my brother's death, white light scanned the sky each night and shone through the window at the side of my bed. I was afraid to lie in the pool of this light. My father called what I saw a "searchlight," and told me it was nothing to fear. I trusted he wasn't lying and could even picture the machine he described a few blocks to the south, where the beam narrowed down to a source. Still, I knew what I knew: This circling light was a pathway, a trail witches rode to their home. I knew those witches wanted me to join them, and I'd lie in their light night after night, eyes open, unable to sleep.

The images and phrases that moved through my head as a child—my reality—didn't lend themselves to the kind of language my father valued. My mind naturally made quick, leaping, poetic connections that could only be explained to my father's satisfaction through a process of what felt to me like reduction. But I loved my father and knew he loved me, knew he had my best interests at heart, so I tried to find words that made sense to him.

In my imagination, though, I was free from this effort of translation. The price of this freedom was hiding behind that Lone Ranger mask: I kept my truth hidden to protect it. However, as I'd realized in that Point Arena phone booth, I know wanted to remove the mask.

During my first weeks at San Quentin, I wrote down the words I heard when listening to officers in Four Post or my students in class. I cherished these found poems: "They don't make dumb convicts, not for a long time;" "Never call your cell home."

I also began to write first-person poems in my own voice, such as the one I'd shared with my students about that moment after class when they entered the dark on their way to the blocks and I walked out of the prison and into a world of "bridge lights and town lights and stop lights and shop lights." "So much light," I wrote, "and still I can't see."

And then, the found poems next to poems from my point of view gave birth to poems in voices neither overheard nor my own. My lifelong tendency to see others' viewpoints more clearly than mine had the upside of allowing me to cross thresholds easily. Now voices of imagined prisoners, imagined guards, and imagined folks on the outside flowed through me. Poems in his voice and her voice and his voice and my voice accumulated to create a long sequence. This sequence made me happy, for I felt I'd been given a form that enabled me to observe through a larger lens and to do as Bresson had asked: "Accustom the public to divining the whole of which they are given only part."

I *was* happy, that's true, but as I wrote, the voice of my old critic, Doubt, hissed in my ear: "You're exploiting your students' lives for your poems!" "You're an outsider; you have nothing relevant to say!" "You're a fraud; you'd better stop writing."

I spoke back to Doubt: "I'm not writing about prison, I'm writing about the whole we're each part of. I can write about that; that's mine; that's how I see the world!" In my argument with Doubt, I imposed two ironclad rules on myself as I wrote: To use nothing personal anyone had actually told me, and never to indulge in irony or distance, but instead to enter completely the world of the imagined speaker so that I spoke fully informed by how he or she saw the world.

When I stated the question bluntly—did those of us teaching in prison have a right to let our own artwork be affected by what we were experiencing?—the answer was simple. To be affected, and then to give witness, was a primary task of the artist. But when Doubt's voice pounded in my ears, I was less sure.

Lynnelle told me about a time she was working in a lockup unit. "Each cell had a window, with bars on the inside, that was kept shut. I would knock on this twelve-by-twelve-inch window, open it, and talk to the guy through it. All I could see was each man's head and these bars. Of course, the bars were about eye width apart, so I never had direct eye contact with the man I was talking to.

"This was such a strong visual image, I wanted to do some drawing. At first these drawings were too literal: a face and the bars. This wasn't really what I wanted to show. Finally I broke through to being able to draw the bars and the face and the man's features with one line, appearing as one form. These were some of the strongest drawings I have ever done.

Lynnelle encouraged me to persist with my poems. She gave me permission to encounter this world we had entered and to let what I wrote be shaped by what touched my senses. Lynnelle and I, and most of those teaching with Arts-in-Corrections, were not famous. But we were people for whom painting or writing poems or playing bass was essential; to create was why we were here on this planet. We had whatever feelings we had about lack of worldly recognition, but recognized or not, being an artist was at the center of each of our beings.

I had read a few of the earliest poems from this series to my class the previous summer, and now I wanted to read more from the work. These poems expressed how I saw the world and I was very excited to share them with my students.

However, the phrase "my students" now indicated a larger group of men. Many prisoners had seen me in West Block during the lockdown, and, when they discovered there was a poetry class, they signed up to attend. Though I'd talked with each of these men individually, we'd hardly met as a group. The officer taking afternoon count on Mondays was new

and extremely slow, which resulted in a series of late counts and, conse-
quently, canceled classes. Though prudence would have had me wait and
let this new grouping of men coalesce, my desire to share these poems was
so strong that on an evening in early March, I just went ahead.

Eleven men sat around the two tables I'd placed together. Elmo,
Gabriel, Spoon, James, Ralph, Glenn, and Smokey were there, as were four
others—Carl, Chris, a new Leo, and Sammy—who had joined class after
the lockdown. Coties was at court.

As soon as the men settled down, I introduced my poems and began
reading "Count's cleared and the guard says . . ." Many men had heard
this one, but I soon shared poems that were new to them. In one a
guard says:

> I know how I'm thought of
> as some kind of Nazi
> a man who takes pleasure
> in control over others.
> You think I'm sadistic
> that seeing men locked in cages
> or a gun on my hip
> gets me off.
>
> Well, I tell you you're wrong.
> Just try spending eight hours
> in one of these blocks.
> Five tiers, steel and concrete;
> odor the essence of dungeon.
> Four gates on each tier
> and I tell you the keys
> must weigh more than the gun does . . .

I read a poem in the voice of a woman on the outside, whose young daugh-
ter had been raped and then murdered:

> I still want to tell her
> Baby, that's not what sex is.
> Sex is good, you'll see.

Halfway through the reading, Elmo shoved his chair away from the table,
rose noisily, and stomped into the hall. I could hear him talking to some-
one out there as alarm whistles—like those that shrieked loudly over San
Quentin's grounds, setting staff running—wailed now all over my body.

When I came to the end of the last poem, Elmo walked back into the classroom and said, "How dare you write about this world that isn't yours?"

Chris had stayed seated during my reading, but he nodded. "Now, you *know* poems like these feed the public's anti-con attitudes. Why would you write poems like that?"

"But . . ." I started to sputter, summoning all my will not to let the catch in my voice expand into the cry now spiraling inside me. Despite my effort, I felt the tears in my eyes spill over my cheeks. I barely knew Chris, so it wasn't his words ripping me open. I felt so close to Elmo, though, and he was clearly upset—not just upset, but upset at me. Was he really so angry because I'd written a poem from the point of view of a decent guard? I wanted to ask, "What about the poems in the voice of prisoners? What about the ones that say:

I've got life without possibility of parole.
Life without.
Life without helping my kids do their homework,
without taking my mother to church . . .

or:

. . . who I am. A man
who once was a boy.
A man with hands that know
how to shape, how to be gentle,
how to touch what they love."

But I didn't trust my voice not to shatter, so I said nothing.

For a long while, everyone else in the room was also quiet. I felt us all doing our best to stay still enough to contain the emotions—anger, hurt, and some others I didn't know quite how to read, though they seemed pointed and ugly—that threatened to overtake us. In that group effort, those metaphoric alarm whistles quieted down sufficiently for some real conversation.

Elmo and Chris wanted to know if I was just another outsider walking into San Quentin inviting them to open up, then using what I saw and heard to exploit them. "Seems to me, you're using our pain for your gain," Elmo said. If Elmo was right, If I was exploiting my students' suffering for my own ends, such an act went beyond betrayal: Such an act was my definition of evil.

Most of the other men continued to be silent. Glenn, who rarely spoke, asked about writing from a point of view not your own. "Could a man really write like he was a woman having a baby?" Glenn asked. "I don't see how he could."

This question allowed me to assume a teacher's voice and talk about the history of literature: There would be no such thing as novels and plays if what Glenn described was not possible. Then Carl asked a question about rhyme, and we were able to spend the rest of the evening talking technique.

Gabriel walked beside me up the stairs after class, but when we reached the top, I walked over to Elmo. He was standing in the corner, alone. As soon as he saw me he said, "I thought I could trust you, that's why I've told you so much. I told you both my parents had died, and you used that line in one of your poems."

"Both my parents have died," yes, I remembered the line, and I remembered Elmo telling me this fact from his life. But I hadn't thought of Elmo's truth when I wrote the poem; I'd just thought of very large loss.

On that Monday night in earl March, I didn't know how profoundly Elmo had felt the passing of his parents and so didn't realize just how much trust he'd placed in me by telling me of their deaths. That Monday night, I didn't fully realize the emotional risk Elmo had taken by choosing to be open with someone in an environment he would later describe as one in which "truth and trust are rare commodities." But I understood that, though I'd felt attacked, Elmo felt betrayed.

I had been as conscious as I could be and had still managed to break my own rule: use nothing personal anyone had told me. I'd written the best that I was able, and had hurt someone I cared for. For a long string of moments I thought, "Well, I'll just stop writing."

But what I asked Elmo was, "I can't believe we've been working together for eighteen months and now, at my first bad mistake, you're not willing to extend me any grace at all?"

"I'm talking with you, aren't I?" Elmo responded. "If it wasn't for those eighteen months, I'd have walked right out; you'd never have seen me again."

Sara was sleeping when I got home, but her sweet face on her pillow gave me enough courage to encounter the night. I put away all the books and papers I'd carried to the prison, placed the poems I'd just read back in their folder, then sat down in that same bentwood rocking chair I'd rocked in that night long ago when Elmo first asked me hard questions. This ordering calmed me—here's home, here's where I'm safe. I settled myself in the rocker and watched what arose.

I knew my body, in that basement classroom, had reacted as though attacked. Alarm whistles had gone off inside me, and not just for me, but for us all: I'm in danger, this group is in danger.

I saw how, as a group, we had managed the necessary stillness and attention to let tremendous passion be held in that room. Because I didn't know well all the men who composed the new configuration of our class, I wasn't sure how to name the feelings precisely. But I knew emotion burned hot in that room and as I sat in my rocker at midnight, I was very much impressed with our shared ability to contain what might easily have burst into flames.

My own feelings felt hurt. My students had questioned my poems, these poems I'd been so excited to share. I'd read these same poems on the north coast on the night of my fortieth birthday. Some in the audience let me know they were offended by my intensity. I knew what they perceived was true: I was driven. Bresson's "Make people diviners" injunction was delivered in the same steady, straightforward tone as his films were. My nervous system was not nearly so stable, and my jumpiness led me to grab folks by the shoulders and shot: Look, look at this.

Now some of my students seemed to be saying that since I wasn't locked behind bars, I didn't have the right to speak about prison. If I had been able to talk without crying, I would have told the men in my class that in my mind, my poems were less about prison and more about con-sciousness. To me, my poems were "about" how what each of us sees is all there is to the one who is seeing, but only part of the picture when looked at from a wider angle. To me, the poems were about the knowledge that there *is* a wider angle, even if we can't measure it by degrees.

Still, at least some of my students wanted to make sure I acknowledged that my poems were also about prison. And if I was going to speak of their turf, I'd better tread with utmost care.

Whatever hurt their words had caused me, I knew Elmo and Chris had raised a serious point: Prisoners were vulnerable to each of us who walked in from the outside. I didn't feel my poems exploited my students; I knew that wasn't my intention, and I didn't see exploitation as being the effect of the poems. However, I understood that simply writing about the world my students endured put me in jeopardy of taking advantage of their suffering.

Something deep in me hated relationships of unequal power, and this aversion often made me pretend that my students and I were all equal in an equitable world. Such pretense was harmful, however, both to me and to my students. For the reality was that, although all these men were big-ger and stronger—and most of them full of more anger—than I was, I was the one with authority. I was the one likely to be believed in any altercation. I didn't want to accept this fact, but I could see that pretending otherwise was a "false innocence" none of us could afford.

Okay. Danger, hurt, sadness, accusations, and self-deception—all these were fairly easy to face sitting there in my rocking chair fifteen miles from San Quentin, my sweet daughter asleep down the hall, our cat in my lap. But the closer I got to looking at Elmo, specifically Elmo and all he had told me, the faster my heart beat.

Elmo's size, forceful male presence, and articulate speech could certainly be intimidating, but it wasn't these that made me want to crawl under the covers to avoid through sleep what I was feeling. Instead, the pain swirling inside me was twofold. First, Elmo felt I'd betrayed him. Letting this fact come close to my heart nearly ripped me apart. Writing was too dangerous: I could write the best I was able, with as much consciousness as I could muster, and still hurt someone badly. In the world of prison, which Elmo had described to me so many times as a war zone, he had chosen to trust me. He'd chosen, despite all the prison rules that made simple human sharing so risky, to tell me a sacred fact of his life. And, though I hadn't meant to, I'd abused this trust.

The very permeability of mind that allowed poetry, also made poems perilous. When I wrote the poem with that line—"both my parents have died"—I didn't for one moment think of the words Elmo had told me. But he had told me those words, and somehow, somewhere, they must have stayed with me. The poem then called on those words. This unconscious process now scared me.

Months earlier, I'd experienced a somewhat similar shock. I was working on a poem, and I was stuck and—as often happens to me in that state—suddenly sleepy. I lay down for a few minutes and woke up with the line "Comprehension of good and evil is given in the running of the blood." I went back to the desk, and with this line, the poem flowed. For months I thought of that line as a gift from the gods.

Then, reading Milosz one afternoon, I saw that the line was his—the first line in his poem "One More Day," a poem I didn't even remember reading. How could this have happened? If I hadn't picked up the book, maybe I never would have known that the line repeating through my poem wasn't mine, but one that had been created by someone else.

In my series, I had felt that one poem was touched by Gabriel's tone, another by Richard's. I'd decided that this was okay; the speaker of each poem was so clearly different from Gabriel or Richard, and I had used nothing factual about either man. But this truth of Elmo's was different.

I sat in my rocker and worried about the nature of poetry. Milosz had also written, in "Ars Poetica?" "The purpose of poetry is to remind us/ how difficult it is to remain just one person,/ for our house is open, there are no keys in the doors,/ and invisible guests come in and out at will." This truth is what I loved about poetry, and what made the form dangerous.

"Ars Poetica?" recognized that "In the very essence of poetry there is something indecent:/ a thing is brought forth which we didn't know we had in us . . ." Milosz was referring to beings within, but Elmo was the one who came through my poem, unbidden.

Milosz continued: "That's why poetry is rightly said to be dictated by a daimonion,/ though it's an exaggeration to maintain that he must be an angel . . ." and, "What reasonable man would like to be a city of demons,/ who behave as if they were at home, speak in many tongues,/ and, who, not satisfied with stealing his lips or hand,/ work at changing his destiny for their convenience?"

Not I, not at this moment. At nights darkest hour, I sat in my rocking chair frightened by how easily other beings spoke through my poems. Elmo had told me something that was crucial to his ability to keep his humanity alive in prison, a place where the odds were stacked against such survival. There had been not one shred of motive inside me that desired to abuse Elmo's trust, and still I had.

So I wanted to stop writing. Which was the second strand of pain swirling inside me. For besides the hurt I'd inadvertently caused Elmo, I recognized that Elmo's voice sounded just like the familiar voice of Doubt. The angry tone of Elmo's words echoed that of my lifelong internal critic, the one who managed to find a multiplicity of ways to let me know I had no right to speak, the one who, all through my younger years, made me discount my own point of view. Tonight Elmo's voice had sounded just like the voice that, my whole life, tried to silence my own. Elmo's powerful voice was making me ask once again: His need or mine?

As I sat in my rocker, I tried to find what, in those years, I continually hungered for: that vantage point from which our needs co-existed. From this viewpoint I could see that Elmo and I shared a strong human desire to be closer, to know each other, to become friends, and all this was controlled by prison rules. Spoon and I needed human connection, too, and we had found a way to be close that didn't resist prison protocol. Elmo's righteous energy wouldn't accept the limits Spoon and I managed to live with. So I always experienced Elmo's insistence that we were two human beings desiring real communication as an in-my-face challenge.

But as night moved toward dawn, I saw Elmo didn't mean to challenge me. I had handed him the role of censor when, in fact, what my body had interpreted as attacks, Elmo intended as invitations. Elmo *wanted* me to respond with my truth, to do my part to bridge the gap between us—to speak, always to speak. What I perceived as a roadblock, he intended as an avenue for approach.

By the time the late winter morning broke over the hills I could see from our window, I knew I could rise from the rocking chair and reenter San Quentin without dread. I stood up, made Sara a smoothie for breakfast, and got ready for work.

Hybrid/Mixed Genre

Raquel Almazan

from LA PALOMA PRISONER

La Paloma Prisoner is a multi-disciplinary play about the reclamation of identity by women in the Colombian prison system. Based on the true story of a group of incarcerated women selected as beauty queen contestants at the Buen Pastor prison in Bogotá, this new play interweaves the ritualistic journey of a "parade of prisoners" within Colombia's social, political, and spiritual history. The play centers on an infamous woman nicknamed "La Paloma" who transcendentally soars beyond physical and societal barriers to avenge the raped women of Bogotá. Her actions revolutionize the women's lives, Bogotá's prison society, and the world beyond its walls.

A PLAY IN TWO ACTS

ACT I—16 SCENES
ACT II—16 SCENES

SETTING

This play takes place in a maximum-security prison in Bogotá, Colombia. The present.

The stage will consist of a series of boxes, cardboard, crates and trunks. The different scenes will be set up with these boxes. All props will appear from within or behind these boxes.

On Stage right there is a box with dirt. Enough for three to sit in, deep enough to step in. Stage left there is a box of water, large enough for three to step in.

There is a screen where select images will be displayed.

THE SPANISH IN THE PLAY WITHIN (PARENTHESIS) IS NOT TO BE SPOKEN. JUST FOR TRANSLATION PURPOSES.

NOTE: Moments when Paloma's key glows and transition of certain scenes-including scenes, where "visitors" and ancestors enter, a spiritual portal opens, that alters the world - opening to another realm- world. These metaphysical moments can be supported by music, movement and sounds.

*A live Latinx musician—percussionist can/ has create(d) live rhythms to accompany the majority of the play.

CHARACTERS

LA PALOMA—Colombian, feminine yet natural looking, in her early 30's. Convicted for killing several men, a rampage against rapists.

ORO (Gold)—A beautiful 20-year-old girl, in for armed robbery, a crime committed with her mother, starting to show signs of pregnancy.

DIANA GOMEZ—Oro's mother, also beautiful in her late 30s, somewhat heavy set. She is also in for armed robbery.

LOBA (Wolf)—The oldest inmate, 65 years old. She is seen as an oracle, known for being able to read palms and the eyes of the future. Convicted of killing her husband with a kitchen knife.

MARILYNN RAMIREZ—Early forties, doctor convicted for aiding the FARC and Para-military activity.

SOLIAR "Reyes"—Mid to late forties, FARC leader convicted for attempting to kill the Colombian president.

MAMA / WARDEN—Early fifties, but appears younger. Attractive and well kept. Paloma's mother. Very religious. Warden is similar to a boxing match announcer.

YOUNGER MAN—20s / 30s - will play the roles of guard #1, guard #3, reporter #1 and Antonio.

ANTONIO ° Soliar's son—military stocky, strong in appearance.

OLDER MAN—40s / 50s—will play the roles of Guard #2, Guard #4, reporter #2, TV reporter and Paloma's step father.

PALOMA'S STEP FATHER—Slightly overweight and strong in appearance.

CITIZEN VOICES AT THE TOP OF ACT II CAN BE DIVIDED BY ALL CAST MEMBERS.

ACT 1

SCENE 1

AT RISE

The stage is dark and bare. From the right corner in the ceiling a small white light starts to appear. An immense sound of a bird's wings flapping is heard. Then an even louder sound of a bird screeching is heard. Suddenly La Paloma sits in a steel chair. She is in a spotlight created by a huge light from the prison yard.

LA PALOMA: Some say I can fly. On nights like these, I can. Me llamo La Paloma. They call me Paloma because I'm gentle and only want peace, flying to other dimensions. The bones of my wings sprout out from my ass, almost breaking my spinal cord every time. All those men I killed . . . I did it out of peace.

I'm pretty femme to be a butch dyke serial killer. It's funny, I tried killing off anything that wasn't good in the world. Men of course. And they stick me in a place full of women. My dream. Malparidos tontos! (Fuckin' fools). I love pussy. And do you know why I love cuca?

You're probably thinking it's because I'm trapped in walls with only women and that eventually I gave in, gave into wanting love and needed to feel the touch of love, intimate love, the kind of love that has you revealing your childhood terrors, kissing in alleyways and making promises to a stranger. That kind of love, true love, can only be found here in a prison - my personal freedom.

Soy Colombiana, and like any good Colombian, amo el pan. Soft, wet, warm bread. I used to knead the dough in my mother's bakery and imagine nipples on that dough. I would leave my imprints on the pasty live dough, satisfied in how I had changed the composition of that bread forever. One day my mother caught me with raw dough in my mouth, salivating on the counter. She slapped me and forced me to start the bread again. And I did. Chanting my own made up incantation when the water, yeast and flour hit together. I could create women.

That's how it felt when I first touched a woman, there was nothing softer, warmer or wetter than my mouth on her life nipple. El sabor de mujer.

I can destroy too.

Soy hija del sistema. I'm a daughter of *this* system. I am loved and hated in this family of steel. They watch me here closely. So closely. They time how long it takes me to shit, to piss, to breathe. They say I'm still out there, killing those rapists. Hijos de puta. That somehow from behind this steel I fly upon them at night on their way home and slice them down the stomach with my nails.

Lights immediately go to black. The sound of wings flapping returns. La Paloma is gone.

SCENE 2

FIRST PARADE OF PRISONERS

The stage is empty as Oro and Diana enter from the left, Soliar and Maryann enter from the right.

Loba enters from up center. Cell bars appear behind them. The women enter wearing nude bras and a simple bottom. Each woman carries a large box. These boxes will serve as set pieces for the remainder of the play. These boxes contain the objects that are most dear to each character and will be used throughout the play.

The following is a choreographed MOVEMENT WITH TEXT, similar to processing when first entering a prison. The executions of the movements and text, RHYTHM must be PRECISE. The sound of water running down a river is heard mixed with footsteps running quickly in jungle. The women will use the dirt and water elements throughout this section.

The text for all women can be divided up between characters, while certain sections spoken in unison.

The women form a straight horizontal line facing forward towards the audience. They all turn their heads to the right. Then to the left. They all then face forward. In unison they set their boxes on the floor in front of them.

Together they open their box and retrieve their 1st object.

THE WOMEN SPEAK THE NAMES OF THEIR OBJECTS, WITHIN QUOTATIONS

DIANA: "A hair brush."

LA LOBA: "A photo of my son."

ORO: "A ripped piece of newspaper."

MARILYNN: "A medical pin with my name and picture on it."

SOLIAR: "A small machine gun."

ALL WOMEN: *Colombia, mi Colombia*. Colombia, my Colombia. I have freed you and you have condemned me. I have traveled your streets, and you have poisoned my veins. I have drank your rain water and you have drowned my spirit. I have fucked your history and you now fuck my future.

The women hold the objects in their hands as if for the first time. They are re-discovering their objects and themselves. Each character turns to the women beside her and they switch objects, look at it, and give it back to its owner. They put their object back into the box. In unison they turn to the left and form a line to walk together, circling in front of their boxes. They return to the same position in front of their box. Each character retrieves a 2nd object.

DIANA: "A makeup compact."

LA LOBA: "A pair of nylon stockings."

ORO: "A silver ring."

MARILYNN: "A nail file."

SOLIAR: "A military metal."

They hold up their objects again, physically using its purpose.

ALL WOMEN: I prayed in your churches, you sent me to hell. I listened to my mother and you fathered me like a dictator. You told me to dream big, *duerma con los angelitos,* and awakened me from my sleep with invisible hands choking my throat.

They repeat the same action of discovery with their object. Each character retrieves a third object.

DIANA: "A shawl."

LA LOBA: "A necklace with a wolf claw",

ORO: "A baby's blanket."

MARILYNN: "Aa pair of glasses."

SOLIAR: "A small evening purse."

ALL WOMEN: Colombia, I love you. Colombia, I hate you. Colombia *por favor amame* (please love me). Colombia *por favor, odiame* (please hate me). Squeeze me, tickle me, kiss me, lick me. Put your hand on my knee. Remember to put your hands through my hair first. *Asi no, asi* (Not like that, like this). Now lie on top of me. Put your weight on me. Let me feel how heavy your past has been. Do you know what to do next?

They repeat the same action of discovery with their object. They put their object back into the box. This time in unison they each step in front of their box and walk upstage. Each step they take is weighted. They are on fire inside. They advance on the audience, a group of calculated bulls charging forward.

DIANA: I want to travel on an airplane again.

LA LOBA: I want to see my dead son.

ORO: I want to eat chocolate until I'm sick.

MARILYNN: I want to stitch up open flesh.

SOLIAR: I want to hug my brigade again.

Once they reach downstage, the edge of the stage, their movements soften and they turn upstage, their bodies floating. They sing together loudly.

ALL WOMEN (canon): I remember the jungle, *recuerdo* the river that curves down into town, dirt clouds that form off the road. I remember tin roofs, pastry shops and lost children *en la calle*. Cars honking, drunks staggering and my mother calling me for dinner. I remember . . .

ALL WOMEN: I remember ME.

The women are now back behind their boxes. The women all begin to retrieve simple shirt tops and simple bottoms and dress themselves in unison. They close their box with the following text.

DIANA: I broke into a jewelry store for you.

LA LOBA: I sliced my husband twelve times for you.

ORO: I took what was rightfully mine for you.

MARILYNN: I healed your sick for you.

SOLIAR: I slaughtered your false citizens for you.

The sounds of the prison world: ALARMS sound. CELLS open and close. The sound of GUARDS ORDERING a group of women to roll call over the loudspeaker.

Guard #1 enters.

GUARD #1: Presente! Presente! Presente! Quien esta presente?!

The women straighten their line.

GUARD #1: Those chosen to represent each of the nine cell blocks for the annual beauty pageant present yourselves.

ORO: Presente!!!!!!! Oro Brillante present! Representante de cell block numero dos.

DIANA: That's your last name now?

ORO: Yes. It's now Brillante.

DIANA: Bueno! Presente. Diana *Gomez* presente. Representante de cell block numero uno.

LOBA: Aca estoy yo, presente. Loba. Just Loba. La mas vieja. The oldest of cell block numero siete. Representing.

SOLIAR (as a military salute): Presente esta Soliar "Reyes." In memoria de Raul Reyes, my dead hero. Representing cell block numero seis. I represent the political prisoners, held in block 6 of this overcrowded place. We demand a humanitarian exchange of political prisoners as a first step for a political solution to the deep social and armed conflict in the country—

Marilynn cuts in, stepping forward. La Loba can't help but laugh at Soliar's extremity.

MARILYNN: Estoy presente. Marilynn Ramirez. I am in opposition with prior comments, as those of us who are innocent should be released immediately. Eso es todo. (That is all). Representante de cell block numero quatro.

Suddenly Paloma enters wearing a large gold key around her neck and joins the line.

PALOMA: Paloma. Everyone knows who I am. Presente. Representante de cell block numero nueve. Each cell block divided by our crimes—

The women look over at her surprised.

An alarm rings loudly. Guard #2 enters.

GUARD #2: Everyone to your cells!

(to Paloma)

Two men sliced down the stomach last evening were found in Medellin 153 miles from here . . . Abnormally large white feathers surrounded their bodies. The victim, she was older, and was cradling the feathers, singing.

The women look over at Paloma quickly.

GUARD #1: Do not stop at the cafeteria! To your cells! NOW!

The GUARDS disperse the women.

The women lift their boxes and place them on stage in creation of the set.

The guards exit in haste after Paloma.

Paloma sits stage right in preparation at her cell.

The women exit the stage in the direction that they entered.

Raquel Almazan

about LA PALOMA PRISONER PROJECT

La Paloma Prisoner Project[27] is a multi-faceted theatre and outreach project about the reclamation of identity by incarcerated and formerly incarcerated women in the prison system. This project takes the form of play presentations, panels, conferences, activist demonstrations, advocacy think tanks, workshops and community partnerships with orgs dedicated to serving people impacted by the criminal justice system. Documentation of the productions and events with formerly incarcerated woman and incarcerated men with La Paloma Prisoner Project are included post essay.

My major inspiration for the La Paloma Prisoner Project comes from my experience as an arts facilitator with Art Spring Organization to incarcerated women at two maximum security prisons in South Florida. This play fuses years of facilitation and activism in the field and continued work that spans South Florida, Bogota—Colombia and New York City.

La Paloma Prisoner: is a multi-disciplinary play about the reclamation of identity by women in the Colombian prison system. Based on the true story of a group of incarcerated women selected as beauty queen contestants at the Buen Pastor prison in Bogotá, this new play interweaves the ritualistic journey of a "parade of prisoners" within Colombia's social, political, and spiritual history. The play centers on an infamous woman nicknamed "La Paloma" who transcendentally soars beyond physical and societal barriers to avenge the raped women of Bogotá. Her actions revolutionize the women's lives, Bogotá's prison society, and the world beyond its walls.

The script has been in development for over ten years, across four countries. Workshop production at The Signature Theatre off-Broadway. (Selected for World Theatre Day: Performing Gender and Violence in Contemporary National and Transnational Contexts Conference in Rome, Italy. Tre Roma University reading) (Women's Playwrights International Conference, Stockholm, Sweden) (The Lark Play Development Reading, New York City) (Labyrinth Theatre Intensive reading) (Staged Reading at La Mama ETC and INTAR). Critical Breaks Residency directed by Estefania Fadul (Hi-Arts). Attendance in Bogota, Colombia, at the (Buen Pastor Prison) for the Annual Celebration and Beauty Pageant.

27. Raquel Almazan. "La Paloma Prisoner." Accessed May 24, 2022. https://raquel almazan.com/latin-is-america/la-paloma-prisoner/.

As a female writer of color, survivor of domestic violence and immigrant to the US who has had close family members incarcerated, I have navigated the challenging power structures of society, race, class, education, and gender. This project was born from my arts facilitation and training that tackled the systematic conditions that lead to incarceration and racial justice in America with women in maximum-security prisons and male youth at Rikers Island. This project has been a fifteen-year commitment for me as an artist/activist with social conscience and builds on collaborations with Just Leadership USA, Close Rikers Campaign and directing performance demonstrations, attended by thousands, including: The Stop Mass Incarceration Network, where I collaborated with Cornel West, Quentin Tarantino, Arturo O' Farrill, Carl Dix, Gina Belafonte, Eve Ensler; and The Prisoners Revolutionary Literature Fund.

The United States has the highest incarceration rate of any nation in the world. Nationally, according to the US Census, Blacks are incarcerated five times more than Whites are, and Hispanics are nearly twice as likely to be incarcerated as Whites. Our major cities are erupting in response to police brutality: as a result, black and brown communities are left to deal with losing loved ones and/or community members being jailed with a record that will permanently impact their future. This creates a ripple of negative effects on these communities causing disproportionate incarceration rates throughout the country.

This piece is an offering to make visible the potential for ending mass incarceration. I am using my full range of skills: art making, organizing, advocacy and facilitating to build knowledge on mass incarceration as well creating platforms on the spectrum of change within several components of the project. This project seeks to end mass incarceration, by bringing together community organizations, the District Attorney Re-Entry Task Force, prisons/jails, women in the system, the public and policy makers.

The play and its programming has been accompanied by post-show activities with criminal justice activists, extending audience engagement and citizen action events; including panel discussions *Unlocking Female Incarceration: A Panel Discussion, Parts 1, II and II.*

LA PALOMA PRISONER (Impacted Women Series)

LPP—IWS—was funded by the Arthur J. Harris Award—Columbia University, combines women who have experienced the criminal justice system alongside performers to engage with audiences with the themes of mass incarceration. On June 1, 2017, excerpts of the play were performed at Greenhope Services for Women as well Queensboro Correctional Facility for Men in New York City; in collaboration with impacted women. These unique readings were directed by Laura Gomez (who is a recurring actress on Orange is the New Black) and co-produced with Mightee Shero Productions, who is dedicated to performing work with formerly incarcerated women in facilities.

An excerpt from the La Paloma Prisoner play, analysis and interview with Alessandro Clericuzio in Performing Gender and Violence in National and Transnational Contexts; edited by Maria Anita Stefanelli; was published in early 2017 by L.E.D. Edizioni Universitarie di Letterature Economia Diritto, Milano.[28]

Connecting the Dots: Intimate Partner Violence Prevention, Healing, and Advocacy Conference

I participated as a panelist on June 5, 2017, for the New York City Mayors office (Department to Combat Domestic Violence) where I performed excerpts from La Paloma Prisoner and spoke on a public panel to the process of working with survivors of domestic violence in prisons and being a survivor myself. In collaboration with Gibney Dance, I also facilitated a breakout session to fifty professionals working in the advocacy field, on the use of theatre, visual collage to create transformative solutions to domestic violence.

This project also has a workshop series with formerly incarcerated women that has been piloted with community partner, Steps to End Family Violence NYC. This project, which employs methods integral to the Theatre of The Oppressed model of community-action, will lead to a public performance of La Paloma Prisoner by the workshop participants; participants have used theater-making as a tool for advocacy, breaking down the systems that oppress them.

Contribution by Brigitte Harris (formerly incarcerated woman, lead performer and consultant/ collaborator for La Paloma Prisoner Project):

> *The main character in Raquel's play was arrested for killing a child molester and when I saw the play I was deeply moved and immediately thought that this play could bring awareness to the horror of child molestation but also about women in prison, people of color and how they end up there, informing people about the unknown realities of lives within mass incarceration. I am aware that not everyone's story is like*

---

28. Almazan, Raquel. "Interview w/ Alessandro Clericuzio in Rome, Italy." Raquel Almazan, February 25, 2016. https://raquelalmazan.com/interview-w-alessandro-clericuzio-in-rome-italy/.

mine but there are a large percentage of women in prison who have been molested and raped. To continue to empower women of color like me, who became part of the system with a history of abuse, this work can change the lives of the women and the perception of those working in the system. This project brings more opportunities for supporting the women in creatively expressing themselves and changing the system through that expression. I also recently experienced Raquel's work again, in HERE TO BE SEEN supported by the Brooklyn Kings County District Attorney's Re-Entry Task Force office, where she wrote the closing piece of a play performed by actors and formerly incarcerated women, for an audience of 300 people, some had experienced incarceration and the majority were people who worked in the criminal justice system in New York City. Watching that play reminded me how important it was to keep advocating for women in prison. Once you finally leave prison and are not constantly surrounded by those women, it is easy to forget the stories and problems associated with incarceration. Too often there is a stereotype and misinformation about women in prison. Raquel's work breaks those stereotypes and puts the truth out there.

LA PALOMA PRISONER Project, A Community Journey:

During 2018, Brigitte Harris became the Impacted Women Ambassador for the La Paloma Prisoner Project leading up to La Paloma Prisoner's off-Broadway premiere with Next Door @ New York Theatre Workshop originally scheduled for April 2020. Due to the Covid-19 pandemic, the production is on hiatus and will be rescheduled.

The following events continued to build the project, including programs designed to uplift the voices and narratives of current and formerly incarcerated women-identified folx of color through performances/workshops in prisons, conversation circles, and panel discussions leading up to the production's scheduled run at NYTW.

September 14, 2019—La Paloma Kickoff event held at The People's Forum, was the launch of a series of events geared toward amplifying & celebrating the community of activists and artists who are actively raising awareness and inciting action toward decarceration. The Kickoff featured performances, including live music, an excerpt reading of the play, and a panel highlighting key organizations within the movement.

October 18–20, 2019—Almazan collaborates with impacted advocates, artists and change-makers creating an original piece addressing civic participation towards decarceration. With Theater of Change Forum with Broadway Advocacy Coalition, Columbia University School of Law and The Center for Institutional and Social Change.

November 2, 2019—Almazan collaborates with PEN America in a series of interviews, featuring Pen America poetry by incarcerated women at Paloma Prisoner events and as a guest at the Writing for Justice Fellows cohort gathering.

November 13, 2019—La Paloma Prisoner Project: "Unlocking Female Incarceration—Part III", Women, Trauma & Decarceration at Kingsborough Community College. Collaboration with Dr. Vanda Seward. Featuring impacted panelist Donna Hylton (Center for Health, Equity and Justice) and Roslyn Smith (V-day organizer).

November 20, 2019—Poetic Theatre Productions Poetic Theater Productions, Judson Arts Wednesdays, and The La Paloma Prisoner Project in association with La Lucha Arts presents:

Ascención: Celebrating the Movement Toward Liberation—directed by Estefania Fadul.

A free potluck-style meal was served at Judson Memorial Church. An evening highlighting the work of women artists of color devoted to advocating for and developing work around decarceration, liberation, and reclamation. With a particular focus on those who have been targeted or imprisoned for protecting and defending themselves, their rights, and those of other women or their families, Ascención created a space for activism, healing, and embracing a destiny of liberation.

November/December 2019—Almazan facilitates as a guest artist at (Rikers Island), East River Academy.

December 18, 2019—La Paloma Prisoner staged reading tour to Incarceration Facilities (Rikers Island) in New York City, directed by Estefania Fadul.

The continued goal of this project is to affect systemic change with citizens and lawmakers. La Paloma Project will urge policymakers to take into account the institutionalized racism when making new laws. Formerly incarcerated people will have a system of support, to re-channel energies to produce systems of solidarity to influence changes within the justice system. La Paloma Project has revealed the power of theater when in collaboration with communities affected by the systems that silence instead of uplift people. I am continuing to seek resources to evoke the need to re-evaluate the purpose of jails: instead of punishment the system needs to rehabilitate people to contribute to society with their particular gifts. I look to a future where there will be a ground swell of active civil engagement towards the realization that it's the people that change and end the system.

Tara Betts

To Keep a Green Branch from Snapping

Editor's Note:

The following is an introduction to *Poetry* magazine's February 2021 special issue, "The Practice of Freedom," dedicated to the work of incarcerated writers. The issue was co-edited by Dr. Tara Betts along with Dr. Joshua Bennett (poetry contributor to this anthology) and Sarah Ross, and features writing and art by prisoners both former and current, as well as their families and loved ones. Each co-editor wrote an introduction to the issue describing their connection to the topic and their approach to editing. In this piece, you will encounter references to writers and poems not included in this book. All referenced pieces can be found on the *Poetry* magazine website.[29] Also of note: this issue of *Poetry* was met with much resistance from literary and activist communities. The controversy surrounding this issue reflects the challenges—moral, literary, ethical, legal, and beyond—faced by those of us involved in "arts in corrections" (whether incarcerated or not). A discussion of this resistance lies beyond the scope of this book, but can be found in many articles and interviews, including one for *Slate* by Dan Kois[30] and a conversation between poets H.R. Webster and Demetrius "Meech" Buckley for *1508*, the Poetry Center Blog for the University of Arizona[31].

Love is contraband in Hell,
cause love is an acid
that eats away bars.
          —Assata Shakur

The editors of this issue read thousands of poems submitted by people who have experienced incarceration, which were winnowed down to the sampling here. We have been working collectively toward publication since

---

29. "Poetry Magazine." Poetry Foundation. Accessed June 25, 2022. www.poetry foundation.org/.

30. Kois, Dan. "Was Poetry Magazine Really Wrong to Publish a Child Porn Convict in Its Prison Issue?" Slate Magazine, February 4, 2021. https://slate.com/

31. Webster, H.R., and Demetrius "Meech" Buckley. "Poetry Is like Water: A Conversation between H.R. Webster and Demetrius 'Meech' Buckley." The University of Arizona Poetry Center, June 15, 2022. https://poetry.arizona.edu/

2017. The contributors, who are often no longer perceived as people in the non-incarcerated world, are indeed human. Many of them have partners, families, friends, and try to help other people. Some of them have made mistakes. Some have faced cycles of violence and abuse themselves. I hope that people come to this issue with open minds, and I'd like to underscore that openness by saying that poets are not members of the jury. No one undertook this project to declare a verdict on any of the contributors therein. Although many of these poems are about the lived experiences of being contained—sometimes indefinitely—by the state, we discovered poems about subjects that some of us hadn't considered. We read the words of poets from across the country and outside of it, from poets of different faiths, races, cultures, and abilities. None of these poems romanticized prison or glamorized aspects of how they ended up there. We were not looking for a poetic noire. We hope that we gathered some work that illustrates honesty and vulnerability. We considered a range of issues that the contributors wrote about, but each poem took on some compelling element that moved us as artists and writers editing this issue.

This brings me to a poem that kept resonating in that electric tissue of my mind. I found myself carrying around Nazim Hikmet's poem "Some Advice to Those Who Will Serve Time in Prison." If you've never heard of Hikmet, he was a Turkish poet born in 1902 in Salonika, now Thessaloníki, Greece. I have always taught this poem in jails and prisons because it often becomes a lighthouse moment. A beacon of awareness swings into view for at least a few students because they realize that someone, imprisoned for a long time for his political beliefs, wrote poetry that speaks with a deceptive simplicity and captures their experiences. They find affirmation that their own experiences are worth writing about too.

The last time I taught this poem was in 2019 at Stateville prison, a men's maximum security prison just outside of Chicago, where I've taught poetry workshops for almost three years. On that cold spring day in the small concrete square known as "the education building," we read Hikmet's poem. There were two moments that the poets reading and discussing it were completely fascinated with—when Hikmet says,

> To wait for letters inside,
> to sing sad songs,
> or to lie awake all night staring at the ceiling
>   is sweet but dangerous,

and when Hikmet advises, after a woman stops loving you, to do the following:

> Don't say it's no big thing:
> it's like the snapping of a green branch
>   to the man inside.

When it comes to the "sweet but dangerous" distractions that exist in such tenuous conditions, the people inside prisons know them and some do their best to dodge them altogether, but that "snapping of a green branch" caught each of the poets off guard. How dare Hikmet describe that kind of vulnerability where a branch can bend and nearly snap. How did he so simply describe an act that could lead to an irrevocable break where a person cannot return to what they were before?

On March 7, 2020, I unknowingly taught my last in-person poetry workshop at Stateville. The students were already murmuring about COVID-19 because they follow the news more closely than many people beyond such confines. I reassured them that I'd be back because I had no idea how fatal this pandemic would be, especially for Black people, Indigenous people, and people of color, who have suffered significantly throughout 2020 due to this unprecedented health disaster and the persistent racism that underpins police brutality. During 2020, and in the years to come, *Poetry* magazine will be dealing with its own legacy and challenges with race and privilege. As a guest editor, I couldn't think of a better time to showcase the brilliance and challenging subjects presented by poets here, who represent so many marginalized communities. I corresponded with some of my students throughout the summer of 2020. At least two of them were diagnosed with COVID-19, and one at Stateville died from it.

As startling developments evolved and the National Guard set up a mobile hospital on the prison grounds, I heard more stories where prisons across the country turned deadly, and many people have protested for medical releases and pardons to help loved ones escape the infectious conditions of prisons and get home to hopefully safer family environments. When I've participated in readings and talks online, I've discussed these conditions because people are often curious about what happens in prisons, but this is also an opportunity to turn analytical and creative eyes toward how these institutions do not address human needs and rights.

As Americans, many people simply think about human rights as an issue in distant countries or as the fodder of strident poems. This issue of *Poetry* magazine challenges both notions. Most of these poems came out of America, where we are now thinking about which workers are essential. Haven't poems declared everyone from all sorts of experiences essential and human? If not, they should. These poems consider the practices of freedom and the lack of it.

Many of the poems here address the "small freedoms" that Hikmet described. Those freedoms are allowed or taken away by people who are deeply involved with what we now call mass incarceration, the carceral state, or the prison industrial complex. When you read these poems and the essays by my coeditors Joshua Bennett and Sarah Ross, as well as contributors Roshad Meeks and Audrey Petty, and look closely at the stunning collection of visual art, think about the poets discussing Hikmet's poem. Consider how they set their pens to paper to offer advice with thoughtful metaphors and tender line breaks. They can speak for themselves. Even if you visit a prison, you may never fully understand that lived experience, unless you've served time yourself.

Eva Chiladaki

Scenes from Ten Years at Thiva

September 2004

She is sitting on the bench with her lawyer going through papers, an expensive looking travel bag by her side. Her little girl in brand new pink tennis shoes, is dancing around in circles, passing the detector every now and then, stopping with a happy smile at its beep. The warden doesn't interfere, she even lets her play with her hand cups. A picture of innocence.

This little girl will have to get used to new sounds, steps down endless corridors, sirens, loudspeakers, bolts withdrawing at the gates like the sound of a disturbed snake. I hope she'll continue to find them amusing.

October 2005

Vaso is over 80 years old; she doesn't remember exactly. She remembers a lot of more important things though: her husband ("my old one") and his two white horses, for which she used to decorate the bridles, and which now only exist on a faded photo together with her "old one" and a happy bride and groom (her son). She enjoys talking about her children (her daughter is in the same prison; her son is out but stays in a closed community for addicts). She also tells us about her grandchildren and her great grandchildren, and of course the little pony, some stray dogs killed, the day they were all arrested— images that appear in many of her quilting works. She is that rare person who never gets into a fight, not even an argument. Everybody loves and respects her and the air feels different when "grandmother" is around. The only thing she sometimes complains about is her one and only tooth. It gets in the way when she eats, and she wants it out. She is also sad that the prison didn't accept her for the reading and writing lessons because she is considered too old. But she makes beautiful embroideries of the letters she learned from us and proudly writes some of the letters of her name, instead of the cross, when she has to sign papers. It takes her some time, but she enjoys it.

February 2006

Vaso is concerned about her old one's health. The District Attorney told her that she would get out on parole without escort if he died. She seems lost in thought.

2007—2008—2009

Vaso is on parole and gives an interview to "Espresso" on October 17. I'll translate some passages:

> *ARTIST BEHIND BARS—the story of the 83-year-old Mrs. Vaso who became an embroidery expert in Korydallos.*
>
> *Four years ago, Mrs. Vaso had been sentenced to twelve years in prison for the possession and trade of Indian cannabis together with her son, who is addicted. She is denying that accusation until now. She lodged an appeal and her sentence was reduced to six years in prison. So, on October 20, having served the bigger part of the sentence, she'll pass the gates of the women's wing of the prison for the last time. . . .*
>
> *. . . "They bring us little pieces of fabric, threads and needles, so we pass our time. Otherwise I wouldn't know what to do. I'm friends with all the girls in the workshop. I love them all and they regard me as their mother." says Mrs. Vaso to the "Espresso" about her "daughters" . . . .*
>
> *. . . Mrs. Vaso lifts her embroideries one by one. Her favorite subject is horses and she can explain why: "My husband used to be a carter. We had two horses, which had driven some of the richest and most famous people of that time. I myself used to shine their bridles. My "old one" has played in well-known Greek films. We have met Jenny Karesi, Lambro Konstantara, and I don't remember whom else. . . .*
>
> *. . . She used to spend her time with her children and grandchildren or in the pen with her sheep and goats. "I used to get up early. There is always work to do, grazing the sheep, looking after the old one, ironing" . . . She is excited that her release is near: "I'll grow wings and I'll fly. Feel how nice the air is here. Inside we don't have enough oxygen" . . .*

On her last time in Korydallos with us, Vaso tells everybody how much she has missed staying with her old one. Maria with a sigh: "It is nice to have company . . ." Vaso: "O no, not just company, my old one is not useless!" Surprised looks, seeing Vaso in a whole different light.

Shortly after Vaso's release, the Women's prison moved from Korydallos to Thiva. Vaso's home is on the way to Thiva, so I see her regularly on Tuesdays. She continues to make her beautiful embroideries, always wondering why people like them so much.

Four months after Vaso came out of prison, her old one died. She told me on one of my visits "I thought he was playing games, when he didn't move at all in the morning."

So she continued to look after the sheep all by herself. I used to help her with their injections and then we would have coffee in her tidy cottage and talk—about how much she missed her friends inside, about horses, and about injustice.

She described to me the day she was released. She was so excited she forgot the bag with her sewing material in the dormitory. She remembered when she was standing outside on the street. So she went back in, although she was afraid to do so, because on her release in the office they had given her 800 Euros, which had made her dizzy and she feared that if they found the money on her, they would keep her in prison for some more years. She seemed still not sure if it was safe to tell me. The money must have been partly from her embroideries we had sold, and I can imagine that the woman from the "Espresso" might have left her something. Anyway, the prison personnel must have been surprised to see her back so soon but were not willing to help her with the bag. After some agonizing hours she managed to be back on the street again with her precious bag and the money.

She was making plans about what to do without her old one now. Her neighbor was willing to buy the sheep and her son told him to come to live with her in the North. Before I left, she gave me her son's telephone number and some fresh eggs from her favorite hen. Somehow I never could get through.

I don't know where the wings she was talking about to the "Espresso" have taken Vaso, to her son in the mountain village or much higher looking for her old one. . . .

March 2010

Maritsa is one of our "celebrities." She sits in the teacher's chair and the rest of them have to check with her if it is ok to talk to me. She has other women do her needlework—strictly after her instructions. Her fingers are useless due to arthritis, her legs the same. After our meetings on the corridors, she hangs heavily on my arm and makes us walk very slowly, resting every few steps, gaining time for talking. Sometimes she gets religious or philosophical about being locked up without a reason. On other occasions she wonders if it wouldn't have been better to confess everything. Eighteen years have passed by now and maybe she isn't sure about anything anymore. She tells us her side of the story—different from what we know from the media—how the bank had confiscated her house (she made an impressive quilt showing all the rooms in it, with a lavish bathroom, fireplace, TV, countless kitchen appliances) and how her daughter's fiancé got engaged to someone else. She admits to taking the donuts to the engagement party, but she says she had nothing to do with the poison. "God is my witness, Mrs. Eva."

She loves to feed people. On one of our endless walks along the corridor one Tuesday afternoon, on a bend where she believed that the camera can't reach, she slipped a sandwich into my pocket. "You have such a long way home; you must get terribly hungry." I didn't want to hurt her feelings. Driving home, I checked on the sandwich at every toll station and it seemed to check on me. I put on the radio, but couldn't pay attention. The sandwich wouldn't let me, so I had to eat it.

February 2011

Maritsa is finally released. The group loses its balance. Sofia is trying to take Maritsa's place, demanding respect and playing it tough. She gets in an argument with Iris, who very politely proposes that a friend of hers be accepted into the group, now that we have a vacancy and Iris herself will be released soon. But Sofia had already managed to pass three friends of hers through the inner control of her wing and now here they are grinning slyly at everyone, especially at Theoni, who hates lesbians. I don't want Theoni to be taken to the hospital again and ask Sofia to control her friends. It seems to work. Sofia makes a speech about her three protégées and their talent in needlework. Everybody seems amused. Meanwhile Sonia is winding the yellow yarn on her used phone card and wouldn't pass it to Sula, who after a while gets really angry. She throws the wool I brought her on the floor and asks me to cancel her name from the list. Not a good day. I cut out some patterns for Sofia's friends to stitch to prove their ability. But when I'm ready they have already left. Efthimia and Sonia take the cutouts gladly. Everybody seems to be tired but peaceful. We cut the old clothes I had brought to handy pieces. Kristina finds a tiny coin in a hem. It is an American cent. She dreams about what she could buy with it if she were in America.

July 2011

My old car is a mess. Our volunteers prefer to take the bus. It's much faster, safer, and less hot, now that it's 40 degrees C. The windows are blocked and permanently closed. The air conditioner works, but if I put it on, the car goes even slower. The only solution is to leave the trunk open and secure the bags with a rope.

October 2011

I finally managed to get a new car. Well, used, but everything works. The first thing I checked were the windows. Natasha asked me if she could have my old one. She was released from prison last year and spent the last six months in a closed mental institution, but now she works at the tailor's shop she set up with her son. She has to take three busses to go to work every day. I warned her about the car, but she is sure that her son can fix it. "You won't recognize it!" she says with a happy smile.

December 2011

Preparations are underway for the Christmas Bazaar at Mairivi's puppet theatre in Metaxourgio, which for the last years has housed mostly prostitutes and drug addicts—and immigrants, because rents are low. Each year there is a discussion about having the bazaar elsewhere, in a safer neighborhood, but it has become a tradition and it's such a beautiful old building.

Maritsa is there too, helping to put up the exhibition. She is putting her dolls everywhere and throwing other dolls back in their boxes. Mairivi invites her upstairs for coffee so I can do my work in peace. When Maritsa is back, she is not happy, but she leaves in a hurry when some reporters show up.

When I arrive the next morning to park the car in the recess next to the entrance, it is occupied by people in sleeping bags. Vasilis, Mairivi's husband, calls "Epemvasi," who arrive with an ambulance. But they all seem ok and pack their belongings into cardboard boxes that they leave in the empty building next to us. The first dealers appear with "breakfast". Vasilis fetches the water hose shouting angrily, while the owner of the Syrian restaurant on the other side of the street does exactly the same thing.

The first visitors arrive, some for the exhibition, some mistaking us for one of the brothels nearby. They gladly accept our refreshments and then leave to look for other dolls.

Maritsa is telling everybody to have a good look at her dolls. It works, people buy. She has a long talk with the "Thursday ladies" who came to see the exhibition. They are called "Thursday ladies" because they used to come to Korydallos with Pater Nikolas on Thursdays to talk about the Bible and bring soap and other useful things. They seem excited to find Maritsa here.

Walking to Mairivi on the second day of the exhibition, someone with a pickax runs past me, crying "where's my money?". Now I understand why the person ahead of me was turning all the time and grinning in a strange way. Now he is running too. I continue on the other side of the road.

Lots of rain on the last day of the Bazaar and very few people. Plenty of time for Maritsa to talk. She is living with a former cell mate. Mairivi and I had helped her with the moving, two cars full of big black plastic bags, no visibility whatsoever. She is sad that she can't go back to her little town and that her daughters avoid her company. Her health seems to get worse. She gives me instructions about what to tell the others inside and what not to tell them.

With our new volunteers and two musicians, we take the road to Thiva for the Christmas party. Efthimia is organizing the buffet as usual, checking that everything is shared equally. We try to make room for a dance floor and for the musicians to take out their guitars. Most of the women dance in spite of the limited space. From the cooking class next to us they sneak in one by one to join us. So the buffet is empty soon, no more melomakaronas. Sofia calls me to tell me that she needs something sweet quickly because of her diabetes. She is looking impatiently at Irini, who had covered her paper plate with a paper napkin. Irini has to let go of some of her melomakaronas and from the cooking class they bring us some samali fresh from the oven. The space is getting really crowded now, but everybody is having fun. Dionisia enters and orders the musicians to stop and start the song from the beginning. "I'll show you how to sing this song." She has a beautiful clear voice, and she knows all the songs people ask her to sing. In the end they bring in the astonished cooking teacher and make him dance in the middle of their circle. Another great party is coming to an end. I wonder why nobody asked me about Maritsa.

January 2012

Despina is much taller than everybody else and wears her gypsy clothes with pride. She has 17 grandchildren. She has never been to school, can't even write down a phone number, totally lost in the system. Nobody wants her in the group, she couldn't care less. She speaks only to me or our volunteers. She has her trial at the end of the month and asks me to pay her lawyer. But she hasn't brought me any work so far. She does beautiful embroidery, but for us she has stitched only one tiny little flower. So I explain to her why I can't pay her lawyer and give her the phone number of Dimitra, who maybe would help her for free.

"Dimitra? A woman?"

"Yes, a woman."

"I don't want a woman, I want Charis! May she burn in hell!"

"But why, Despina? Dimitra is a great lawyer."

"Last time I had a woman and she got me six years. May she burn in hell! Charis knows me since I'm a little girl."

She gave me his telephone number and I called Charis. But the person that answered didn't speak any Greek. Despina must have mixed up the numbers.

March 2012

Two weeks before Easter, Despina calls me at home. She orders red fabric with flowers for underwear.

"Despina, next Tuesday we'll have our Easter party and I'll bring only orange juice and cake . . . and Antonis."

"Who is Antonis? A priest?"

"No, a psychologist."

"A psychologist? Do they give money?"

"No, only cake."

April 2012

Despina has lost her trial; she doesn't know exactly how much longer she has to stay. I'm trying to lure her into doing some needlework. She doesn't seem impressed. She likes the little black horse I cut out for her, but decides to keep it plain, no princess riding on it, no wagon, no flowers. Efthimia bets against Despina ever finishing the horse.

Nobody believes Sula anymore. But it's fun to listen to her stories, how she drove her truck around on Mount Athos (a place strictly forbidden for women and with access to the monasteries mostly by boat), distributing spaghetti to the monks, or the story about the shipwreck near Brindesi, where her truck went to the bottom of the sea, but a dolphin saved her life by carrying her to the shore on its back, great motives for her quilts. They are very imaginative but stitched in an awful manner. She says she had never used a needle before, and this is about the only thing I believe.

It's Despina again on the phone in a strange whining voice:

"I'm a poor old Christian woman and I'm in the prison of Thiva. I have 17 grandchildren and no phonecard . . ."

Last time she asked me for Onesimos' phone number (a Greek Orthodox charity for prisoners) and now she had mixed up the numbers again.

Onesimos told her to apply to the Social Department, where she didn't have any luck either. Maybe there is a chance she is going to stitch that horse now.

May 2012

Natasha calls in a broken voice. She wants to talk to me, but not on the phone. We meet in a little tavern on the beach. She wears huge sunglasses and there is a big bag in her car. She doesn't want to go back home. I notice some bad bruises on her face. "Andrei. Fortunately people can't see my back." We try to eat.

Tears are running down behind the sunglasses. She had been sewing far into the night, but hadn't been able to finish the order for the theatre and the last pieces were defective, so Andrei had cut them into pieces with those heavy scissors and somehow he must have continued to give vent to his rage on his mother. Her main concern had been not to become violent herself. Now she is here with no place to go. We finish the wine and the squid. She leaves the car near the beach so Andrei wouldn't find her.

At home I call various shelters without success. One shelter tells me they take only women beaten by their husbands. Law and order rule our life. We finally find a shelter ready to take her in, but it's only two blocks from the little apartment where she lived with Andrei until last night. She is afraid to go there, so in the end she stays with us.

Half the night she talks about crime and punishment and black magic; she is convinced that someone with supernatural powers has made her his victim. I try to follow her. When she comes to the point, her voice gets feeble and she turns to Russian. I only get a vague picture. In the end we decide to go to sleep. I must confess, the dogs sleeping next to my bed made me feel more comfortable.

I try to digest this black magic theory and remember encounters with Natasha: jogging together in the park of the mental institution, where she had to stay for six months after her release from prison, and the day we went for a swim after her release from the mental institution. Natasha was getting out of the water and I feel something like a heavy blow on my whole body, while lying on the beach chair and talking on my cell phone. All our clothes and things are floating at a distance. The only thing left is the cell phone in my hand. In all these years I had never experienced something similar on a Greek beach. I am lying in the middle of a circle of strangely intermingled umbrellas and chairs. Outside the circle life goes on as if nothing ever happened. A lifeguard comes running and asks if anybody is hurt. Everybody seems fine, just a little perplexed. A mother with a little child on her arm is shouting: "I will denounce you! I want my money back! Where is my bag? You are liable for damages!" Here we are again, law and order . . . We help her collect her things from the water together with ours.

I'm too tired to decide what to think about all this and try to get some sleep. In the morning Natasha is happy when we find an adaptor that fits her cell phone among my old stuff.

She has a meeting with the priest I met at her daughter's commemorations. In the evening she calls me. She found a little apartment. The priest paid the deposit, and her Bulgarian friend brought her some blankets.

The next day she buys a newspaper and visits people to look for a job. No luck so far. She also sees Antonis at the office and talks to somebody from Epanodos. Some Buddhist friends from Austria bring a bed, some chairs, and a hot plate. So now there are two psychologists and priests from various religions looking after Natasha. She doesn't seem confused at all; she is grateful to all of them. "When I was released, I felt like I had reached zero. When I called you last week, I was way under zero. Now I'm climbing up steadily."

Dimitra, the lawyer, offered to arrange things with Andrei. Natasha just wanted Andrei to know that she was fine, so he wouldn't start a general alert for a "dangerous maniac" as she put it. Andrei seems to continue the tailor's shop without Natasha. He would like to have her back but doesn't insist. Natasha says she would only work there with Andrei's girlfriend present. She is afraid to be left alone with him.

Natasha calls me on the phone. She had a "wonderful" Easter at the internet café, talking to everybody in Uzbekistan. She invites me to her new apartment. It turns out to be very tiny but freshly painted and decorated with the paintings Natasha had done in prison. We have Vodka and delicious sweets made of dried sugar melon that her niece had brought from Tashkent. We talk about her plans. She would continue to work for her son but is planning to have her own line too. She shows me her sketches, school uniforms for Uzbekistan and dresses for older ladies. Becoming one herself, she says that you can't find anything in the shops. It's either very trendy for young girls or awful grandmother stuff. I tell her to keep my sewing machine but advise her against opening her own place.

June 2012

While I'm working at the zoo with the pony, Natasha calls me. She seems breathless.

"I'm sorry, but it's something serious."

I take the kid off the pony to talk to Natasha. She had gone for a swim at Loutsa and spotted a desperate puppy in the waves. But she can't get near to save it. It seems to be drowning. I inform Nadia, a zookeeper, who runs an organization for rescue dogs in Loutsa. She calls her friends there, and, in the end, they manage to get the puppy out alive. It seems to be a pit bull mix again, like the one I've got from Nadia last year. Nadia is furious. I ask Natasha to bring it to the zoo, so we can try to find it a home. But she says she is going to take it to her place, and I can take it from there.

The next day she calls. "What a smart little puppy! I named him Marat! He is so happy here!"

I call Antonis. He also thinks that I should try to convince Natasha to give me that puppy. But this seems difficult. I tell her about damaged furniture, veterinarian expenses etc. She doesn't seem to listen much.

When I arrive at Natasha's place, I find her table turned to enlarge the tiny balcony, with a cleaning bucket next to it. Marat is chewing happily on the table's leg. Natasha declares me his god mother. She tells me about the other Marat, her first love at school. The same beautiful eyes. She can't give him away. She takes him for a walk every day. "A lot of people have dogs here."

Natasha pushes the table aside and Marat hops in and gets on her lap, as if he's known her for ages.

"I gave him a bath."

"Hasn't he had enough of a bath already?"

Marat comes to greet me. He smells of orange blossoms.

Natasha puts her Marat in a bag and takes me to the car. I can't do anything but give her some advice on puppies in general.

July 2012

The corridor looks different today, neat and tidy, even flower arrangements. But the big surprise is the open door from the corridor to the garden with the apricot tree, the rabbits, and a happy hen with her chicks. There is a table set for coffee, like a picture from another world. They tell us they were expecting the ladies from the YWCA of Thiva. Our women come walking up the corridor. One by one they step on the threshold and enjoy the picture. Nobody dares to step outside, not even me.

After our visit, loading bags full of dolls into the car at the second gate a young woman in a fancy black dress comes running pulling a huge suitcase and holding two 20 Euro notes in the other hand. "Are you all released?" We explain. She has to catch the 5 o'clock bus to Piraeus to be on time for the ship to Corfu. So we load her suitcase in the trunk and squeeze ourselves into the car. We start calculating, wondering if the 40 Euros, she got from the Social Department, would be enough to get to Corfu, especially if she couldn't catch the last boat, and decide to give her ten more. At the external gate they check her name. Anna Liakopoulou. I take a good look at her, so this is the little Anna, I knew from Ano Liosia, the Roma settlement, where I was working for "Save the Children" long time ago. She had been one of the few kids that lived in a real house, a little princess, her grandfather being the "Baro". I remember, they even had a doorbell and a wireless telephone. Anna remembers our caravan and everything. She tells me that it had been Chrisovalanta who stole my sewing machine. Waiting for the bus, I admire Anna's tattoos. "Is Costas your husband?"—"No, my son. My husband's name is Dimitris." She pulls down her shirt and shows me proudly his name, decorated with a heart, flowers and a flying pigeon. I hope, this Dimitris will wait for her at least on Corfu.

On our next visit Theoni comes late, her eyes on some of the gypsy women who are fighting over the clothes we brought. She calls Kristina an ignorant gypsy. Now Sula calls them both ignorant Albanians. Theoni leaves without a word. A few minutes before five, when most of the women have left, she appears again and shows us a bag she had made, carefully stitched with a cat, a mermaid, and lots of stars. After we admire her bag sufficiently, she starts telling us her opinion about the whole program. It can't continue like this, we should be stricter, organize it better, and sell more. She asks for more productive lessons and better team spirit. We discuss team spirit, mentioning that hiding one's work from others, so they can't copy it, is not "team spirit." But we promise we'll do our best to sell her beautiful bag.

Ruska had changed her useless scissors for one of ours. So at the control of the inner gate, we didn't show four black little round scissors, as when we came in, but three black and one pink held together with little pieces of wire, yarn and a yellow ribbon—a great piece of art. The employee checking us seemed amused, she didn't ask questions.

It's the last time before the summer holidays so we bring two musicians again who play mostly songs from the islands and Rebetika. Our volunteers start dancing and the women join one after the other. They open some space for Iris, who gives a great show and is applauded by everyone. Sula stays seated, she whispers in my ear: "Look at her, she has killed her husband and look how she dances!" I tell her that you can dance whether or not you've killed your husband. She's not convinced.

It's a great party; our Albanians, Bulgarians and Rumanians have no problem with Greek dances, not even Olena from the Ukraine. Judid from Hungary doesn't join in, but it's mainly because of her feet.

Sofia has occupied the teacher's desk and orders others to bring her refreshments. She enjoys watching and picks the songs for the musicians to play, mostly forbidden Rebetica. She insists on one song our musicians don't know. So they ask her to teach them. She tells them rhyme by rhyme and they sing it enthusiastically after her.

September 2012

Our first visit after the summer holidays.

There seems to be a wind of change for the worse. The search at the entrance takes much longer than usual. New faces at the control. Among other things we carry a bag with cotton, as we have before, to stuff the dolls. There is a long discussion about cotton. In the end they let us take it in.

Efthimia distributes the cotton in smaller bags for everyone. Some of our women had to leave early but come back without their cotton and tell us the warden had asked them to hand it over. I was accompanying them to the chief warden's office when we met a group of prison personnel with one of the new faces following at a distance, distrustfully.

"Since when is it allowed for the inmates to take cotton with them?"

"Since 2001."

"We have a problem here, a very big problem."

"But you always scan the cotton."

In a loud voice, so the new face can hear: "That's not the point. We thought, you use it during your lesson. Don't you understand, there is no way inmates can keep cotton in their wing."

"I have not been informed of this. I'm sorry if I caused trouble. From now on we will stuff the dolls with little pieces of fabric."

All together we go to the classroom, where the personnel collects the cotton to the last piece. They make a list of who else might have left with a bag of cotton and inform the respective wing by walkie-talkie to collect it. They find an empty thread bobbin in the waste basket and tell me, never to leave empty bobbins. They want to see all six bobbins we have brought in when we leave, empty or not.

When they are gone, Theoni starts shouting:

"We won't stand this. They can't take away our rights. We make dolls and we need cotton. We'll write a complaint to the Ministry of Justice, and we will all sign. Whoever doesn't will be expelled from the group." Theoni has never made a single doll.

"Theoni, there are more important things to complain about. We can stuff our dolls with pieces of soft fabric."

She gives me one of those looks. "You represent our group, and you have to tell those idiots (she uses another word) your opinion!"

"If I acted like that on every occasion, this group wouldn't exist."

"Mrs. Eva, you are a coward!"

She continues until she has no more breath left. We sort out the soft cloth and cut it into tiny pieces.

On my next visit I try to show them a rolling technique to make dolls without stuffing. As our volunteers had to write their examinations, I am alone and not quite in control of everything. At a certain moment I can't find my glasses and tell them so. Iris takes them out of her bag, she hadn't noticed they were mine in the middle of all those pieces of cloth. They had all tried them on, but they didn't fit anybody, they told me. Then Efthimia takes my spectacle case out her bag with a smile. They are not excited about my new technique. "Don't worry," Kristina tells me, "We still have a lot of cotton."

December 2012

Another Christmas bazaar at Mairivi's. Natasha comes by with a grown up and very excited Marat. I try to make him calm down in the yard while Natasha talks to people inside. When she comes out, she tells me that Maritsa had visited her last month. She had finally moved to her little town and was in Athens for a few days. Natasha had offered for Maritsa to stay at her place, a bigger one now because of Marat. But Maritsa was afraid of the dog. I can imagine.

July 2013

Soika has managed to be accepted in Elena's inner circle and feels obliged to join Elena in her permanent complaints. Up to now she has been mostly timid but friendly.

Soika: "We don't have cloth to make dresses for our dolls. We can't use the rags you brought us."

"Let them stay naked; they will love it with this heat."

Soika smiles, Elena looks at her sharply. I make a note on my list: glittering cloth for Elena & Co.

The group has issues with Elena. Her wool trade with the whole wing had caused the prison personnel to be stricter about the quantities of wool we are allowed to bring in. Maybe this is why Elena is building her circle with women like Soika and Sonia. Sonia used to be her interpreter, but Elena is learning fast, her complaints are in an almost perfect Greek now.

Iris was her first interpreter before Sonia. Hungarian and Bulgarian, they both learned Russian at school. Iris was the one to bring Elena to the group, but soon began to avoid her; she didn't like Elena's greedy ways. She became friends with Keti and they founded the angel corporation. They produced hundreds of tiny angels for Christmas every year, always trying to hide them from the others, so they wouldn't copy them. But Elena had managed to get a glimpse and is making the same angels just with a fiercer look in their eyes.

When Iris is finally released, Keti looks for a new partner for her angels production. Violeta accepts the deal. I'm curious about how they will look, now that they will have Albanian blood, instead of Hungarian.

Theoni comes in shouting: "I've taken two Lexatonil, TWO of them! Look at me, I'm still shaking!" Sweat is running down her face. She hadn't been at the last group meeting with Antonis and wants to know exactly what they have been saying about her. "EVERY WORD!" But she wouldn't even listen to anybody. "I don't belong here! I'm a lady! What is it with you all?" She goes on and on.

Sofia: "What are you babbling about murderers?"

"Who said 'murder' (φόνος)? I said 'envy' (φθόνος). But you are all illiterate, nobody understands Greek."

She insists she knows what they have been talking about.

Stella: "We were talking about the wool and that Eva has to make an application now for every single ball."

Kristina shouting angrily at Theoni: ". . . and you told them that they were trading wool and now Eva can't get anything in anymore, no wool, no cotton, no beads . . ."

Now I'm practicing this choreography again where you try to stay on a straight line between people shouting at each other. The trick is to get them interested in something else really fast. I show them where Bruno the camel bit me when I entered his enclosure in the zoo to take a photo of his newborn daughter. It works. We even cut out some camels.

Theoni is the last to leave. She says she is sorry, then she tells us that she had problems with her bowels in the morning, but the warden wouldn't let her in from the yard to go to the toilet, so she had to walk all the way back in her soiled clothes. No wonder the Lexatonil didn't work.

September 2013

Sofia calls me on the phone and asks me to call her mother. She wants to find out if she is still angry with her, or if there is any chance she would let her stay with her for five days on parole. If her mother doesn't sign the paper, Sofia can't get out. She would call me back in ten minutes. So I call Stella. She wouldn't stop telling me ugly stories about her daughter, about her travelling around as an "artist", her illegitimate son, who Stella had brought up, her "agent", her "gypsy husband" and her behavior when she is on parole. I had visited them last Christmas, when Sofia was out and they had seemed happy. I tell her so and ask her who is going to sign now for Sofia to come out. Stella doesn't promise me anything, but she asks about Sofia's health. When Sofia calls back, I tell her the last part of our conversation.

October 2013

Sofia is in a bad mood. She doesn't want to talk about her days on parole. She wants the piece of red felt I brought for Olena. Olena ordered it last time because she wants to make a very special Santa Claus. When Sofia doesn't wear her teeth, it means she is really angry and you better stay out of her way. Olena agrees to cut the felt in half and gives Sofia a piece. Now Stella remembers that she needs red felt to decorate her tobacco bags with lips. No way to ask Sofia, so Olena gives another piece of hers to Stella. She looks sadly at what is left. It's going to be a tiny Santa.

Now everybody has their bag, with the things they ordered last time. I'm left with only Nikolitsa's bag. She is in hospital. Kristina looks at the bag thoughtfully and asks what is inside.

"It's cotton perlé, I'll keep the bag and give it to Nikolitsa when she is back." Cotton perlé is expensive and I can't get it in my neighborhood. I squeeze the bag under my desk. Irini is trying to get my attention, so Kristina can get the bag. I tell Kristina to stop this, without looking in her direction. Kristina finds this very funny. Somebody from the Social Department calls me outside to talk. Before I go, I place the bag in the center, so everybody can see it. When I come back, it is gone. Now Kristina is angry: "Nobody is going to leave! WHO HAS THE BAG?" Froso in a menacing voice: "Me, do you have a problem with that?" I explain to Froso about the cotton perlé and she hands it over to me.

After all this fuss, a friend gives me a big heavy bag, full of cotton perlé somebody didn't need any more. So for the next visit I prepare little bundles of ten for everyone. Fatmira is new. She leaves her cotton perlé on the table, while everybody else had hidden it in their pockets. Zvedsda didn't want to miss the chance, but Fatmira was quicker with her fingernails. Blood is running from the back of Zvedsda's hand. Sofia gets nervous when she sees blood and newcomers get on her nerves anyway, so she calls Fatmira and everybody else names. She tells me to take care of the three dolls she brought. "I don't want them to get harmed!" They are huge, carefully dressed in a fancy old-fashioned way. I make them sit down on a desk with their backs to the wall and they follow the whole scene with astonished eyes. I explain to them what is going on, talking to them as if they were the ladies of the YWCA. They are speechless. In the end the one in the purple dress and the flowers on her hat tells us that we should take Zvedsda to the infirmary immediately, so we do.

November 2013

Chrisa, the "needle eater", found a way to join us again. She's not in our group because of her habit of swallowing needles (among other things). Whenever she appears, we hide everything in our pockets. Now Chrisa searches the table for something interesting. Not spotting anything, she sits motionless with a blank look in her eyes. Her face gets even paler, and she begins to breathe with a strange noise. As I have only Andreas with me, I ask him to take her to the infirmary. After a while we hear Chrisa's triumphant laughter from the other end of the corridor. Andreas comes back alone. We don't discuss it.

January 2014

Keti had an appointment at the infirmary too. She comes back when we are collecting our things. She seems to be waiting for the rest to leave so she can speak to me. But Sula seems to have the same thing in mind and won't go. Glances are cast at each other, at me, at the ceiling . . . after a while Sula decides to start talking. It's the gypsies again. She says it's a good thing they are all together in E wing. But in E they have only Greek gypsies. "The others are everywhere, even in our group. It's against the Human Rights to put defenseless Greek women together with those wild animals in the same room." Eftichia, today's volunteer promises to look it up in the Human Rights, but she believes it will be hard to find such a paragraph. I agree that it's not always easy to live with people from a different background, but that I find it interesting to come to know other cultures. Easy for me to say with just two hours a week here.

Keti is getting nervous. There is not much time left for her to talk to me face to face. Sula must know exactly what's going on. Eftichia knows too and tries to make Sula leave with her, but we underestimated her stubbornness. Keti finally starts to talk, first about irrelevant subjects. Then she begins to cry. Now Sula gets really interested. Keti shows me a piece of paper they had given her at the infirmary. She'll have to order the medicine and pay for it herself. She complains about the women smoking in the dormitory. It's getting cold now and the windows are closed most of the time. She says that she's going to die. Then she talks about her daughter, who has been without electricity for three months now, because she can't pay the bills. She is desperate that she can't help her. Sula follows our conversation with huge eyes.

We take our bags and leave. All along the corridor I listen to whispers to one ear or the other or both and try to make sense with my answers.

Getting near the check point, Keti gives up and continues for her wing.

June 2014

"I'm going to roast him (or her) with potatoes!" I had heard this from Sofia many times when she was angry about somebody. Now Kristina tells me that Sofia had actually done that with her husband and had offered the dish to her mother-in-law. Kristina loves horror stories. I don't know and I don't want to know . . . but I remember Dionisia from Mani who used to tell everybody proudly how she had buried her husband in the backyard and planted onions on top of him. She had caught him with her daughter and killed him.

We often talk about husbands in general. Kristina usually didn't talk very respectfully about her husband. But now that he is in the hospital (of another prison) she is concerned about his health. "What am I going to do without him?" She can't call him directly. It's complicated to get his news and she is constantly out of units on her phone card.

July 2014

I call Natasha.

"Natasha, do you have time for a swim?"

"PLENTY of time, but swimming is not possible."

Natasha is at the Dromokaitio (mental institution) for at least two months.

"And what about Marat?"

Andrei had left him with a friend, but he can't keep the dog any longer. Marat is getting aggressive. I consider taking him, but it's not easy with my own dogs, especially with Marat's temper. I make some calls but without success.

The next day I bring some Tiramisu—Natasha's favorite sweet—to Dromokaitio, as I used to do a couple of years ago when she was in Dafni. Things are much more relaxed at Dromokaitio, no need to show my ID or sign papers to take Natasha for a walk. She is free to go anywhere in the huge park with its big trees and romantic old buildings. Cicadas are singing everywhere, hardly any security.

Natasha tells me her story. Andrei had informed the authorities that he was concerned about his mother because she wouldn't take her medication regularly. The first day was more difficult. During the night she was chained to her bed. Natasha says the important thing is to always be polite to keepers to avoid injections. The keeper even shared his breakfast with her, because she wasn't on the list yet to have her own.

Vivaldi. It's Valentina's ring tone. They allow cell phones here.

"Oh, I'm sorry, but I'm not in Athens. I've found a job elsewhere. I'll be back in two months. I'll call you."

On the next visit Natasha seemed to have made friends with everyone. She takes me to her room and shows me the Acropolis with a gorgeous sunset she had painted on the wall next to her bed to cover a stain.

A young girl sleeps in the second bed. She wakes up and asks me if I were her mother. "Not exactly," I answer, and she continues to sleep.

August 2014

I meet Natasha at the entrance holding Marat on the leash. We walk the whole park, meeting other dogs, strays who seem to feel quite at home here but accept Marat.

Unfortunately Marat can't stay here for long. He had started chewing things up and some people were afraid of him even when he was chained to the car. Andrei decided to take him home and seriously start training him with the help of a professional.

It's Anka's birthday and Natasha spends all the money she has left on candles to burn in her daughter's memory. I have difficulties finding the right words. Natasha says: "Children don't die, they just don't grow older." This year she is not allowed to go to visit her grave. She usually goes with friends to clean its marble, talk to her daughter, and leave flowers and a cigarette for her to smoke.

Natasha is ready for the transfer to the courthouse, where they will decide about what is going to happen to her. In the evening I get her on the phone (no cell phones allowed on transfer). She sounds exhausted and doesn't really know what they have decided.

February 2015

Natasha is still there. Papers. Public shelters cannot accept her because she has no insurance. Finally they seem to have found a solution. She is not allowed to drive anymore, so Andrei keeps the car. I help her move to her new home. Two big bags, one filled with clothes, the other with painting material. She likes it there. Later we bring the sewing machine and other things. On her birthday they tell her that she can bring Marat to live in the garden behind the shelter. Andrei seems relieved and Natasha feels blessed. She tells me that Marat is behaving much better now.

March 2015

I never thought I would hear from Mirka again. She was one of the first in our group when we began the program in Korydallos. Mirka had "only" eight months left in custody. The dolls she had made were unique, mostly little brides in very fancy dresses and with frightened looks on their faces.

So Mirka calls me. She has no job and wants to sell me some dolls she had made so she can buy a ticket for Bulgaria. I meet her in the evening at the metro station. She gets in the car with her plastic bag.

I have a look in her bag, an impressive company of brides and one little bride groom.

"Mirka, there is only one man, whom are they all going to marry?"

"Oh, they are so beautiful, they will find grooms."

We count them and tell them all how lovely they are. Mirka is wearing a thin dress and is in no hurry to get out in the cold wind. She tells me her story. Now her Greek is much better, and the story makes more sense. Maybe the main reason she wanted to see me was to prove her innocence to me.

She starts with her grandson, who is going to get engaged. I remember him from the TV news, where they showed him as a little boy sleeping in a cardboard box at the entrance of the women's prison. They wouldn't let him see his grandmother nor his father or his uncle, who were in the prison on the other side of the road. He had escaped from the orphanage they had put him in, and had been living for a while alone in their old apartment, but it didn't have electricity or running water anymore.

Mirka tells me it all started with that Gypsy girl, the daughter of a neighbor in her hometown in Bulgaria. Her mother had sent her to Greece to find work and Mirka had let her stay with them. This girl seems to have fallen in love with one of Mirka's sons, who was engaged to a Bulgarian girl and wouldn't listen to the Gypsy. So she hid some drugs in Mirka's home, went to the police and told them that she escaped from this terrible place, where they had locked her up, given her drugs and forced her to receive men by the dozens. She gave them the address and disappeared.

When the police arrived, they found only one of the sons. They made a mess of everything, found the drugs and hit the son. The other son was warned at the kiosk not to go home. But he wanted to help his brother, so they hit him too. They took them to the police station.

When Mirka arrived home in the morning from her shift at the hospital, she thought that burglars must have made all this mess and called the police. They tell her to wait there. She can't get her sons on the phone. After a few minutes the officers arrive and arrest her. At the police station she meets her sons.

At the inquiry the woman from the bakery near Mirka's apartment declares that she knew the young Roma girl, who was living with Mirka, and that she had been coming to the bakery every morning to buy bread, so she can't have been locked up. They told Mirka that they can go home now, just a little paperwork to finish. Waiting outside the office they see the two policemen who had beaten up Mirka's sons. They talked for a long time with the district attorney. Maybe they were frustrated that they had done all that beating for nothing. So they finally brought the sons to the hospital under custody, Mirka to prison, and the kid to an orphanage.

At the trial eight months later, they were declared not guilty. So Mirka can stitch her dolls in peace at home and prepare for her grandson's engagement.

Caits Meissner, with Zeke Caligiuri, Jevon Jackson,
Sean Thomas Dunne, Justin Rovillos Monson,
B. Batchelor, Charles Norman, Rahsaan Thomas,
Sean J. White, Louise K. Waakaa'iganj, & Spoon Jackson

On Why "Prison Writer" is a Limiting Label: What Incarcerated Writers Want the Literary Community to Understand

Through the piles of white envelopes stacked on my desk, each marked with a red correctional institution stamp, an unusual cut n' paste package called my attention. The oversized envelope—featuring a xeroxed photograph of a sky-high mohawked punk—reminded me of my younger days of snail mail, and the giddy anticipation of discovering a handmade zine or mixtape stuffed into a similarly-designed sleeve. Inside was a letter from someone named Sean Thomas Dunne, written to his newly assigned mentor in the PEN America Prison Writing Program. Listen, he warned, "I'm not really looking for some highfalutin' jack-off on a philanthropy trip to pat himself on the back because he donated his time to an aspiring unfortunate."

This is the way it would work; Sean wrote: "I send you the stories, 'cause I want you to see I have the goods. If you don't think I do, okay, fair enough. I'll continue with my own agenda [and] promote myself and my stories through punk rock publications, street performances, online venues, and open mics, and consign at stores whose proprietors meet the expectations of my ethical standards. At least that's the plan."

The letter went on to say that if, indeed, he did have the goods, this was the kind of exchange Sean was looking for—real feedback, connections to publications, an epistolary relationship of mutual sharing underscored with the word *substantive*. I turned to my colleague to share the missive aloud. And then, with Sean's permission, we staged that entire letter at PEN America's annual literary gathering in New York, the 2018 World Voices Festival, as an unconventional—funny, crass, effective—expression of our pedagogy: connective versus charitable.

Sean's written voice, a mix of raw vulnerability and barking candor, feels like both an assault and a gift, and it certainly draws attention. Sean doesn't want your pity, your charity, or your faceless feedback. And, like the rest of us who scratch words in the night, hoping someone might one day read them, he wants his work to matter. If you're going to be in touch with Sean, one thing you've got to know is that he hates, I mean really *hates*, the label "prison writer."

With the shameful problem of mass incarceration elevated in the national conversation, it is easy to make a case for the sort of pseudo-genre of "prison writing." It names a body of work that challenges public perception of "prisoner," illustrates the capacity for personal transformation, calls out the system's gross inequity, uncovers root causes of violence, and brings the failings of the criminal justice system to light. Our PEN America Prison Writing Awards program serves an additional purpose by judging writing exclusively from those currently incarcerated. I've been told that simply seeing the contest name advertised had opened whole pathways of possibility for incarcerated writers. *This is for me. I am not forgotten. I am welcome here.*

On the flip side, nearly every serious writer in prison I've encountered grows a similar disdain for, or at least frustration with, the label *prison writer*—one that slaps on a special qualifier of romanced danger and warped intrigue, invites immediate background checks, sets up expectations of particular content, and potentially turns off an entire readership. This phenomenon is expertly expressed by writer Elizabeth Hawes—also currently incarcerated—in her short nonfiction *Exposure*, a piece we commissioned for a recent event of the same name. She writes:

> *Every time a prisoner submits their writing into the public sphere they are subjecting themselves to an audience who can easily look them up and be told a prosecutor's version of a story (true or untrue) about their conviction. This is in juxtaposition to all a prisoner desires: To put the past behind them; To lay low and quietly merge back into society; To reconnect with those they love in fresh circumstances. . . . While all artists/writers question the value of their work and wonder who is viewing it and how it is being perceived, a prisoner who is an artist or who writes always carries the added burden of having to apologize for their past.*

Our program works to balance naming and celebrating excellent writing coming from the prison environment, while also envisioning an expanded horizon—one that stretches beyond the silo of "prison writing" events and one-off prison-themed lit mags. But when working to bridge inside/outside divides, we always run into the same problem. Prison, as a concept and physical institution, is doing an exquisite job of punitively suppressing expression, creativity and connection. Significant labor is needed to support even one writer in helping their work be seen in the world beyond the walls, and thus, baked into every interaction, regardless of intent, exists the power dynamic of "helper" and "the helped."

This summer we engaged in a lofty experiment. In partnership with The Poetry Project, our Prison and Justice Writing Program team at PEN America asked all the local reading series we could dig up in New York City to host the work of a currently incarcerated writer during the month of September—a nod to the Attica uprising anniversary, the inspiration for our program's founding more than 4 decades ago. In these venues, writers in and out of prison will be featured side by side for an audience that gathers in the honest pursuit of inspiration, community and good writing. Incredibly, over two dozen reading series signed on (with a handful across the country) to receive and stage a uniquely curated set from the most active writers in our network.

Writers. Who happen to be in prison.

Paradoxically, in order to move the needle, we first must call on the writers as spokespeople, taking ownership of the incarcerated label in service of sparking conversation on a larger scale. What's the call to action, we wondered, in staging this event series and in sharing this information? To raise awareness always feels like a cop out, but taking action feels largely philosophical, not to mention, difficult to resource. For the first step, I think, we begin by listening.

We invited a handful of writers featured in the BREAKOUT movement to answer three questions about the experience of being a writer in prison. Here are their answers:

What do you want us to know about the experience of being a writer in prison? Or being a writer outside of prison (the label, the stigma, the space)? Or both!

ZEKE CALIGIURI

The story of incarceration is not a singular one. Just as the story of marginalization or the dynamics of power do not follow a singular linear moral pathway throughout our history. That is why it is important to broaden the spectrum of voices being held in the great captivity business. Whether free or encaged, we all live with some kind of stigma—that's the nature of making decisions you can't take back. We have to temper our own regret with our belief that our work matters at some deeply philosophical or social level, that cannot be represented by anybody else. So, as writers, we are conscientious that a sense of self-value can only be created personally. If we are looking to be redeemed at some greater social level with our work, I'd say that is an undue expectation for our art. We only get short windows of time on this earth to be and create, wasting it because we want other people to love or like, or forgive us is a lot of pressure to put on our art.

I would also say that writing is hard, and it can be so much harder when it comes from a place where it isn't supported by anybody. There isn't always typing opportunities, and so much of the editing and revision processes are excruciating. And honestly, people who run these places don't care if you are a writer or the greatest living artist on earth—they want the facility to run as simply as it can be. Individualism is stifled. Then there is the censorship. Anything can be deemed threatening.

So, we become so protective of our art, and so much of our energy goes into protecting our ability to create. It's a whole second level of survival that we are constantly aware of; one, our own, two, our work.

JEVON JACKSON

One of the most important things to know about the imprisoned writer experience is the difficult balance we have to strike in separating our grievances and our gripes from our Art. If it is pure grievance disguised as Art, then, I believe, it is unlikely to be truly absorbed or appreciated by the reader. And our everyday lives are overwhelmed with grievance—not just the superficial grievances that are a consequence of imprisonment itself, but the earnest human rights grievances that are the catalyst for reform and revolution.

Just within the past week, I've personally experienced a week-long lock-down which was initiated with a unit shakedown (rooms tossed asunder) by 70+ rookie guards, as over 260 inmates stood idle, crammed onto a small, muddy rec. field for four hours. How do I make such an experience relatable to a middle-class father of three from the financial district of New York or to a 60-year-old retiree from a low-crime cul-de-sac of Connecticut? That is the balance. To go beyond the individual agonies to tap into the collective humanity that we all can identify with.

SEAN THOMAS DUNNE

I want you to know that I absolutely fucking hate being a "prison writer." It makes my allergies flare up just thinking about it. It's like every editor's desk at every literary journal, publishing house, annual writing contest, and school newspaper is just inundated with submissions from "prison writers," or something. And these cheezedick motherfuckers are really driving down the value on my shit. I try to decorate my envelopes in a spunky way so as to distract my recipients from the bullshit parental advisory label that the cockknocker who reads the outgoing mail stamps on there. But nothing's doing. It's come to the point where I'm certain that "STATE PRISON GENERATED MAIL" is interpreted as "THIRD RATE TRIPE FROM A PILE OF HUMAN GARBAGE." Oh, man. You gotta know how much I hate it.

Does it ever occur to me that the summary rejection with which my work is customarily received could be based upon its lack of merit rather than a discriminatory act of classist passive aggression? No. It doesn't.

Now, as pertains to the second part of your question about being a writer outside of prison, I will admit to this much: I've spent 1/4th of my life in prison, it's true. But what the fuck was I doing the rest of the time? If I was so worried about the horrid connotation of being a prison writer then I shouldnt've spent the other 3/4th's shooting up and masturbating in a bush.

JUSTIN ROVILLOS MONSON

Seeking out thoughtful, honest feedback on my work has often felt impossible, let alone submitting anything for publication. This lack of accessibility to a viable literary community has made me feel perpetually alone, like it's all pointless. On the other hand, if you put in the work, you can have some successes. The danger comes, I think, when you feed into the idea of being a "prison writer." I've heard quite a few times of the romanticized notion of the poet, working with fire and fury, alone at their desk. Though probably unconscious, I think this notion is often attributed to the poet in prison, by both the poet and the outside literary community. This image isn't necessarily a bad thing—it can be what drives a poet to write and what generates a hunger for their work—but I think it can also lead to false ideas of what it means to grow and thrive as an artist.

Of course there are exceptions, but I really believe that writers—like any other human beings—need community more than they do a sense of personal legend. The writer in prison faces a paradoxical dilemma, one of working against both carceral isolation, and romantic arrogance; of both attempting to transcend the "prison writer" label, and taking advantage of the literary community's hunger for marginalized voices.

B. BATCHELOR

I am lucky enough to be part of an amazing writing community with the Stillwater Writers Collective (a large group of inmate writers who support each other through writing) and the Minnesota Prison Writing Workshop. I think that I am much more fortunate than many incarcerated writers around the country who are not afforded this opportunity. From the very beginning I have been nurtured and supported and given the creative space to spill myself on the page.

It is tough dealing with the internal issues of the prison environment (the noise, the constant hassle, the inherent negativity, etc.), and in the past we have not been given much of a chance in the publishing community, whether with literary journals or independent/major publishers. The landscape for us has completely changed. I feel that the "inside" and "outside" writing communities have blurred the stigmatized lines and there is growing support to have our voices heard.

CHARLES NORMAN

Prison officials in Tallahassee (headquarters) frequently republish my work on their websites and even Facebook. Many guards tell me they enjoy my writings, and learn from them. Others, who have the chain-gang mentality that all prisoners are scum, subhumans who don't know their places, who need to be taught lessons, are the ones I avoid, since there is no room for positive dialogues with such closed, hateful (mostly ignorant) minds.

I have experienced retaliation from prison staff for my writing, and been locked up in solitary confinement for my work. A corrupt mailroom supervisor had me locked up over a poem I wrote (a PEN prizewinner), and when she brought my legal mail to my cell, she told the escorting officer, "He's a fucking poet." I won a federal retaliation lawsuit against her, and she lost her job for lying, filing false disciplinary reports, and stealing postage stamps, but that didn't give me back the time I spent in solitary.

RAHSAAN THOMAS

Being in prison allows me the time and space to focus on a writing career. I don't have to worry about lousy pay for beginning writers or crushing bills that may have forced me to pursue a career other than this one I love so much. However, without email access (which we don't have at San Quentin State Prison in California) or a full-time secretary on the outside, it's difficult to submit work to most organizations because they only accept stories sent through Submittable, which requires going online. The days of handwriting or typing up stories and mailing to a magazine editor are nearly at an end. Unless the prison system makes some changes, writers who are incarcerated may soon be heard from very seldom.

What are your hopes for how your work is received by literary community on the outside?

SEAN J. WHITE

Bright lights, big city. I aspire to fame inasmuch as most people do. Who in their life has not entertained a daydream of being a high-profile artist?

I want to someday do an interview on *Fresh Air,* and be featured on a segment of the *PBS Newshour* Such things, however, do not occur without people. That is, if no one hears or sees my work, the work will remain confined to the limits of my existence. Of course, I had better put together damn good work if I want recognition.

I want notoriety and acclaim within the literary community because I have this dream that if my work becomes significant enough it will help me get out of prison—be it commutation, or parole, or whatever. Is that realistic, or does it fall within the theme of David Hammons' "Higher Goals" sculpture? At the same time, anything I achieve affects the collective. With a spotlight, prison and the issues of mass incarceration appear in the background. Any level of fame I gain also gives me a platform to highlight prison issues.

JEVON JACKSON

My hopes for how my work is received by the literary community outside is that it connects simply to the point where it is not passively embraced as work from an "imprisoned writer," but from a writer who writes about his pain, his imprisonment, his joy, his relationships, his life. My hope is also that the literary community out there can see themselves in some aspect of my shared experience.

CHARLES NORMAN

I really have no expectations. My hopes are that I can continue to "bear witness" and express the truth about my experiences, communicating those truths to those "out there," who would not otherwise conceive of the realities we live through. When a prison guard read one of my poems, she said, shivering, "It gave me goosebumps, it made me cry," that may have been the highest praise I'd received. Months later she was brutally murdered by another prisoner, which haunts me to this day, recalling conversations we had about my writings, and the loss.

B. BATCHELOR

I hope my work is received the same way that they would receive their peers in the literary community. Not as something less than or something marginalized, but as something equal, or something striving to be equal. We are all artists; the only difference is our space and circumstances, but that is external. All writers share a similar internal landscape that we visit, maybe fall asleep under a weeping willow, muse in a clover field, breath vitality from the breeze that loves us enough to caress our face with cool hand. All I ask from the outside literary community is to read and listen to my/our work with complete mindfulness and openness. You never know when we will meet each other on that same internal landscape.

JUSTIN ROVILLOS MONSON

I hope that readers can digest my work with intent and appreciate my writing without falling victim to the tendency to tokenize or romanticize the "real prison experience." If there's any beauty in the language I put into my work, I hope that the focus can be placed on that beauty, rather than some stereotypical benchmark of "rawness" or "realness." The people in my work, including myself, are real human beings who endure real consequences for their actions; I hope readers will focus on that.

LOUISE K WAAKAA'IGAN (AKA KAROL HOUSE)

It is my hope that the literary community will see me as a woman, a writer, a voice, not as a prisoner holding a past.

SPOON JACKSON

Hope can be a strange word at times for hope, especially for lifer prisoners in California, is often hopeless. My hope is that the literary community know they have fellow writers incarcerated who would welcome their exchange with letters and critique—I mean there is so much, so many depths an incarcerated writer can take the outside literary community to enhance their writing, and it can be a two-way street. There are such intense and to-the-bone experiences that can be shared with outside writing communities, and art and writing suffers without fellowship.

In what ways can you envision a lasting connection with literary community outside the walls? From your perspective, what can we do to be more inclusive, or to help shift the narrative?

JUSTIN ROVILLOS MONSON

The most exciting part of receiving the Writing for Justice Fellowship from PEN America was being the possibility of being a part of—and less apart from—the literary community. I sincerely hope, as time goes on, I can further feel not only that I belong, but that I am making meaningful contributions of work to that community and tradition, beyond being recognized and appreciated mostly—or solely—for my contributions as a "prison writer." I think, if you want to change the narrative surrounding writers in prison, programs and organizational mechanisms and practices need to continue to push us to write beyond prison. By that I don't mean the content shouldn't be centered in the institutions that have shaped our lives so tangibly, but that the bar should be set high enough to demand quality work over the possible tokenized inclusion of marginalized voices, and the resources made available to us should reflect that demand.

The literary community as a whole should continue to ask tough questions about its role in responsibly cultivating and giving audience to the voices of incarcerated writers. Some of these questions might be: How can we make it easier to find and submit to our platforms? What can we do to match up the work of incarcerated writers to publications that will appreciate the individual works? And what steps can we take to push incarcerated writers beyond the "prison writer" label and into the mainstream literary fray, while still honoring the stories and content that come from the prison experience?

B. BATCHELOR

Personally, I would love to be able to have access to more writers/poets on a one-on-one level, creating possible relationships with my contemporaries as if I were an MFA candidate making meaningful connections along the way. One of my favorite things to do when I receive a new poetry book is to find the acknowledgements page and read all the names the poet thanks for their friendship and partnership in creating the poems in the book.

RAHSAAN THOMAS

If possible, create a Submittable assistance program where incarcerated writers who sign up are notified of publishing opportunities and are assisted with editing and sending in their work.

LOUISE K WAAKAA'IGAN (AKA KAROL HOUSE)

There needs to be more conversation with prison staff and administration for them to see the value and importance of writing opportunities, classes, computer time, support groups. I am fortunate to have a strong supportive network within the facility here, yet I know not every writer on the inside has this.

ZEKE CALIGIURI:

The simplest way to be more inclusive of our community is to read our work. Don't necessarily segregate us from the rest of the literary landscape as a specific body with specific politics and culture. The incarcerated are just as nuanced and different from each other as artists and personalities as the spectrum that exists in free literary circles.

CHARLES NORMAN:

Encouraging those in the literary community to write letters or emails to prisoners, if nothing else, to say they enjoyed that person's work, or offer encouragement, could be meaningful to someone locked in a cell with no other human contacts. By making the prisoners' addresses available, and encouraging citizens to write them could change someone's life. I've had an email address for over 18 years, a website and blog for over 11 years [that my wife runs], and that has been life changing for me.

I've received comments from readers in 100 countries over the years. A 25-year-old single mother in South Africa wrote that she'd been reading my blogs for three years, that life was hard in her country, but if I could survive and live a positive life under my circumstances, she could, too. That makes a lot of suffering worthwhile. Give the prison writers some positive publicity, send them copies they may use for their freedom efforts.

SEAN J. WHITE

The incarcerated are famished for connection. Outside of prison people go to where the literary community congregates—readings, bookstores, workshops, et cetera. We have little of that here, and that which we do is typically brought from the outside. I feel it necessary to say that although some in prison have less than ideal intent, most have a genuine desire to have a reciprocal relationship (I use that word in the broadest sense) with those who communicate and connect with them.

Additionally, gatekeeping (in the literal and metaphorical sense) creates issues. Prison staff deny access at times to those wishing to say, run a workshop, and impose numerous restrictions on those they do let in. From the literary community, gatekeeping occurs because of the sheer volume of requests—insufficient money, insufficient time. For anything to succeed requires grassroots development. That is, if a non-incarcerated writer "adopts" one incarcerated writer into his or her circle, or a bookstore "adopts" 25 to 50 incarcerated writers, eventually the majority receive the connection they need and desire as enough people and venues participate. The problems always develop because the desire/need for connection by the incarcerated exceeds the capacity of any one person, organization, or venue.

I have three suggestions to make a more lasting connection between incarcerated writers and the literary community. First, bring more workshops and reading to jails and prisons. The poet Bruce Dethlefsen visited New Lisbon Correctional Institution several times while I resided there. Unfortunately, he is one man, and there are over a hundred prisons, correctional centers, and county jails in Wisconsin alone. Second, a regular compilation of news and notes for and about incarcerated writers.

Finally, I would suggest something akin to PEN America's mentorship program, though on a grander scale. Unfortunately, anonymity costs money. However, in a system operated by, say, a bookstore, such correspondents could pay for postage and use the address of the venue that a person might visit regularly any way. In those cases where a prisoner has access to Corrlinks (an electronic messaging service—growing more frequent in application) or something similar, a postcard could be sent with a name and email address. The likelihood of potential crimes perpetrated against a correspondent seems minimal. Writing a cross-country prisoner would diminish that further, as most blue-collar crimes involve drugs, and what drug-addled mind drives hundreds of miles to burglarize a home (Truman Capote's book offering an outlier).

SEAN THOMAS DUNNE

I hope my work will be received with the unyielding enthusiasm of a fucking Beatlemaniac at Shea Stadium in 1965. I want so many people to be screaming in ecstasy that you can't even hear what the fuck I'm saying. I want to be invited to spend the night at your house and I wanna drink your beers and smoke your bud and I want to be DJ and Master of Ceremonies all night long for the meaningful experience that we're gonna have.

I want to be written letters of love and hope precipitated not by some bourgeois charity agenda but predicated instead by the value of my personality and talent. I wanna take L.S.D. with you. I wanna ride bikes with you. I wanna Facetime with you. I wanna lend myself to care about your problems, and when shit goes sour between you and your old man I wanna be the alkaline base that uncurdles your funk. I wanna talk to you about punk rock. Fuck, man. I shoulda put that first. Aw Christ, I been thinkin' about this one a long time!

Great Heavens to Mergatroid! I wanna listen to new bands with you and cut and paste collages and write zines with you on your bedroom floor. I wanna hold your hair back when you puke, girly. Wanna buy you a corn dog, girl. You gotta check out my double kickflips and my pressure flips. Fakie pressure flips. Pressure flips for days, girl. And seahorses fuheva.

We could totally watch all the horror movies I've missed these last five years I've been upstate. Aw, man. You don't even know. This one time I sat there and watched all the Halloween's with this beautiful gothic girl named Crystal. I sat through ten hours of Michael Meyers, and don't get me wrong, I was fully into it cause I love horror movies, and plus we had just narrowly escaped the iniquitous obsession of methamphetamine possession and we ate and slept finally, and her dad came by and took us to rent movies, so we were just smoking long bud and feeling the serenity of 1980s horror creep into the synaptic knobs of our overused dopamine receptors, and just doing it grande.

But inasmuch as I had a lifetime lasting episode of joy to reflect upon and look back on in the real-life horror movie that would ultimately envelop the rest of my life, I also had a monumentally miserable experience 'cause I wanted her so bad. But Crystal just didn't feel that way about me. One by one. Halloween 1, 2, 3, 4, 5? The whole time flailing in the dichotomy of joy and abject torment as she sat there in her tiny boxer shorts on her futon, beside me. It was awful.

But maybe it won't be like that with you. Maybe this time you'll just look at me the way I always wished she had, and we'll go and put bottles of dish soap in the fountain at city hall and we'll start an acoustic punk band and we'll hang out at Tompkins Square and Battery Park and when the cold weather comes, and when the rain comes, and when the dope runs out, and when the cops come and take us away and we wake up on the holding cell floor and we have to kick, at least we won't be alone. That is what I hope to accomplish when I put my motherfucking pen to page.

Maybe it's hard for you to imagine this, but I have tears in my eyes cause no one has ever thought to ask me that question. So, I would like to yield the floor to the little blue-eyed boy inside me, staring out the window, waitin' for mom to come home at three am: the answer to your question is I just want to be your friend.

You Can't Have it All

Black and white comic with combination of collage, handwriting, and typed text, with pen sketches. Top panel contains the title, YOU CAN'T HAVE IT ALL, in white text on black background. Additional text reads: After Barbara Ras, written with/for the young women on Rikers Island, summer 2016. The text is set atop black and white squares that look like bricks.

Next panel is a sketch of a notebook; on the left page is a sketch of a school desk with plastic seat and swing-over writing surface; right side has text: YOU CAN'T HAVE IT ALL. But you can have a window, a light switched on, a door to close. YOU CAN FIND A CLEAR POOL IN THE MIND TO DIP YOUR TOES CLEAN AS A FISH. A sketch of a fish follows, and a sketch of toes holds the notebook open.

Bottom panel is a collage of sketches—a figure with long braids flying through the air; a moon risen over the Eifel Tower; a highrise apartment building; and decorations for Dia de los Muertos. Text reads: YOU CAN FLY AWAY ON DREAMS, I AM TOLD.—to Mexico or Paris or home's sweet memory, for free.

Caits Meissner, "You Can't Have It All", 2016.

You can share a table with young
women with invisible wings,
        who flap through a hot cloud of yes
        and don't even ruffle their feathers.
    You can   have   their
                    smiles   breaking across
                the day like a band of   horses
                running towards water,
and you can make a
world of poems and step in
like a snow globe, all the glitter
sticking to your body like a disco ball wetsuit.

Black and white sketch of four human figures riding Pegasus-like creatures to escape a barbed-wire fence. They are galloping on clouds. Text underneath is white on black background, with little white geometric shapes spread out like confetti. Text reads:

You can share a table with young
women with invisible wings,

who flap through a hot cloud of yes
and don't even ruffle their feathers.
You can have their
smiles breaking across
the day like a band of horses
running towards water

and you can make a
world of poems and step in
like a snow globe, all the glitter
sticking to your body like a discoball wetsuit.

Caits Meissner, "You Can't Have It All", 2016.

You can't have it all, but you have the slow broom ticking time and a poem culled from the mouth of the corner drunk like a magician's scarf.

You can have sorrow's twin sputtering in the basement of your chest and you can put your fingers on its struggling pulse and strum its strings and sing the blues.

Black and white sketches atop lined paper. On top of the image is an older woman with an apron raking, and a bunny surrounded by flowers. Layered underneath these figures is a side profile of a man with bushy eyebrows and stubbly beard, with a snake coming out of his mouth. The snake circles down the right side of the page, and the flowers sprinkle the inside of the snake-loop. The bottom of the snake loop meets a frowning scarecrow. To the left of the scarecrow, at the bottom of the page, sits a guitar player with a large-brimmed hat, instrument rested on his knee, hands clasped. Text reads:

> You can't
> have it all, but you have the slow
> > broom ticking time
> > and a poem culled
> > from the mouth of the
> > corner drunk like a
> > magician's scarf.
> You can have
> sorrow's twin
> sputtering in
> the basement of your chest
> > and you can
> > put your
> > fingers
> > on its
> struggling
> pulse
> and strum
> its strings
> and sing
> the blues.

Caits Meissner, "You Can't Have It All", 2016.

You can write your best friend to share a dream where you
entered a secret garden, or saw a statue covered in pristine snow.
You can photograph beauty with your internal eye, you can write
poems of beauty and someone might read them, and even
if they don't, YOU can understand that beauty is a choice,
and you can choose it, even when the halls are slick
and dark
as a womb.

A winking moon-face with suns on its face peers out at the reader. A notebook page transforms into a sketch of a naked femme figure with a wrap tied around their pelvis. Windows are open, walls covered with ivy. Long reed-like plants rise from a stream underneath. A feminine figure on the right with long curly hair stands holding a lotus flower, wearing a long flowing dress. At the bottom, lined paper is cut to look like clouds. Six eyes are open and looking out at the reader. At the bottom left, a person with long hair and closed eyes has a wide open third eye, with rays shooting out. Text at the top of the page reads:

> You can write your best friend to share a dream where you
> entered a secret garden, or saw a statue covered in pristine snow.
> You can photograph beauty with your internal eye, you can write
> poems of beauty and someone might read them, and even
> if they don't, YOU can understand that beauty is a choice,
> and you can choose it, even when the halls are slick
> > and dark
> > as a womb.

Caits Meissner, "You Can't Have It All", 2016.

When someone has
crushed the tiny bird
of your spirit under foot,
you can hear the bones crackle
like radio fuzz and make a new anthem.
Yes, you can choose beauty. Hold beauty.
Know beauty, even when it is so dark you
cannot see, you can know that
darkness is renewal, and feel the life
growing inside your body, the vibrating
atoms of your own good body, and the
touch of your very own skin,
that rough/smooth truth
that no one, no one
not anyone, not ever
(so long as you are
breathing, you are
beautiful) can take
from you.

A cityscape is sketched above a piece of lined paper covered in starfish. Under the page are three more starfish and a human figure curled up, smiling, looking safe and comfortable, surrounded by four more starfish. Text reads:

When someone has
crushed the tiny bird
of your spirit under foot,
you can hear the bones crackle
like radio fuzz and make a new anthem.
Yes, you can choose beauty. Hold beauty.
Know beauty, even when it is so dark you
cannot see, you can know that
darkness is renewal, and feel the life
growing inside your body, the vibrating
atoms of your own good body, and the
touch of your very own skin,
that rough/smooth truth
that no one, no one
not anyone, not ever
(so long as you are
breathing, you are
beautiful) can take
                    from you.

Caits Meissner, "You Can't Have It All", 2016.

Idra Novey

from Exit, Civilian

Civilian Exiting the Facilities

Each week my body is fist-stamped and triple-scanned before it lands again in the electoral world. My mind takes longer to leave, stays in the elevator considering the kind of crime it might be capable of. Would I have to be hungry. Could it happen over nothing. Could it happen nightly. In the shine of a car outside the prison my reflection gets wider until it splits. In one likeness the face I recognize. In the other my face.

Recent Findings

after the cells of Louise Bourgeois

I

Studies show the difference between legs and arms is in what tends to come before them: hands or feet. As the difference between teaching in a prison and the Ivy League is a question of attendance and if you can tell the weather from the wall.

II

This tiny spiral staircase in the corner appears to be moving. Some experts say it is not. They say getting a degree in prison is like this.

III

It's not uncommon, doctors concur, that while gnawing on a stone you can discuss the nature of dependent clauses with two sisters incarcerated in the same prison and gnaw a stone to stone.

IV

Recent polls note a breakdown in language when people say incarceration over generations, a hesitation and.

V

Too many enclosures make people cold, new data shows, and when it's cold it's going to be cold. As for the spider, she's feeling for an open seam between the walls.

All Ceremonies Start with Inspection

A dress pressed into a dented metal box. Bodice and satin balled for pas-
sage then a passing of body into dress and vestibule and then the picture.
After the vows, it all happens again.

                        Backward—out of the vestibule, out
of the dress, a re-balling of bodice and back to the far island where the only
bread is a photograph, hands touching in it, wedding band stuck at the
knuckle, to stare at that finger as if your eye were a mouth and could eat it.

Eighteen Hours of Daylight

A woman offers me a pamphlet called *The Miraculous and You*. We're in a city famous for its glaciers and I say no thank you. A chunk of ice calves into the water and the sound is like a bullet. Later, the same woman is in our restaurant. She offers me the same pamphlet and I wonder if this will keep happening. My mission is to convert the imprisoned, she says, you wouldn't believe how many are awaiting the Miraculous. Around us, the sound of bullets is still the sound of bullets but also the sound of where we are—ice crashing with a smack into the sea, the melt of eleven thousand years unsettling the water to a startling lazuli blue.

Riding by on a Sunday

Nothing shatters.

The day around the prison gleams like the clean face of a spoon.

To the man on the bike beside me, I say, see how it blends in, the same brick and height, disappears after a mile like any other high-rise?

Only A still sits inside, denied parole again for an assault twenty-three years ago.

And Officer M sits in the Annex until ten, stacking the women's ID's according to his ideas of beauty.

The faster we go along the river, the more the city tips into background.

The blocks become ellipses, each building possibly a prison, possibly a warehouse full of pinwheels.

I want to stop longer.

But keep pedaling.

I tell myself prisons are inevitable and inevitably awful.

Tell myself this thought is just another way of looking away.

All day the river beside us streams the silver of dream hair.

Parole

I'm going straight to a graveyard, Lena said and Janet said me too, all that grass and no one, a stone bench and some wind—no one belting breakup songs on the radio, no ricochet of shouts just for the sake of it.

In a photo of bones what you notice are the bones: the only things left after the gristle's gone and a voice. To be quiet in a prison, Janet said, is to admit that you're there.

The Lava Game

We invented a volcano so it would chase us and erase the backyard empire we called The Land. As the lava got closer, whoever was emperor had to race around the tomato plants and toss the plastic tiara we called The Crown.

Once The Crown was in the air, the rest of us got to dive for it, claw each other's faces if we had to. That the only crown in The Land got stolen every disaster seemed as natural to us as the scabbing-over of skin.

If you fell in the dandelions, that was Lava Death. You had to lie there and die a robber till the next emperor said c'mon, c'mon, everybody get up.

I cried once from too much dying in the dandelions. Limp on the ground, that stillness was enormous, acorns printing into my arms, the other voices growing distant, and it would occur to me, *we are children.*

We all died as robbers sometimes; I don't know why the emperor always lived. Just before the lava spilled, invisible and everywhere, whoever had The Crown got to describe it.

And whoever couldn't describe it, died too.

The Metaphysics of Furniture

I picture wood for the finished look of vio-
lence—the narrow and unforgiving walnut
chair nobody remembers buying or haul-
ing inside.

> The guard asks what we're reading today,
> says he'd like to get a degree, wishes he could
> get one free the way they do here.

A chair with no purpose that remains for
decades like pain in a phantom limb or the
wreck outside that was once our splendid
new swing set.

> You keep coming back, he says, what's it you
> like so much about this prison, you live
> real close?

Today one of us collapsed in the narrow
walnut chair. Our panic spattered so fast
there was no way to trap it.

> In the slowness of the elevator, I press and
> press the buttons. He says you know those
> lights have never worked.

Go, go, whispers the little boy who has built
a tent for us, has filled it with buttercups
and mittens.

Riot

Call lockdown call the lapdogs call for backup and God. Call broken pipes and flood risk what all the guards predicted. Call it overcrowding or a cloudburst the loud undoing of done time. Call the sound what it is: shouting and alive.

The Ex-Cárcel of Valparaíso

And so it was agreed the empty prison would be reopened for festivals, that a pony would be tethered to a table and children would pay for rides along the walls.

The same hour, off in the pampas, a llama was found trotting among the horses and an astrologer in Santiago saw the cosmic future in the crushed bristles of a toothbrush.

At the very same minute at the prison a man began to tune his cello in one of the emptied cells and someone else limped past with timpani drums and children started to follow, children, somebody said, who would in time build a prison of their own, and maybe empty it, maybe fill it again—

The Last Beep and Door

I hold my breath, step into the wet mouth of November wind, arrive at the river moving up and down in its rocky bed, the new art museum that blinks its watery eye. I line up with the others waiting for the M23 bus, which stops for us and we enter it, have the pleasure of choosing whether to sit or stand, which tan and blue-rimmed seat, which window and moving view.

And the ride begins, gradual as a carousel. And all of us inside take on that carousel stillness, as if forty invisible horses were beneath us, and lifting.

Poetry

—

Buzz Alexander

Charlie Mack's Glove

Most dear to me are the things I cannot touch
or speak,
        the fragile framework of the butterfly wing,
the lightly freckled blue of the robin's egg
in the nest of twigs on the wall lamp
that lights my back porch, the brown body
of the sparrow spitting water off its back
a few steps away, the wind of the forest path
around the enormous roots of a fallen tree,
the wind of the snake through old patterns
of fallen leaves, old autumn grass and dying moss,
the swift seconds when the thick oak
comes with stunning force to the ground,
the unusual softness in our eyes
the delicate edge in our voices
the leanings of our limbs
as we talk at the kitchen counter,
and the way the door closes when you go,
the touch of your tear as you already mourn
those taking their last leave,
I cannot touch or speak the final bloody tips
of the cluster of razor wire
or the glove of Charlie Mack
still clutching the prison fence
where he died
or the site
where murdered children are sealed
in the psyche of Dick Cheney
and in the psyche of the American voter.

Buzz Alexander

The Shape of the Tear

hard gray stone, diamond, boiling edge,
ancient formation, glacial agony,
volcanic fire, racing blood, anger
beyond words, layer on layer,
it shapes itself where it wishes,
in my chest, upper center,
in my throat, my brain, my kidney,
my bowel, beneath my left kneecap,
a new lump in my hand,
tear in my eye, tear in my ear,
in my breath,
in the beating of my heart,
another another again and again
it shapes itself
in the form of unfairness, of chance,
of childhoods that led to these places,
in the form of the brutality of a system
that punishes
carelessly,
it takes the contours of numbness,
pulses like the tightened heart
is pocked with cavities once filled by friends,
has lonely eyes beneath deep pools,
looks like a barren womb,
shapes itself perfectly,
like every tear, bulbous,
tapering to a tip,
the tattooed image on a convict's eye,
hardened, a lump, not liquid, permanent scar.

Raquel Almazan

Here to be Seen: A Choreopoem

I'M HERE TO BE SEEN

THE VOICE/CHARACTER OF STRONG WOMAN: Can be Afro-Dominican and or identify as Latinx- multi-racial.

CHORUS OF WOMEN: THE ONES WHO CAME BEFORE: Voices - chorus of women can speak underlined words, phrases with strong woman, continue repeating certain words throughout the piece.

STRONG WOMAN

I'm here to be seen
Here to be seen for this interview
For a job that I'm overqualified for
Yes, I'm Denise Jefferson
The one you called in after reviewing my resume
That sheet of paper you're holding in your
Hand
I look great on paper don't I?
I can do the administrative assistant position
In my sleep
Why is your head turning sideways?
Do I not look like Denise Jefferson? Like myself?
You're looking at my hair aren't you?
It's cute right? Just had my braids done, and my
Big hair stands out at the end
You can look down at my resume again
On paper I have high grades-
HIGH IQ
Went to all Catholic schools
An honor student
You're looking at me a certain way—
Do I look a certain way to you?
Jefferson
Should I be wearing a white wig instead?
With a quill in my hand to draw up a constitution that
Doesn't serve me

Women we are America
You can see my dress is work readiness
A society that dresses a certain way
My culture's way is not good enough?
My hair- a certain way
A better me? Hair is what? A better me! Let me bring my full self and
     my full hair to the job. I get the hair I want
You get what you asked for
Are you examining my attitude and behavior?
You don't know our culture

Yet I'm about to conform so I can fit into yours
In hopes of getting this position
To position myself outside your paradigm
If I let the voices that hold me back
Tell me
"You are the enemy - trouble maker - going against the norm"
I'd start to believe that I'm not capable,
Not represented
The way they got black and brown people subconsciously
NOT attempting the largeness of life
Getting their minds on fashion
Materialistic desires on advertisements
Pulling them away from their roots
We don't think like white America
We have our own cultures
And our kids have their own culture
Society is built one way
For us to fit into that one way
It's not inclusive of us

Yes I'm here to be seen—
Just checked this box off right here
I just openly disclosed my past record of being incarcerated——I was
     honest on this application.
You honestly going to tell me that you will
See me
For this position?
You could ban the box
See me
I'm here to be seen
Coming out of incarceration

You see the world differently
Re-habilitation
But in prison- you have time- to heal yourself
Away from the world
Inside
You see what the world is
A world of systems that we don't even know we're in
We fight back with
Open eyes
Small but powerful groups- addressing issues—
Grass root rehab

On street dealing,
You're not thinking of the world
Survival
Sell drugs for $
Crack got dropped off -
In urban areas - where it was dirt cheap,
$3 $5
Chemicals in there to stop the thought process
All the social movements stopped
Black progress stopped!
People of color were at a standstill
Children were on crack
The dealers were on crack
Even the elders were on crack
It knocked out entire families
With a community dealing with the trauma of Slavery,
Abuse
Rape
You could crack it all away-
Weed, Marijuana, Yerba Buena
Was connected to consciousness
Now they got K-2 chemicals in our herbs
Self medicate?

Inside I got the time to think about equal rights
A spiritual solitary confinement
Inside there are
Beatings- rape- self regret-
Taking women's
Dignity

At night alone- you got nothing but time
Minorities we are changing the world
Systems are designed for 95% of us to
NOT apply for these Jobs
Those opportunities - we can't afford it - afford retreats?
MY ASS
Afford to go back to school
Not a dime for education -
I re-designed my life through my own research

When I write my address on this application I can't ignore
Segregation of economy - a racial segregation
Riding the bus and train
We can't afford to live here
Get to the good schools

How are those colored kids, doing better than white kids?
Close the charter schools!
Don't want to pay for our books.
They trying to tell the
Mexican, Colombian, Dominican
Kids- to pick up a trade,
Learn plumbing or repair carburetors,
They have made the
GED even harder to pass, like it's impossible to pass now
They're trying to make it impossible to get an education
I use to teach GED prep classes,
But now they added all this
Comprehensive reasoning?

John has a boat that he is transporting animals on,
A small boat
That can only hold a few animals.
If he has a goat, a chicken, a turtle, a panda, a bird,
A chimpanzee, a squirrel, a pig, a skunk and a cat:
How many trips across the river does John need to take in order to
        get them all across?
SHIT like that!
Who can comprehend that?

I'M HERE TO BE SEEN
If you take a look at my fluency skills—
Yes I speak Spanish

Suarez is my maiden name
I could be Cuban, Dominican, Puerto Rican
We all the same to you?
Right now English-Spanish is dominating
We're the people who speak both of those languages
If all of us in the 5 boroughs came together
Minorities
We will outweigh those with privilege
Minorities we are changing the world
We're not a color
We're a people
Same blood in our veins.

In between the lines - the lines that don't exist on my Resume
What you don't see
Is me
Me getting beat by my cop husband,
I gotta create my own Domestic Violence Act
I gotta create forgiveness?
I gotta create protection
For myself, my children, the future
Understanding every moment that keeps me alive—
That lead me to—
Me calling 911

Me calling for help
And having cops tell me, "I gotta work it out"
Man is the king of his castle.
Women were the bad ones- elders say if he don't smack you around-
    bash your head in, he don't love you
Women have nothing?
Men come from us though
Our passages that give life

                        Chorus of women start to hum.

But if I listen to another voice . . .

CHORUS: I'm here to be seen.

STRONG WOMAN: The voices of the ones that came before, long
before . . .

CHORUS: I'm here to be seen.

STRONG WOMAN:

> Las mujeres que me cargan
> Las mujeres unidas
> Las mujeres que cantan y me levantan

CHORUS: I'm here to be seen.

STRONG WOMAN:

> The ones that came before, the women of my
> Lineage, they see me
> Then I see myself,
> And then I see you,
>
> (can be with chorus)
>
> Seeing me
> Seeing me
> Seeing me

Sarah W. Bartlett

PASSAGES

. . . floating in a frigid blue stream
arms clutched to her body
for warmth

warmth that would cover her
if only the gold were sun, not
last seasons' leaves

leaving her to float along
like time, neither pausing not returning
but moving

moving as she cannot, lodged
as she is under a rock ledge wedging her
tightly

tight as the birth canal she once knew
though forgot, how she needed to push out
to the light

like the light spreading before her now,
fanning from swollen breasts outward, an invitation
of color

blazing color of autumn's amber - that pine resin frozen in time -
but not she, here, now - no, a life force
pulls at her

pulls her from that tight passage
between then and now, the passage
that transforms

transforms as water shapes rock, as leaves ripen and fall,
as life cycles through the body
of earth

earth-bound, air-borne, water-channeled -
light and dark, birth and death - all cycling through
the tight spaces

spaces we construct from what we think
or think we know, believe - and yet, true space
is wide open, floating . . .

Note: Poem created with an exercise using Deborah Koff Chapin's *Soul Cards* as inspiration.

Black and white (originally color) painting of a nude feminine figure holding her head in her hands with fallen leaves cascading from between her breasts. The woman's figure is clearly outlined but paint strokes of different shades begin at the top of her head and waterfall down to the bottom of the page.

Deborah Koff-Chapin. "Soul Card 065." Washington: Center for Touch Drawing, 1996.

Ellen Bass

Bringing Flowers to Salinas Valley State Prison

When Mr. H saw the little meadow blooming
on the steel table, he bowed to the starry faces of jasmine.
This is the first flower I've smelled in twenty years.
And when I slid each man a bouquet in a paper cup
Mr. M said, I'll have such a short time with these.
We spoke, then, about Beauty and Loss,
the great themes of poetry.
And when our time was done
and the guard said they had to leave the flowers,
most of the men acquiesced. But Mr. S
insisted he had, as a Native American, rights
to his rituals—sage, sweet corn, tobacco—
and no one could stop him—it was the law—
from taking these sacred plants back to his cell.
Then he raised his cup and drank
the water the flowers were drinking
and a small wind stirred in that windowless room
as we watched Mr. S quietly bite
the heads off the Peruvian lilies,
crushing their pink sepals and the gold
inner petals flecked with maroon, swallowing
the silvery filaments, their dark
pollen-laden anthers, his mouth frothing with blossoms.

Joshua Bennett

On Blueness

which is neither misery
nor melancholy per se,
but the way anything buried
aspires. How blackness becomes
a bladed pendulum swaying between
am I not a man & a brother
& meat. How it dips
into the position
of the unthought,
then out. Trust me.
Foucault isn't
helpful here. I am after
what comes when the law leaves
a dream gutted. The space
between a plea & please.
A mother marching in the name
of another woman's dead children.
Not the anguish she carries alongside
her as if it were a whole, separate person,
but the very fact of her feet
addressing the pavement,
the oatmeal she warmed in the microwave
that morning, sugar & milk
& blueberries blending in a white bowl
as she reads the paper, taken aback
only by the number of bullets
they poured like a sermon into him.
How despair kills: too slow to cut
the music from a horn, or set
my nephew's laughter to dim.
I am dying, yes, but I am not the marrow
in a beloved's memory just yet.
Who can be alive today
& not study grief?
There are bodies everywhere,
but also that flock of cardinals
making the sky look patriotic.

Joshua Bennett

Teacher's Aide

My father showed up to school that day dressed up
as a man with a son with a rage problem; that is, a boy
whom violence—as if rumor, fresh from out of town

—followed everywhere. Ms. Hollinger never mentioned
the more practical elements of this ongoing conflict,
that I fought the other students because I liked my blood

very much & wanted to keep all of it inside of my body
once the playground went feral, as it was wont to do.
From his first day on the new job, my father

would bribe the bullies as only a Casanova of his stature
could, butterscotches & dirty jokes quelling all prior conflict.
The shift was immediate. Now baptized in the flame

of an older man's beauty, the war on the wise guy
was no more: a cease-fire forged by sheer esteem,
the stuff of corner-store science fiction it was,

this lovely Marine standing watch, half smile
drawing both teachers & seventh-grade girls
to him like lightning to a god of gold.

Sharon Charde

Field Trip

The guard wants us to line up in twos
says, It's easier to see bad things happening
this way. Coatless in late March air
we shiver on the prison pathways, walking
to our first event. Cinderblock-women
in handcuffs shuffle to other places
in this monstrous compound, each with
their very own guard. Our women wait,
all seven—Jennifer, Juanita, Jillian, Brenda,
Sue, Lisa, and Tabatha—in green plastic chairs,
the kind you put out on a summer patio.
They form a half-moon, and we set up
the other half carefully away from theirs
though I would have gone closer if I could. Their eyes
never leave us; we are their recreation today,
their break from lock down.

I settle into my molded chair, the girls fanning
out from me into a dark half-circle. The stories begin—
the stories I can't get enough of—Jennifer's baby born here,
she in shackles. Tabatha's children seen
only through the thick glass of the segregation cell. She worries
they're on crack now without her. Brenda slouches
towards us—Huh, my gang, I'd take a bullet for them
but where are they when you're in here? she glares hard at the girls—
Nowhere. Jillian's eyes snap each one naked. One guard to 76 of us,
so we take what we want. They sell roommates here
for rape, to do your laundry. Juanita, a big woman
in for murder, tells of 24/7, years of it, meals shoved
through slots in the door. Sue, her blonde hair pulled
high off her narrow face, prison uniform loose
on her lanky frame, shares of selling herself, being beaten, broken,
high on heroin. Lisa says, There's no comfort here.

I don't want them to stop. I want to stay here,
eat with these sisters, share their cells, their touch. I am home,
safe in the house of my childhood, in its long narrow hall,
all the doors slammed shut.

Benjamin Cloud

Prison Letter

A nigga gets a lot of time to think,
Nigga being him, her, you, me, anybody,
Bits get done inside,
And on the other side of barbed wire,
In or out, niggas find themselves,
They find what they're really dealing with,
Niggas sit, bored as hell, staring at four corners,
Recollecting on the good and bad, inflicted and experienced,
Niggas sit back humbled and sincere,
however circumstantial that may be,
A pen meets paper, correspondences indited,
Niggas get apologetic, guilty, confess, lash out in anger,
Those four corners are a bad motherfucker,
That piece of mail is a bad motherfucker,
Genuine expression at a nigga's best, worst, strongest, most
    vulnerable,
Between friends, family, special someones, enemies,
Niggas disappear, pop up after a hiatus, fuck you mentally, and show
    much love,
A nigga truly finds how calligraphy influences such joy and pain,
Words through the eyes that can build or collapse a relationship,
The type of shit that can make and break a nigga,
Composed and contained within the pages of a prison letter.

Chella Courington

At the Maximum Security Prison for Men

Columbia, South Carolina

Students come to me from solitary confinement
concrete oven set on high—
they come to me
a young woman from the University
who wants to talk about *Paradise Lost*.

They want to talk too.
Tony says when he broke in, he spotted a dog
and shot a man. *Thought the house empty.*
Billy Ray says he just needed money from the girl
at the ATM. *My hand shook and the trigger went off.*

They know why Milton's God
clips Satan's wings and kicks him out of heaven.
The man can't take much lip. Just like my own daddy
knocking me three ways into Sunday when I say no to him.
Knuckles kneading my cheek blue till I cry stop.

The students ask if Satan's the hero. And I wonder.
Did he endure that heavy hand one too many times?
Punched and mauled like a yard animal
taken behind the barn
left in darkness to find his way back?

Brian Daldorph

The Coin Toss

In the end it all comes down to a coin toss
between God and Satan
to decide who gets my soul.
See, I did some good in the world
but as it turned out I did _exactly_
the same amount of bad,
so it all comes down to God tossing the silver coin
high, high into the air.
he devil makes his call
and we all watch that coin loop up
and up, stop and tumble down.

Ian Demsky

Already There

After the incident a female approached me
And asked if I saw what happened
I told her that I had

She asked me if I knew they were having trouble
I told her that I initially did not
But eventually figured it out

She asked me if I was going to report it
I told her that I was not
Because there was nothing to report

I told her that I write reports on crimes
And that there was no crime

She asked me what I would have done
If they had gone under

I told her I would mark where they went down
And call the dive team

She asked me why I would not jump in
And try to save them
I told her that my life was more important
Than theirs

She asked me if I called 911
I told her I did not
That seemed redundant to me, after all
I would be getting the call
And I was already there

Ian Demsky

Critical Incident Report

to N. Budnick

SERGEANT ROBERT ANDERSON
At approximately 1130 hours, C/O Leal
Stated "there was a Hanging in FB 12"
I told C/O Davidson to go in the control booth
To assist C/O Norberg. C/O Mildon felt
For a pulse and stated he felt no pulse

CORRECTIONAL OFFICER WILLIAM MILDON
I grabbed the bed sheet off the TV stand
We moved him face first onto the bed
We placed handcuffs on him
And tried to get a response from him

CORRECTIONAL OFFICER WILLIAM DAVIDSON
I came out of C-Pod
And went into the F-Unit control booth
I assisted with answering the phone
Radio, and operating the unit sliders

CORRECTIONAL OFFICER STEVE LEAL
I lifted the offender by the waist to relieve
The pressure of his weight and to remove him
From the television stand
I removed the bed sheet from his neck
And placed it on the floor

CORRECTIONAL OFFICER ANTHONY DIBENEDETTO
I performed chest compressions
C/O Mildon performed rescue breaths

NURSE KATHERINE FISH
I performed a wellness check at 1015
He had a kite stuck in his door
It was addressed to mental health

He said he hadn't slept in two or three days
I asked him if he was in pain
I told him I would make sure mental health
Got the kite and that I would check back
With him on the noon pill line

FIRE CAPTAIN MATTHEW SEBASTIONELLI
Fire crew did a great job maintaining the airway
He had some "bad stuff" come back up
So the tube was pulled back

HEALTHCARE MANAGER BOBBY BAKER
Response sounds like things went very well

ASSOCIATE SUPERINTENDENT SEAN MURPHY
Good job! People of his family
Have been calling and seeking information
Do not disclose information to anyone
Refer them to Judy Hubert

INMATE DUANE LYNCH
I woke up when the cops yelled medical emergency
FB-12. It's at this time I seen it was Rich dog
A guy I have known for 7 years
The officer kept pumping his chest
While the other officers and sergeants watched
No one gave him mouth to mouth
I only seen a cop give mouth to mouth twice

Brian Gilmore

philadelphia (for d.j. renegade, ta-nehisi coates, darrell stover from landover, and the prison writers, lorton reformatory)

history will absolve me . . .
—FIDEL CASTRO

like fidel after raiding
moncada barracks
we face history like
seed removed from
soil
no longer waiting on
america
our eyes open now
curtains on tropical
sunday mornings
peering over horizons
around corners
desperately seeking road
that leads to
sierra maestra
until then

pens must move like
scalpels
slice through layers of
lament
challenge headlines
handed down through
history
       that which forces us to gather
       here, though even outside these
       walls we are linked: gravity to earth
       needle to thread, each of us

free beyond barbed wire
and bricks, spill our souls on
these floors, like scattered
pieces of puzzles.

Kate Glavin

Letter from Lansing Correctional Facility

Thank you for the magazine. I made
a painting from that picture of the swans
over the Marais des Cygnes,

flying north. I've been to that river
but never seen a swan flying over me.
But I haven't seen much the past fifteen.

In my youth, I went north
five years after Mount Saint Helens blew
its side. That was a lot of devastation.

I remember on the television, Jimmy Carter said
it was more desolate than a moonscape.
Moonscape. That's a pretty thing to call it.

Renny Golden

Ode to Cook County Jail

What is broken is blessed
——JIMMY SANTIAGO BACA

To Jose and Darnell shackled at the waist,
Houdinis trapped in a sinking trunk.
To their relatives who climb courthouse steps
holding pain like paper lanterns, helpless when
the judge throws away the padlock keys.
To those who swagger past the uniforms
moments from their brother's or sister's doom.
To the defeated mothers who spent two hours
on the bus to sit in a paneled room
and watch their sons go down.
To the pimp idling the motor of a Lexus
waiting for the suits to cut his woman loose.
To the guards who pat down weary grandmothers
passing ghost-like through metal detectors.
Move forward, the guards repeat, eyes empty of light,
empty your pockets, raise your arms, Ma'am.
To the bailiffs who call for order from spectators
so tired that only the surprise
of justice could stir any commotion.
To the City Councilmen who never set foot
beyond the high gloss wood of the court room,
who never walk a catwalk, gag from the sour smell,
hear a 20-year-old sob at 3am when they rip off his belt.
To the officers who push boys into cells of muscled rapists.
To the guards in the pen who strip-search women
caught with four ounces of crack, *Squat lady, squat!*
To the prosecutors who bring their voices up
from way down in their throats and never move their lips,
who speak through public defenders who say, after five
minutes with a twenty-year-old facing an inferno,
Do you want the deal or not?
To the district cops who bring in the captives every bone

aching night, cuff them, ignore eyes filling.
To the detectives who interrogate, kicking chairs out
from under them, their mouths to the scum's eardrum,
screaming, *You piece of shit.*

Nancy Miller Gomez

Growing Apples

There is big excitement in C block today.
On the window sill,
in a plastic ice cream cup,
a little plant is growing.
This is all the men want to talk about:
how an apple seed germinated
in a crack of damp concrete;
how they tore open tea bags
to collect the leaves, leached them in water,
then laid the sprout onto the bed
made of Lipton. How this finger
of spring dug one delicate root down
into the dark fannings and now,
two small sleeves of green
are pushing out from the emerging tip.
The men are tipsy with this miracle.
Each morning, one by one,
they go to the window and check
the progress of the struggling plant.
All through the day they return
to stand over the seedling
and whisper.

Nancy Miller Gomez

Invoking the Muse in Cell Block B

There is a heavy sucking
when the door swings open
and a dull clank when it locks.
The men file into the fishbowl
and open their notebooks.
Javier taps the table, nodding his head
to a soundtrack no one else hears.
Sol covers his eyes and yawns. Daniel paces
as if on a flight path. It takes awhile
for the men to settle, and then
the stories come out: a child's face
shoved into a bowl of oatmeal; baby shoes
tossed out for the dogs to chew; a bat
cracking across a small boy's arm.
They gather these images like kindling
to try to ignite the darkness. Inside,
the air hangs dank and mossy,
the walls sweat like a submarine. Outside
guards come and go, their shapeless voices
and the odd doppler shift of footsteps
rise and fall in the halls. The fluorescents
hum and glow off industrial green paint
slopped onto cinderblock so thick
it looks like moldy cheese.

Sean holds the cockeyed frames
of his broken glasses and scans the dictionary.
Raven noose, he says, and writes it down,
Ravenous. Juan draws black crosses
on the palms of his hands. The alarm blinks
its red eye. What is true about a swastika
etched into a man's forehead?
Why does it matter if he still dreams
of nights in a cold stairwell, pallets burning
under a bridge, the sound
of his grandmother singing?

They are all waiting in this moonless place.
Children still waiting for mothers,
waiting for children now grown to have children
waiting for them. They are waiting for someone
to visit. They wait for mail, for meals, for class.
Most days there is nothing to wait for. And still,
every scar is its own dark fact. What if
the thesis is a bottle smashed on a body?
What if the body can't grow wings?

Tristan, with the teardrop
tattooed on his cheek, holds the ink tube
of his pen as if it is breathing, and stares up
at a skylight so dirty
it might be night.

Dianna MacKinnon Henning

Absorption

Much like Saint Bartholomew in Rembrandt's painting,
the incarcerated man has become so intent that his pencil is nearly
a finger as he bends over the drawing of his daughters Sofia
and Sonia. Were it possible to accurately portray the man,
his skin mapped in tattoos, I would start with his eyes, tell you
how I see in them the brown loaves of bread his mother made,
his mouth about to form what he is unable to say. If there is
a heaven of words, or at the very least storage of some kind,
what remains unspoken must go there. It's nearly yard recall
and the man still draws his daughters, his head so close
to the paper that he could be outlining himself—the shapes
of their lovely mouths, butterflies with spread wings.

Prison Portrait

Housed in a cell, the soul
squats in a cement corner.
It hums like the defunct hanging
alcoves of Old Folsom.

Some men break down,
go mad, while a few,
mostly the young, make do
on the salt and bread of labor;
each day a gray wipe-out
in the State's fortress.

Outside, concertina wire twangs.
It's no dance tune. Prisoners know
work boots aren't made for dancing,
nor do shackled feet shuffle
to any old razzamatazz.

To Nuance or Not to Nuance

I
The men I worked with at Folsom Prison
walk single line
down the knife of night,
their eyes averted,
their blue jeans and shirts
baggy as pajamas

They could be on their way
to chapel,
Bibles in their hands
and who knows what
in their back pockets

II
My drama instructor knows the poetry
of the body, each nuance a shift of expression
as he lifts the sloping shoulders of a prisoner,
teases the his mouth into a frown and asks he recite:

". . . .I could be bounded in a nut-shell and count
myself a king of infinite space, were it not that I
have bad dreams."

III
In my dream, I am a frog leaping into heaven,
a moth perched on my tongue—
cool lake water glistening
off the green which is my frogness

O, Holy Father of leaping things
give me dominion over myself
Please bless these men who remain
chastised by public curse, by accusations

IV
I once thought trouble
a blight on the spirit,
but trouble is a shape-shifter;
it smiles like an angel
and dresses in shadowy garb,
a shank hidden in its back pocket

V
"Hamlet is like ballet,"
the drama instructor says.
"How so?" the prisoner actor asks.
"It's all such delicate stuff."

Note: Italics in section II from Shakespeare's *Hamlet*

You Li

In Champaign, Illinois

Up the stairs coiled around the hotel
my new friend Steve and I are lamenting that there is no gym
after all—he lamenting—I going along—

At my door I half stick the key in,
he asks again about how to iron his pants,

I have these pants with a crease—
he uses his hand to saw the air between us

So I'm kind of tired flash a smile, nod
jetlag ha-ha- but I can just tell you how to do it

it's really self-explanatory or
YouTube is the best teacher
on and on, until *ok good night*

I go in and from both sides
make the curtains meet.

Tomorrow he tells me he is on curfew,
has to get home by nine pm
from his first special-approved trip away from home,
six weeks out, when he first ate strawberries
after twenty years locked up he cried.

In the night, beyond the curtains,
out there, he touches all the things in his hotel room,
cold sink, coated hangers, blade of the blinds,

grabs his keys and hops in his rented car
drives to the gas station.
The moon sits where the sun
had half rolled half smeared itself,

the smell of gas, radio vibrating through his palms,
his black footsteps inking the black night,
many directions pointing from him like arrows.

I will wish I had been out there with him,
and the night rolling in from all around,

I could have taken what the night
swallowed, cupped his heels in his inky footsteps.

Take the freedom, I'm here,
Look around, night all around, for
the taking.

You Li

_____

New Map at Garden State

Inmates can't be near tools!
Go sit on the other side, the teacher yells to the men, over
the drill tunneling through the slow slough

of drywall toward the more yielding blue.
Ian walks over and asks, hands vast and heavy as moth wings,
        That missing airplane, it's gone, right?

Yeah, her hands float up, *of course.*
It's been a week, her palms buoyed by the heavier backs.
        And the people, they dead, right?

Yeah, yeah, of course.
He looks down, nods, walks back.
The strange blip had been folded away.

In that moment,
when the vast nothing
wrapped around the world's only room

kneads into its body a new wad of nothing,
what you remember is wind.
You picture rake lines in the sky.

This classroom will finally have maps! The teacher
pounds the world into the wall. USSR. USA.
There is a country on this map that doesn't exist.

Katharyn Howd Machan

He sends a letter telling me

I inspired him to write a story
about Jack the Ripper's final victim,
one nobody ever knew about
because her parts weren't found.
He says I helped him clearly imagine
late summer London 1888, a woman
with dark unwashed curls, tight
whale-ribbed bodice, long fringed shawl,
making her way to earn a few shillings
until the plunge of the knife. He thanks me
for giving him the idea that evening
I visited the prison, guest poet in careful
dowdy layers, no makeup, dull flat shoes.

Katharyn Howd Machan

Little Bear is Dead

Little Bear got killed last night.
Just last week
he pulled out his own front tooth
because it hurt him so much
and the bastard guard
wouldn't even give him an aspirin
though he begged hour after hour.
And now he's dead
with blood drying on the outside of his throat
and that crazy smile gone.

He brought only a few poems to the workshop.
One about a green meadow
full of laughing children.
One about a dream
in which he was a red and white arrow
shot astray into the bushes.
The last about a bright blue bird
circling higher and higher
towards a vague, luminescent love.
They weren't very good as poems,
but they said a lot about Little Bear.

Now he's lying with an old sheet
draped crookedly to hide his body,
the shaggy hair, the torn bandanna,
the chin that always needed a shave.
They'll never find who did it,
who hated his notebooks enough to kill,
hated the pride that strengthened his voice,
the crazy dark light that shone from his eyes
when he sang his poems out loud.

Katharyn Howd Machan

On learning that my daughter's rapist has been taught to write a poem

about his sadness.
About how the moon hung full
that morning, every morning

his fist felt like a beast
tethered and tied against its need
to howl and hit and hurt.

About how he needed
the good dope, too, and how she
stared at the gleam in his eyes

with mockery, goddammit, taunts
he wasn't full man enough
to bend the bars of their gray

days, this city of sunless grins.
About how good it felt to take
her pussy, her twat, her tight dark

hole and turn her inside out
like a star (oh, his teacher talked
of similes) and how he hasn't

seen a sky from edge to edge
since somehow he got put in here
where metal clangs and cotton clings

and generous souls who offer classes
have to leave their belts with buckles
behind them at the wordlessly locked door.

Jill McDonough

Joe Hill's Prison

The Historical Society in Salt Lake still has
some letters, a pamphlet called "Joe Hill's
Remains," even though he made it clear
he wanted his ashes scattered in every state
except Utah. Not wanting to be caught dead
here. The prison where Joe Hill died
is torn down now. Now there's a Sizzler. Neon
and brick at the foot of mountains he must
have looked at through bars. They're beautiful
mountains. They look like America, all majesty.
Rising purple up beyond the wall where he was shot.

Jill McDonough

Poetry Class in a Massachusetts Prison

Turner's lips twitch, his eyebrows go
crazy while he reads Jack Gilbert. I tell
Matthew to think olive, not motor, on the *ooze*
of oil crushed. Paulie's a skinny white guy, blond
beard, blue crocheted kufi cap, going to town
on Robert Hass's "Meditation at Lagunitas."
Which is hard to do! I ask Carl who's the "you"
in "One Art." Ben's shaking his head, erasing
all thought on John Clare. Butch just says *outstanding*
when I ask how he likes Gail Mazur's "Baseball."
He beams. They are men alone with poems, last day
of class in jail. Ken saying *Jill I can't do this, I'm no good*
with poems. And me saying *Ken shut up you give me that*
crap every time I give you anything to do. Ken laughs,
admits he gets the poem's loneliness, knows
what lonely's like. *I broke up with my ex-girlfriend*
when I caught this sentence. I roll my eyes and he gets it,
gets that he gets the poem. Last class. Goodbye,
my gentleman felons. Goodbye to their sentences, locked
cabinets of books we're not allowed to use. Goodbye
dark clothes two sizes too big. Men trying their best, their
beat-up desks. Their glasses and watches, all of us
working together, in the time we have left. Shrugging
at pages, holding their heads in tattooed, winter-dry hands.

Jill McDonough

Prison Education

When the fat asshole who's my student
starts bragging about how he stabbed
his wife and her lover in his bed, I interrupt
and ask how this is relevant. I tell him
we have three hours once a week, and we need to talk
about people's poems, not their pasts.

He's a dick, and I did the right thing,
and the other students are glad. They have
all the time in the world for who killed who.
Once he shuts up we sit in a circle, praise
a sonnet about a daughter in a white coffin,
rearrange a villanelle with sapphire eyes
and solid gold hair. We scan quatrains
on Ramadan filling your soul with light, laugh
with pastorals that end up in beloved
honkytonks, compare translations of Villon
pleading *please don't harden your heart.*

Jill McDonough

Women's Prison Every Week

Lockers, metal detectors, steel doors, C.O.
to C.O., different forms, desks—*mouth open, turn*—so
slow I use the time to practice patience,
grace, tenderness for glassed-in guards. The rules
recited as if they were the same rules every week:
I can wear earrings. I cannot wear earrings. I can wear
my hair up. I cannot wear my hair up. I dressed
by rote: cords in blue or brown, grey turtleneck, black
clogs. The prisoners, all in grey sweatshirts, blue jeans,
joked I looked like them, fit in. I didn't think about it,
until I dreamed of being shuffled in and locked
in there, hustled through the heavy doors.
In the dream the guards just shook their heads, smirked
when I spelled out my name, shook the freezing bars.
Instead of nightly escorts out, I'd stay in there
forever. Who would know? So I went to Goodwill,
spent ten bucks on pink angora, walked back down those halls
a movie star. When I stood at the front of the class
there rose a sharp collective sigh. The one
who said she never heard of pandering
until the arraignment said *OK, I'm going
to tell her.* Then she told me: freedom is wasted
on women like me. They hate the dark cotton, jeans
they have to wear, each one a shadow of the other their
whole sentence. *You could wear red!* she accused.
Their favorite dresses, silk slips, wool socks all long gone,
bagged up for sisters, moms—maybe Goodwill,
maybe I flicked past them looking for this cotton candy pink
angora cardigan, pearl buttons. They can't stop staring, so
I take it off and pass it around, let each woman hold it
in her arms, appraise the wool between her fingers,
a familiar gesture, second nature, from another world.

Michael McLaughlin

The Avenal State Prison & Larry Rivers Died Draft Two Blues

Avenal State Prison, Avenal California

The white number 70 Larry Rivers stencil
Me running Late On 46.
The white number 70 Larry Rivers stencil
Me running Late On 46.
A speeding ticket
With my workshop At 7:00.
Should've known there'd be some kind of hitch.

Cop gone, ninety a hundred, maybe that will save the day
Cop gone, ninety a hundred, maybe that will save the day
Tumble weed, piled up stubble,
Barbwire They call hay.

Plastic chair, Styrofoam cooler,
three hubcaps 'gainst a ditch
Plastic chair, Styrofoam cooler,
three hubcaps' gainst a ditch.
Jet plume snaky
turquoise; the foothills.
Pink flaked particulate.

The joint's lit up
like a bathroom
Every bit of it.
The joint's lit up
like a bathroom
Every bit of it.
Doesn't matter
what size the dinner.
I wouldn't risk taking a shit.

Tomato onion Bear Claw chlorine
Yard Four, where they live.
Tomato onion Bear Claw chlorine

Yard Four, where they live.
Next time you pass one of the homeless
Make that instant. Of your life. Their gift.

Sonny Kurt Enrique Jamie
Forcellini.
Neihart Lamb.

Sonny Kurt Enrique Jamie
Forcellini.
Neihart Lamb.

You wouldn't 've kept coming
'Cept it hooked you.

Now you know.
Poetry's
No Hallmark scam.

Praise Poem

For the Poets at Bedford Hills Correctional Facility

The circle's purpose is to see each other
our unspoken rule: commit to looking.

We were born and we will die, everything
in between is filler, debatable, for example

we have hated a woman for snatching
our man away like morning eggs.

We stay awake at night counting
constellations of guilt.

We both feel menstrual today
don't talk to us.

We call our mothers for comfort
and if they answer, tenuously

measure the distance between truth
and the length of rain.

We read books to remember stories
not of our own making or mess

and thank god, they are good
and thank god they are tragic.

Tragically, we both wonder if we deserve
anything good at all, to feel beautiful

or enjoy the pleasure of another body
when we've screwed or screwed up

we dream of undisturbed sand
covering each track and vanishing.

But in this room we crawl through
the window inside, dig up from burial

the dusty banjo of memory, we play
on childhood's climbing tree,

branches shedding crab apples
snatched up by the deer.

We can praise the fawn for cleaning
the lawn with her hunger.

We can name her prints in fresh mud,
we can call her kin, coo the name

we've crowned her when she shows
her face in the damp morning grass.

And though some of us didn't have
backyards or a steady bed or a tree to love

we can write a porch into the scene
or a birdhouse or untie a hurt until

it stretches its arms out wide as the sea.
We can invent this common history,

waking up what is green and tender,
lit deep inside our body's vast night.

We can remember, it has been proven
that we are made of stars, always vibrating,

sparking, even if it cannot be seen
by the foolish eye and each era, there we are,

unmistakably, a presence growing larger.
Yes, we are spinning: the giant revolving sky.

A Cold and Trembling Thing

It is the darkness of my cell
at night that finds me clinging
to a sip of prayer and a crumb
of hope. What if I opened my
eyes after 27 years only to
discover I could no longer cry?
What then?

There are laws that must be
broken like stones. I am Mandela
a prisoner on an island.

Why is freedom sometimes
a cold and trembling thing?

E. Ethelbert Miller

If My Blackness Turns to Fruit

Dear America, my love.
If my blackness turns to fruit
do not pull it from the vine;
let it grow from earth to sky
untouched by hateful hands.
So sweet, my juice, my jazz,
my blues, so sad but true.
Dear America, my love.

Look behind your prison walls.
Count the black seeds behind bars,
the cells where nothing blooms.
Can hope flower from despair?
Yes, America, my love,
resistance comes and then the rain.

Malik

Malik mumbled Arabic
over his plate like someone
adding salt before tasting.
Islam had been good to him.
It was light slipping
between prison bars,
changing shadows into prayer
rugs.

When Malik thought about the
murder he had committed
his hands tightened around his
Quran and Mecca seemed as
far away as freedom.

A few guards and prisoners
thought Malik's new faith
was a gimmick, a safety device
or a wall to protect one's back
from a punch.

Renee who called herself Malik's
girlfriend still wore short skirts
when she went to see him.
It was her way of slapping the face
of God for taking her man away.

Observed

There is so much I wanted to say to you
before you slipped back
into your cell-block,
where I am forbidden
and where you are

engulfed in schools of yellow fish.
Guards in gray watch you on a silver screen,
memorize your movements,
the symbols swiveling down your arms,
the star engraved on your shaven head.

I don't spell so good, you said to me.
It doesn't matter, I answered,
but you didn't believe me,
getting up so soon from your chair,
never returning to our table.

I can't remember what you called yourself
or if you said you dreamed the night before.
I only remember the anguish in your eyes,
beams of a flashlight on your face,
as if cornered in some dark alley
where the dreams you'd had or hadn't had
came to swallow you whole.

Workshop

base-level anxiety births comfort in a conference room
i am safe at our oblong table, a fish tank to quiet my mind.

a brush of lives too different to care
so let's tell stories and find solidarity in our brief meeting
my most genuine grins greet salty sorrows with you,
remember that.

i am at a loss to explain us.

but please, let me share my soul
with you, whose free years predate my birth.

my words are for me, but when i write
and find flecks of freedom painted
between our paralyzing pain,
it is always with you in mind.

Najee Omar

How to Use Pencils on Rikers Island

Adolescent Housing

- Before stepping inside. Before placing each one in a circle and counting them. Before the 15 of them gather, say a prayer for yourself.

- To start, place each one in the slit at the top of the desk. You'll want them still. Unsolicited movement can cause harm.

- Next, face them. Counterclockwise.

- Notice them, small. A sort of fragile brown and worn and scattered around the room. Same shape. Same size. These types are not built to last very long. There's no room to get creative in here. Remember to watch for lead piercing through sides. Try not to bring attention to any bruises.

- Some will be marked. Chewed on. Exposed like the ends of a detached limb. Catch them before they're forced to bleed. Then,

- prepare your grip. This will ensure no lines are free to stray. Keep enough distance. A close encounter can cause them to splinter. They are known for breaking through the skin. Prevent this.

- When locked between your fingers, surprise them with sudden movement. Tell them how/when/where/if to go. Remember you are in control. Adjust pressure as necessary. Then, watch how they scribble. Misspell. Smudge.

Warnings

- Pencils can be deceptively sharp. Always be sure to point them away from you. They can be dangerous in the wrong hands.

- The officers will tell you to number each one. These little things are never reliable and hard to keep track of.

- If pressed too hard, they will break. Just toss and replace.

Gregory Opstad

Condition Red

Only once in ten years
did I push my man-down alarm
as the guard moved
he others out of the classroom.
The man didn't get to me before
the SWAT team arrived
but my hands were still
shaking long after
the lock-down was cleared.

I cancelled my next class
thought about retirement.

Gregory Opstad

End of Trimester

Like strangers gathered in a bus depot
or laundromat wondering if they're waiting
for something or if they're really just dead
and have to figure that out for themselves,

therapists and nurses and patients drift
in and around the Octagon, clutching reports,
checking grammar, clocks, data, waiting,
waiting for attorneys, social workers,
family, waiting for something to
begin, waiting, waiting.

Such is the stuff of institutions—
working, waiting, drifting,
waiting to find out who is
really dead and when is the next
meeting going to start?

Janie Paul

For a Sculptor Who Left South Africa:
My friend, Isaac Witkin

A man I know takes solace in his farm.
His horizon—a low and wide circumference
surrounding and circling the fields.
The metal pieces take their place
rooted into the ground
like trees.

At night he falls into sleep
lumbering next to dark tree trunks,
the weight of his hands growing large, larger,
even larger than his body.
A sensation he had as a child that no one could calm.
Huge hands growing out of proportion,
so it was hard to touch.
His father went crazy and got shock treatment at a hospital in
    Johannesburg.
His mother talked too much and was terrified of birds.

There now—a piece of light through the bedroom window.
But that's not a dream—that patch of green color
held gently between two branches.
It was cradled, cradling that color,
that surface over which has hands travelled,
carving, first the head of a beautiful woman,
then bronze-casting
and now these low blueberry bushes,
the flat horizon that brings back sensations of the Transvaal
that brought him here to this farm.

His head tumbles forward and he bends over to get up.
His feet get planted directly on the hard planks of the old farmhouse.
Is he old?
Verticality is hard to achieve.
He rises into the studio to work.
It's all so heavy,
Making metal fly.

Joy Priest

A Personal History of Breathing

We woke to life in the 80s. The air dying
from industry & industry dying. Train brakes
groaning to a stop & that singular scent
of horses, their muscular lather & manure
moving down river to Mississippi. Our grandfathers

chain-smoked Viceroys in the house
& we developed asthma before vocabulary,
read books & held our breath, spelled
but didn't speak. In our bodies, humidity thickened
into an argument with speech. When we joined

our fathers' households they trashed our plastic bags
packed tight with medicine bottles & inhalers
curated over the years by our mothers, who smothered us
our fathers said, mumbling something under their breath
about being a man. We were daughters. We were Black

& so, sons too. They vowed to make us stronger,
big-lunged, lit our cigarettes, handed us grip-pleated
paper bags in place of pills. In the 90s springtime,
we suffered through neon particles of pollen
suctioned film-like to all blooming surfaces,

innocuous in natural purpose, but perverted
by a chemical monopoly modifying plant sex
& the work of bees—we became allergic to apples
because we were allergic to apple trees. At the plant
our fathers were talking their coworkers out of the ku klux klan

while we hooped on our still-segregated basketball teams,
outgrowing childhood over an iron-rimmed summer
at parks oxidized to rust. At 14 we went to work
at drive-thru windows, fried batter air settling
in our hair. Black n Mild smoke breaks

freaked to extend time. & some of us
went off to college with polluted memories.
& some of us ended up at the school clinic

with anxiety & traumatic stress, acid reflux
& lactose intolerance, the nurses said was genetic,

we didn't have the phrase environmental racism
yet. & sometimes we just forgot to breathe
or realized we'd been holding our breath.
We tried kombucha & herbal teas, yoga & meditation,
signed up for classes with suburban moms

on Xanax & Ambien & we acted brand new.
Until a man hawking cigarettes, second shift
side-hustling like our fathers, stopped breathing
on a sidewalk. A man who talked to plants
like our fathers stopped breathing

in this state-sanctioned chokehold. & we found ourselves
pacing the brainyard on a cocaine flight
unable to locate our lungs, left arms going numb
saying, *this is it   this is it*
with our heartbeats running out,

leaping & whinnying & lying down long-nosed
in the grass, huffing, panting out. The train
of our childhood chugging backward
to a slow stop in our minds, come to take us
to the afterlife. Its ghostly porters,

mask-less, finally, leaning over us
with our father's faces, reaching toward us
with a bag to breathe into. The trail
of white buttons down their uniforms
like blinding current peeking through.

Nightstick

in Kentucky you are a Black girl, but don't know. you sleep
next to it. crooked bone, split-open head. patrolling through the night.
don't even know you should be trying to run away. it rests
in your night terrors, in a bureau between your grandmother's quilts,
with her thimbles & thread & dead white poems. don't think
for a moment your grandfather won't pull it out, make a cross of it
with your arms, gift you its weight & crime. do you believe?
what if he said its name was *Justice?* would that be too much?
if he was the only man your childhood saw hauled away in handcuffs,
pale & liver-spotted & stiff in limbs sharp enough to fold into the back
of a cruiser? you. this bruise of irony. the only two Blacks ever allowed
in his house. & at night he be singing you to sleep while it sits invisible,
sentry-like out of sight. he be humming hymns—*i come to the garden
    alone*
while the dew is still on the roses—knowing how much blood it has seen &
whose. he be holding you to himself like a secret & every song be a
    prayer
for your daddy's sunk-in head. you breathing one for his whole face
before you. bullying a shit-shaded boy's head is what it's made for,
he say, your papaw, while you hold it, not knowing enough about
    yourself
to understand the cannibal nature of chewing on his words with no riot
inside. no baton twirling in the air of your stomach. no notice of the
    grand
wizard & his wand when he appears in your nightmare. you be
    closed-eye
& it be there, Black as who it means to beat

Paisley Rekdal

Saturdays at Reynolds Work Release

I remember never being afraid, because they said
the crimes they committed were small,
because when they locked each man alone
in the room with me—nineteen, thin as a child
beside the smallest of them—with his book
and pads of paper and sharpened pencils, only
a tiny window that looked out into the hall
where no guard stood, I could see

the boredom and the shyness on their faces, these men
fresh from prison but still waiting
in one building, in Pioneer Square, in Seattle, in winter,

where every Saturday it rained, a fact
we hardly saw ourselves but heard
in the drumming against the roof's beams and in the wet
squeak of someone's soles down the hall

where I would teach them words
they would or would not use; going over
with one man, who was twenty-five but read
as well as a fourth grader, pages of Genesis
so he could learn the terms

firmament and *plentitude*; his agate eyes
flicking over pages that looked
recently unearthed: phrases to be practiced
at his new job, which was to drive a forklift
for Weyerhaeuser, because it was the Bible

he wanted first, as another man wanted Louis
L'Amour and a third asked for the back issues of *Time*
someone left in AA on the chairs. And it was

not frightening, no, not even when one man said
he'd made tapes of letters that he would send me, recordings
of his thoughts that spooled in the dark
in the dormitory where he couldn't sleep, it's locked doors

but open windows, the insomniac moon
peering in on the skinny desk clerk who checked him

in or out, who called the CO if he missed
a meeting, learning to move
from bed to work to group to lights out, but not
to outside the building to stand alone
and smoke a cigarette. And what did he feel

those nights, listening to the rain a wall away,
the cars that drove by in the dark, each steered
by someone smoking, singing, driving until morning

came with its cramped rooms, its yellow book to stutter over:
firmament, the men spelled out, *plentitude, gunslinger,*

working until the locked door rattled open
and I got up because it was time for me
to leave, the sounds of cafés and movie theaters
welling up behind me. *So close,*
I told them, when they got a word

less wrong, as if discipline
made a difference, stopping only when one man,
furious, slammed a hand to the table

and began crying. And even then
I wasn't scared because
I didn't have to be, listening to the thread
of the sentence he hadn't finished. *Brother,*

he'd begun, *thee shall rise again,*
while the rain spat, unseen, against our building.

Karla Robinson

Reprieve: A Testimony

Horizon Juvenile Detention Center, Bronx, NY
2011–2013

For the young womxyn

in the state-issued orange sweats

who gave me serious side-eye

90 minutes at a time

every Monday and Wednesday

for 3 months

before asking-

> *Why you always call us Beautiful?*

To whom I replied—

> *Because I think you're beautiful.*

> *I think all children are beautiful.*

Who then replied

in a less than complimentary tone—

> *Yeah-*

> *You seem real genuine about that shit.*

I write this poem for you.

I call you beautiful,

not because of the way you look,

but the way you look at me

as I flip through my folders to find your writing.

Lips apart, hands on hips, shoulders near your ears.

Part excitement, part terror, part cocky.

I call you beautiful,

not because of what your body

can do, has done, will do,

for others.

But for what your body

can do for yourself.

The way your breath

transforms space.

You decide if it's a sanctuary

or Satan's lair.

I call you beautiful

not because of your

fresh flat iron,

but because of the risk you take to put pen to paper.

Etch ink into wood.

You choose to use your time inside wisely.

Spiral inward and

lose yourself for a moment.

Reclaim a space

designed for your demise.

I call you beautiful

Because you are.

Full of beauty,

and light,

and choice,

in this dark, dank place.

Karla Robinson

Swathe

Back-of-the-bus

front lines.

Battling

Bandaging

Brandishing tools from weapons

designed to destroy us

In all ways,

the best of American life

is a

monument

to

Black Vision.

Antonio Sanchez-Day

My life story (13 years)

Here's a couple numbers I'm gonna throw at
ya. I was born on the **21st** day of the **7th** month
of **"74."** That makes me **2** years shy of **40**.
I lost my brother when I was **7** years old,
and lost my sister when I was **8**. In the
3rd grade at the age of **9**, I **1st** smoked
marijuana. (It is said a person stops maturing
mentally at whatever age they start smoking
weed. So that makes me a **9**-year-old
emotionally). I was placed in
Alcoholics Anonymous at **10**. When I was **12**,
in the **6th** grade, I watched my father die,
2 days after meeting him for the **1st** time
after he dedicated himself to **7** years of
sobriety, to be able to see me. At **13** years
old I began therapy. When I was **16**, I
was kicked out of Lawrence High, and ran away
from home. I caught my **1st** felony at **18**, **4** years
later at **21**, I received my **2nd** strike and was sentenced
to **10** years. (Another stated fact: an individual ceases
to mature emotionally at the age he is incarcerated).
So according to both theories, I am mentally **9**
years old, and emotionally **21**. When I went
through D.O.C. in **"96,"** I became **#63803**.

In **2006**, **480** cheeseburgers later (cheeseburgers
are served for lunch every Saturday in Kansas prisons)
I was released: **2** months later my mother
passed away. Her **1** and only dying request was
that I stop drinking. **7** years later, I have
left that **1** promise broken, resulting in
another **3**-year bid. All that adds
up to **13** years I'll have given the Department
of Corrections when this is all over. **1** day
I hope to get it together.

One of the Girls

You! Stop! Wait!

Who are you?
What are you doing here?

I'm the manifestation of
Your greatest fear
Coming now is the change

Look at you,
With that nappy hair
I'm confused by those street clothes
That you wear

You come in here with style and grace
I said it was your face
But we all know,
It's because of your race
That staff mistook you for an inmate

But you are. . . .
Who do you think you are?
Walking around me, free
Unchained
Unbarred
Unbound

I found strength
In the realization of my crown
I see the guards' eyes staring
Locked on my feet
Searching for a way to capture me
But you cannot stop the change
I am forever untamed

Amani Sawari

Pink Painted Nails

I don't usually paint my nails
I keep them bare and dry
But there are days I will indulge
When I do get the time

I admire the feeling
The gloss, the color, the shine
But today I feel no admiration
I wish I could rewind

As I type the letters on the keys I think
Why would I paint my fingernails pink?

It reminds me of the separation
It reminds me of past segregation
It reminds me of this divided nation
The world of distance between my student and I

I don't want to represent any divisions
Regardless of one's previous decisions
My pink nails represent the distance
My pink nails represent the privilege

It makes me uncomfortable to type
So now with clean nails I write
Trying to close the distance

Matthew John Schmit

Prison Snow

Not the frosted vanilla roofs
of Hansel and Gretel's Home
sweet Home; not the iridescent
shells of eggs,
the blanket on mountains
beneath swift skis; not the promise
of a day away from school, nor whipped
cream beneath a cherry; not neighborhoods
powdered with street-light sugar;

no, this snow is
salt blocks, curing
in the freezer, this snow is
hardened by the whip of wind
that bolts across the Yard;
the mounds collecting in the corners
of the icebox, a flash
like broken glass; the winding
electrified fence, rods
of Freon.

The prisoners sing while they shovel:
the hum of the refrigerator
late at night, lulling a child to sleep.

Patricia Roth Schwartz

Hat Poem

From a skein of pale green yarn
and a plastic hook, Poppi's making a hat.
He's so good now he doesn't even look
as hat or scarf or shawl grows
and grows, billowing down in strips
from the dipping, hooking tool
that's got a rhythm of its own now,
like poems. Poppi's making a hat
while he and Chris and Sundiata sit in the back
of crochet class and compose triptych poems
they'll warble out later in poetry class.
How lucky they are and lucky they know it
to get these scant chances here in Hell
or Oz or whatever you want to call it,
to meet and sit and learn to make something
to keep a loved one they can't touch or see warm
on a walk they can't take, then
to stand, belt out their own precious words,
hooked together, before the group
we've started to call family, home, Holy
Ground. Poppi's making a hat.

Patricia Roth Schwartz

Max Jail, Monday Nights

Oh, Woody, I say, what is it? You look unhappy tonight. You're
    bored? Want to ship out again? Go kick some more Iraqi butt?

Sure thing, he says. No future here. I'm ex-marine, Naval Reserves.
    Why should I risk my sweet patootie policing these hard-ass cons
    when I could be going after Osama?

Suit yourself, I say.

So you're a po-et? He says. What's that?
Kinda like a librarian? Nice and sweet, a lady?

Oh no, I say, a poet's a revolutionary.

No shit. You mean like Dr Zhivago?

That's right! And we walk together across the yard.

Five months later he's come back, thinner, quick face now dull.
    Quietly he searches my Lands' End briefcase for contraband,
    rummaging amidst random ball points, inmates' poems.

How was it? I ask.

He won't answer. Later I walk down the hall to teacher's lav. He looks
    up full at me, almost whispers. Mass graves, he says. Mass graves.

Patricia Roth Schwartz

Some Nights Like This

start out mild, stirred with the scent
of earth rising somehow over razor wire
from the creek that runs along the cement cliffs
that wall in this city of trouble, city of pain.
When you walk out of the main building
from the command post into a corridor
that leads through an iron-gated passage into the yard,
it smells just like anybody's dinner cooking,
homely, hamburger with onion maybe,
and Marge, the C.O. who escorts you over,
sneaks a smoke crossing the yard
on the way to the school, where weekly
you and your caged poets struggle to learn
what is the weight language can bear?

Over by the guard's hut, Marge hands off
her ciggie to her buddy, then, just so she can brag,
pulls out of her I.D. wallet the hospital photo
of her newborn granddaughter: the baby's got
spiky black hair, face like an old apple,
and she's still smiling that milky smile.
Her eyes are not yet opened.

Christopher Soto

The Children in Their Little Bullet-Proof Vests

Each week we
Walked through
Metal detectors
Gossiping guards
 Mothers
  A basketball court
   A blackbird
    Barbed wire & more
    Barbed wire
   To be here
Where

We prepared
Poems
For incarcerated boys
Ages 15 to 19
They are
 Fathers &
  Brothers &
   Boyfriends &
  Together we
  Learned
To write
To wrought
The pain & make it
Beautiful

When class began
 Televisions turned off
  Chess boards were
  Put away // Put away // &
 Boys dreamt with us by
The stainless steel
Lunch table in this

Grey brick room
 Everyone looked the same
 Grey
  Cotton sweatpants
   Grey
   Sweaters sharpied with numbers
  Grey
  Wolves
 Most heads were shaved
 Some tattooed
We asked about
 The boys lives outside
The detention center
Every sentence ended with
The word *prison*
Every prison began before
The sentencing

Our mother	prison
Our father	prison
Our nation	prison
Our language	prison
Our race	prison
Our gender	prison
Our laughter	prison
Our dancing	prison
Our clothes	don't fit

Clothes were our
Cousins covered us
Like a tent

In Unit Y2
None of the boys
Knew we're faggots
Before each class
We'd wash #C003
Rustic Red paint from
Our nude nails then
Exchange our black dress
For slim blue jeans
Each body disciplined

For its difference
For its distance to
State power

Julian started to us *Carnal*
He spent the first weeks of
Our poetry class
Schooling us
He would lift up his shirt
Showing the name
Of his gang
Of dead friends
Etched in ink // On his stomach
We'd tell him to
Drop his shirt

d
o
w
n

He'd keep pulling his
Shirt up

Julian told us he
  Wasn't afraid of death anymore
    He was in solitary against
      His will

He // Sat
      Stood // Sat
           Stood // Sat

Twenty-three hours
A day alone

He couldn't even scream
Without being pathologized

Anything
To open the doors

The first time
We were arrested
We aged to 15
A neighborhood
Watched through the
Svelte smell of
Cow shit as
Our elbows bent into
The backseat of a
Police car
We were wearing
  Only our boxer-briefs
   We were handcuffed &
   The faces looked like
Security cameras
Capturing just one scene
In the movie

                    The brown boy
                    The police car
                    The tow truck

After arrest
For stealing
Our father's car &
Driving away
From an abusive house
Nobody saw the
Cigarette burns stubbed
  On our shoulder
   Nobody noticed
     Our father's chaffed psalms
       The way his grip tore
         Our clothes
         How we sat

              Mute   &   minute

              Like   his   lapdog

In Unit Y2
Julian was finally
Released
Let out of
The detention center
On probation
With an ankle monitor &

We heard the herd
The news said
The federal govern
Men would start
Using these
Ankle monitors
To track movements of
Undocumented Im
Migrants
Migrants tracked like
Wild animals
Our family of
Migrants
Of course
We run from poachers // There's

A
Whole
White
History of
Human zoos

In 1895 // Cree
In 1896 // Sicangu Lakota
In 1906 // Ota Benga
Displayed

We celebrated Julian
For his release from
Caging in Unit Y2
Confetti & balloons but
We felt uncomfortable
Proposing
He was *free*

He was *human*
  Or *citizen*
    We wanted to ash
      His ankle monitor
        We wanted to tell him

Everything
's changed but
The government's still
Tracking
      Felonies
           Peonies

Nothing's changed
Not // Him // Changed
Not // Him // Chained
Nothing's // Chained
Knot // Him // Chained
Knot // Hymn // Chain
No // Hymns
Nothing

        J
        ulian
        He isn't free
        They just rearranged
        The boundaries of his cage

When released
Julian was on a
Couch in his
  Mothers' vintage
    Room watching
      Cartoons after
        Drinking cereal
      Milk &
    He felt
  Lazy
Wondering if abs
Are a personality
The blankets are wool &
Laid lightly

Over his shoulders
Sun tilting through
Cotton curtains
He yawned & stretched
Swiped slumber
From his slants
He hoped for no rain
With his head made
Of chalk

Deborah Tobola

Hummingbird in Underworld

While the prison band sings *I Shall Be Released,*
a hummingbird hovers near the barred window
sucking through its needle-beak nectar from
the fuchsia's red mouth. The sax player
makes his instrument cry, a sound sadder

than the kid weeping in Receiving & Release.
Anyone can fashion a shank from a toothbrush,
use a piece of wire or tin to terrorize his fellow man.
It's easier to give in to *ennui*, to believe you've got
nothing coming, nothing to give, than to pick up

brush or horn or pen and begin. Some people
will journey only with a cross-hatched map,
unlike the hummingbird, who travels flower
by flower, heart beating twenty times a second,
flying sideways, backwards, straight ahead.

A prison poet reads his eulogy for the young man
lost in Viet Nam, voice breaking
forty years of bondage. Men can't live without
war, just as the hummingbird can't live
without flowers. There's a compass

in its head, magnetic particles pulling it back
to its sweet home. In one legend, the god
of music and poetry became a hummingbird and
flew to the underworld, where he learned
the secrets of transformation. A prison artist

paints Jesus in yellow, halo askew, one hand
clutching his robe, the other cupping a red petal
of blood. The artist loves Jesus and the blood
flowering in his palm, and the paint
that makes him creator. When Aztecs see

a hummingbird, they see a quick-hearted warrior
who beats back the darkness with iridescent wings.
Hummingbird sucks the evil out of men, leaves them
with a thirst for beauty and the trick of flying
while appearing to stay perfectly still.

Deborah Tobola

Milk and Cookies

The poets perform in three classrooms, riding Neruda's river
on a little boat of nostalgia, on a craft of black pride,
in a shipwreck of loss and longing. Some poets make
the other prisoners laugh, some cause the teachers
to pause and look up. We pass the guard shack
with its metal detector the prisoners must pass through
daily. *What about us? What if we want to hear*
poetry too? one guard asks. Still high on performing,
the poets look anxiously at one another, step back. Slowly, they form
a semi-circle around the shack, each stepping forward
when it's his turn. The new student paws at the ground,
fairly snorting his contempt. Like a prizefighter,
he delivers his punches with fluid elegance,
reciting from Che Guevara: *Don't think*
that they can make us tremble, armed with gifts
and decorations. We want a rifle, bullets, a stick.
Nothing more. A guard raises his eyebrows.
When another poet exhorts the guards not to
go gentle into that good night, silence hangs on to *night*
and for a split-second, the business of prison—
prisoners shouting, a barked order, wheels and welding
torches and prison intercom—fades to this silence held
by guards and poets, who have never talked,
never listened this way. Stiff thank-yous and the poets turn
away, relieved to be done. *Wait a minute,* says a guard,
and bending down for a big box, he invites each poet to take
a carton of milk and a cookie. Recalling the lines he's just recited,
the fighter cries *I don't want no milk and cookies! I ain't their bitch!*
The other poets pull him aside, tell him to eat.
Later, he will christen himself Big Bad Ass Poet,
walk the yard reciting his own words, taking his listeners
to the raw wilderness he discovers inside. But now he takes
one bite of cookie, an uneasy communion in the chapel
of the metal detector, guards watching as he eats.

Michael Torres

From My Classroom Window at the Prison, Before Students Arrive

Because the blinds stay open, I see birds. I watch how
men watch those birds. They monitor flight paths
and a soaring appetite for the crumbs they shouldn't've

pocketed from chow. The indifferent birds ask for nothing,
yearn for nothing, except perhaps the sky, which is nothing
to them but magnetic blue wind-their one great war

of journey. I've been thinking about mine lately. My own
great war. Once, I met a man who'd been waiting hours
for a storm to hit. At the park, he told me how difficult flight is

for birds. He stared at the humming sky and disappeared. Later
that night, I could not fall asleep. Not with a fact like that. Instead,
I sat at my coffee table and fed a dying rubber fig tree

filtered water and the eggshells I broke apart, calling them
my little countries. I thought of being president. Then I asked
myself, why can't I be king? When I arrived at the idea

of God, I began to float. When I woke, I understood
my only burden is that of a simple life of a man who can go home
and think and care for plants that do not know

he is their father. If I am no one to these leaves, to whom
do I belong? Thus, my great war is with myself. A wingspan
of stirring thoughts that ask what's next, that wait for my response

like the men beyond this window. Breadcrumbs, tiny questions
for birds. Each man tossing a piece at the air anticipates a swooping
answer, tries not to think of what goes uneaten, of what falls

toward death. Wet and certain. That patch of grass they walk,
its cold blades. It's late October. Every step stiff and speechless.

Michael Torres

Teaching at the Prison in December

When the evening sky loses
its blue, the dead trees blossom
                        namelessness.
                        We become what
            we endure.
                        Today
I study maps. Routes to return me.
                        How odd, this necessity
my unending study
                        of the past's magnitude.
Each of us carries a kind of scale.
                        Once a week
I gather in a room full of mean who measure
the lives they wanted
                        —and still want—
by writing it down, men who do not know
they remind me of nicknames and handshakes
from back home. Despite this or because of it
                                    we laugh.
                        We talk poetry, and do not
bring up how we got here.
                        Beyond, a barbed fence carves the wind
countless. Only snow enters unquestioned—without ID,
metal detection, hand stamp—
                        parachuting through
            cyclones of razor wire.
How solemn each blade
                        must be. After class
                                    I want nothing
                        more
than to stray from my escort's side. His proper stare
and pepper spray.
            I understand this infraction.   And yet
I imagine my glove tossed

                                     so that I may graze one blade

with an index finger

                                     warm and crowded
with my blood.

Vachine

Homie

Smokes a Camel and spits on the hot asphalt. He
raps his story out the side of the mouth. Wife-beater
under a hoodie, gordo brother's pants, legs cut to fit.
Holy Mother of universal exultation holds cathedral's
door, but there's no road in the shadow of her wings.
Mama's cancer cure, relief from Dad's belt buckle,
unanswered prayers. He must blaze his own trail across
Zanja Madre. Sun roasts the air above LA River bridges.
Smog hangs with charcoal smoke from the San Gabriel's
wildfires, acrylic sunset paints the Heights in oranges
and lemons, like crime scene tape. Colt 45 night-cap on
moist night grasses of Plaza De La Raza in twilight, he curls
down on the damp sod. Dream song lyrics punctuated
by chingada between syllables. Hollenbeck Division putos
sweep the park in rubber gloves, Waistband 9 his only peace.

Marine Biology 101

We learned that sea water heals wounds faster.
I leaped into Monterey Bay with my heartbreak,
and drowned.

Erin Wiley

Any container that is roughly cylindrical in shape

Everyone forgets
their slights but
never forget
being slighted,
like taking a match
to salt, like burning
salt with a match
it burns slow

it burns slow then
it's gone it
burns slow then
it's gone it
wasn't worth it
in the first place
you know,

Everyone forgets
to smile.

Sidewalk
walking,
face down,
watching,
feet predict
when to look up
if a smile or a wave is of worth,
thinking about it
too much and
I'm thinking about it too much
will I ever see you again
probably not and isn't that
peachy.

There is a reason
people don't smile.

I walked into a bookstore
didn't know the time,
didn't know the time
picked up a book and
started laughing I
picked up a book and started laughing
and he wasn't amused

the owner,
he started changing the radio
changing the radio in and out
around the block he stopped
at ella
fitzgerald and kicked us out.

He asked if I was going to
buy the book
can you believe it
he asked if I was going to
buy the book and I froze
negative twenty to twenty
I went
negative twenty
to twenty wiggling
between two poles
and that's
what gravity feels like.

Whatever happens
I'm going back,
Whatever happens
I'm going back
to this dystopian
bookstore and
only to laugh because
isn't that what it's all about

Isn't that
what
it's all about
laughing
throw me out and
bring me closer throw

me out
and bring me
closer hopefully
my voice will always
be here.

Everyone thinks
it's all a game,
waiters floating a
duck that is swimming
swimming underneath
but floating on top
swimming underneath
but floating
on top and
I'm talking about your dinner.

I'm talking about
your dinner
and in more ways than one
I'm talking about your dinner
the duck is your waiter
floating
and you've forgotten
about the ants
you've forgotten
about
the ants
marching west
it's despicable
you've forgotten
about
the ants and it's all just a game.

that's a
nice dress thanks
that's a nice dress
thanks
that's a
nice dress thanks
and I'm sick of hearing
that because you say it
every day.

I'm sick of hearing that
because you say it
every day
I'm sick of hearing that
because you
say it every day
how many
repeats
constitute a loss
of meaning everyone
should know.

How's your day
hun
good.
How's your day
hun
good. I've been better
you should move to
Arizona.

Any container
that is roughly
cylindrical in shape
and that's it.
A canister any
container
that is roughly
cylindrical
in shape.

Can you
help me dry
my tears
today
I'm sorry sir
I cannot
I'm off alcohol
and drugs all
I'd like is a beer
and a sandwich
I'm off alcohol
and drugs all

I'd like is a
beer and a sandwich
how about a cigarette
instead

forget the slight
let the slight
linger in
a canister
linger with a
canister

Burn salt
with a match
how about
a cigarette
instead.

Erin Wiley

exploited village

I
notice the proprietor

atmosphere of the household
population slow-moving men
military neutrality
future automobile
fast as possible
extra women
spare parts
hundreds
authorities for the day
notice the proprietor
old and large

II
there was a cliff

mystery
ten puzzled grandmothers
well groomed
remarkably wrinkled
at least pleasant
slim shoulders
high-backed furniture at home
dining table displayed softly
gossip around self-absorbed draperies
there was a cliff
his grandparents attack
an overnight guest

III
Joseph at thirty-nine

stocky
balding and bothered
bloating with glasses of milk

rarely in public
presented
a man of five languages
he stood on a box.

Erin Wiley

touchless automatic

would you rather
endure a wash cycle
    or a dry one?

consider the attendant old and wet

like the man that fell asleep on his book nobody will steal it i promise
the car will lock itself and when the lights go out you should be afraid

the ocean came sudsy its waves dry like cotton
tumbleweeds suspend themselves from hooks
    a caterpillar descends
        a spider frantic and loud (i don't know if they're friends)
        i am the gun

Erin Wiley

_____

Reaching, with the I

a Parisian man once said that you
Americans take a bite out of every word you say.

oh-ho-huggh he hé imitations on language you like
to eat it too maybe read it on

televisions say *ffzzupffzup* on beds
of broken springs for swimmers

sound underwater wiggling for future
air.

esses in scanning
with the eye. what about combinations of same
ness like there there
child this is this
what's what (that's that!)
what is that you ask.

we ask. as in the future we. we of settled idealism. we the
Aztec robots.

I think that what it was was that it was

a way for us, as in the us that was then, to have faith
without believing in it so that he can rest, temporarily, before
we were not on the same wavelength

you forget you are your default, Erin. Stop
forgetting that you are not in there, in him, and he is not in you,
and everyone is not on your page of the magazine, you have to try to keep a
friendship for
futures
are uncertain like

walking outside for the first time in hours and breakfast has
already been served.

Let us go back.
to language it isn't it is it?
a story both you and I know so well about cards

them day and bible then pile keep next your you or them away a a
    the Cards. you find onto in them then you Cards. you hold to
    you your verse them some some verse them attached find a
    without or there and hold and onto then pile then onto and find

Aztec robots.

Don't dislike it, our story here,
just because you've forgotten the verse

creativity is a muscle and you haven't done your daily stretches

now we are living in a motor-home, travelling
drifting milky down on Montana
high-ways or hi(!)-ways good-bye-waves

we are lost now. like the kid who went in search for his spirituality,
    and his father in
search for him, a homonym. Where are we going. Why do we seek.
    Which way.

Afterword

Devastated and Busy: Prison Arts Programming in the COVID-19 Pandemic

I write from the middle of a global pandemic on a scale we have not encountered in a hundred years. Nowhere can the devastation of COVID-19 be seen more plainly than inside prisons. The incarcerated cannot socially distance, have inadequate cleaning supplies and personal protective equipment, and receive some of the worst health care to be found in anyone's country. Many who become ill in US prisons do not wish to be discovered because they will be placed in solitary confinement as a form of quarantine. There these unlucky patients are stripped of their meager possessions— even reading materials. They have nothing to help occupy their anxious minds. They must cope not only with the illness that could kill them but also with limited or nonexistent access to phone calls to loved ones in the free world. Like others throughout the world in this nightmare pandemic, those who die will do so alone without the chance to say goodbye to their families. The COVID survivors in prisons eventually leave quarantine to return to a life of perpetual lockdown. Educational and recreational programs and visitation with loved ones remain indefinitely cancelled.

In this new fugue state that has been our lives for the last four months, none of the prison arts programming described in the rest of this book can happen, and none of it will be possible again for many months, or even years, to come. As artists, we must adapt to our new reality and continue to meet the challenges of the world, no matter how impossible they may feel. I am fortunate enough to be part of a global community of prison arts practitioners, and as we scramble to find ways to remain connected to our incarcerated collaborators, we have been reaching out to one another for advice, good ideas, and moral support. The Shakespeare in Prisons Network (SiPN)—an alliance of prison theatre makers from around the world—has been holding a series of online panels and discussion groups in lieu of the in-person conference they would have hosted this November at Notre Dame University.

Through this network, I learned of a youth facility in the Midwestern United States that entreated the volunteer who leads a theatre program there to come back to work with the boys even as the pandemic raged around them. The boys so desperately needed some creative outlet in this time of crisis that the man felt compelled to be with them and do the work they had intended to do, despite the fact that he knew that this put his health and theirs at greater risk. (This hateful disease is carried in and out of prisons via free people—mostly prison staff—leaving and returning every day. Prisons then serve not just as death traps for those who cannot escape them but also massive vectors for disease transmission in the free world, as prison employees infect those in their homes and communities.) This man asked a group of us from SiPN if we thought he was wrong to go to work with the boys under these circumstances. We felt that, like many teachers in this crisis, he had been put in an impossible situation. What is worse: to abandon frightened and trapped people who need you or to risk further deadly contagion for them and yourself? No good answer to this question exists.

No one else I know who does this work has had the opportunity to make such a choice. The rest of us are entirely shut out of prisons, most of us without any means to communicate with the incarcerated folks who have enriched our lives and our artistic practice for years or even decades. My friends who make theatre in prisons in Brazil have absolutely no sense of the infection or death rates in the prisons that hold their collaborators because the carceral system there refuses to release any information at all about the pandemic. Where I live in Michigan, sixty-eight incarcerated people have died inside our state prisons—at least these are the figures officials have released. Twenty-three of those souls lived at Lakeland Correctional Facility, which those familiar with Michigan prisons think of as the old folks' home for the incarcerated in our state.[32] So far, no one has died at the one women's prison in Michigan, but we suspect that something truly nefarious is happening there. Our office at the Prison Creative Arts Project (PCAP) receives a constant flood of mail from the thousands of incarcerated people who participate in our programming. The numbers of folks writing to us rose markedly during the pandemic, but we have not had a single letter from Women's Huron Valley Correctional in over two months. We have no way of knowing whether this is due to short staffing in the mail room or a deliberate censorship of what the women want to tell us about what is happening inside that prison right now.

In concert with the activists who have brought revolution to the streets throughout the US in the pandemic summer of 2020, those of us who care about people in prisons are working to harness the energy of this crisis for profound social change. The pandemic reveals what we have always known—that prisons are public health disasters; that prisons harm us all, including those who believe they have no relationship to incarceration; that prisons and police function as a theatre of security without actually

---

32. "MDOC Takes Steps to Prevent Spread of Coronavirus (COVID-19)," Medium (Medium, April 26, 2022), https://medium.com/

keeping us safe. Never in my lifetime have I heard people speaking openly in mainstream venues about disarming the police. People who are not seasoned activists finally want to know what Angela Davis means when she talks about prison abolition. A wave of progressive prosecutors who want to enable decarceration swept into office in the last election cycle, and many more are running campaigns right now.

The potential to shake off many of the chains of institutionalized racism feels present, though its fulfillment will take much labor and a great many miracles. I can hardly sleep most nights in this pandemic because the need to do more work toward these goals haunts me. We must find a way to do more, to get people out of prison before more of them endure sickness and death, to stop the plague of incarceration from taking further generations from their families and communities. Whatever we can accomplish now will not make right what has already been suffered, will not restore the years and lives that have been taken from so many people—just as the victories of the Civil Rights Movement did not make up for the cruelty, death, and devastation of Jim Crow. Yet we cannot let people in prisons slip back into obscurity, where too much of the public can ignore the human rights violations occurring every day inside the walls.

The work we do as artists has the ability to keep these struggles in public view. The murals of George Floyd and other victims of police murder springing up in cities around the world enable us to see and not forget the cost of state violence. In May 2020, a theatre organization called the 24 Hour Plays did a special edition of their online Viral Monologues series on "COVID and Incarceration" in which famous playwrights wrote monologues based on interviews with currently and formerly incarcerated people and their families. These were performed by high profile actors, filmed, and shared on Instagram.[33] They brought national attention and personal stories to the public representation of COVID inside prisons. We need many more public venues for this work, and the digital age brings with it much possibility for visibility and also for our creations to be easily lost in the constant media barrage.

All of the prison art makers I know on both sides of the walls want more than anything else right now to stay connected to one another—to find ways to keep our creative energy and sense of community alive while sickness and death surround us. Rowan Mackenzie, a theatre maker who does Shakespeare programming in British prisons, devised a way forward that has inspired many of us in other parts of the world. She sends activity packets based on Shakespeare's plays into prisons to keep her collaborators

---

33. "Special Edition: Covid & Incarceration," The 24-hour Plays: Viral Monologues, accessed June 3, 2022, https://24hourplays.com/.

engaged in the work through correspondence. We at PCAP are developing something similar. Our program facilitators will work in small teams with groups of about twenty incarcerated people in a given prison, exchanging correspondence that will lead over the course of about fifteen weeks into a collaborative project in creative writing, theatre, or visual art. The PCAP theatre workshops will also have an opportunity to have some of their collectively generated material translated into Portuguese and shared with university students and incarcerated theatre makers in Brazil as part of an ongoing exchange we have had for the last seven years with two programs doing similar work in Florianópolis and Rio de Janeiro.[34] This shift to doing everything in the mail is new for our program but in a way feels deeply familiar to me. For the twenty years of my father's incarceration in Texas, our family lived most of its life in letters because that was all we had. When everything else shut down in our world, we kept each other close by writing.

Though we cannot escape the terror of this moment, we at PCAP are finding a few unexpected gifts in the necessity of our pivot to remote programming. Historically, we have only been able to offer weekly programming in prisons within about an hour's drive of our Ann Arbor campus. Now we have the ability to reach folks in distant parts of the state with the same frequency. We hope to find a way to keep our correspondence programming running at faraway prisons even after we can resume our in-person workshops. In Fall 2020, for the first time in PCAP's thirty-year history, formerly incarcerated people, including those still on parole, can facilitate weekly workshops inside adult prisons because we are not actually going inside. This opens up deep opportunities for collaboration and helping to build an even stronger network of support for currently and formerly incarcerated participants. Our alumni who have moved away from Michigan can also return to facilitating workshops remotely, and in yet another first, we can share the final celebrations of our workshops with a broader public outside the prison. We hope that our correspondence workshops in visual art and creative writing will produce magazines or chapbooks that can be printed and sent back into the prisons and also shared online. Our theatre workshops are aiming toward collaborative script writing and filmed performances by our facilitators which can be shared online for the families of the incarcerated participants to see. We would love to be able to send the filmed performances into the prisons as well, but that remains to be

34. Ashley Lucas, Natalia Ribeiro Fiche, and Vicente Concilio. "We Move Forward Together: A Prison Theater Exchange Program among Three Universities in the United States and Brazil," *The Prison Journal* 99, no. 4 (September 2019): pp. 1–22, https://doi.org/10.1177/0032885519861061.

negotiated with the powers that be. Nothing can replace the level of meaningful interactions we can have with incarcerated people by working together in person, but like so many communities that have endured incarceration, we resolve to make the most out of everything we have. Neither prison nor pandemic will stop us.

—Ashley Lucas, Ann Arbor, MI
December 2020

Acknowledgments

Thank you to Lynne and all the superstars at New Village Press, for diving in and believing in this book.

Thank you to the contributors, without whom this book would not exist. Thank you especially to Kate Glavin, from whose poem this book's title is sourced.

Thank you in particular to the late Buzz Alexander, for creating the Prison Creative Arts Project; Ellen Bass, for your early enthusiasm and help in spreading the word; Phil Christman, for your unwavering belief in me; Ian Demsky, for your thoughts on ethical editing; and Erin Wiley, for your infinite patience and wisdom as we navigated those first writing workshops at Cooper Street Correctional Facility in 2011.

Thank you Riley Hewko, Doran Larson, Vikki Law, and Judith Tannenbaum, for early guidance regarding the socio-political considerations of a project such as this.

Thank you to my friends and mentors Renee Gross, You Li, Will Leaf, Heather Martin, Robbie Moore, Catherine Pikula, Gabi Shiner, Bennett Stein, and H.R.Webster, for listening and advising.

Thank you Daemond Arindell, Reginald Dwayne Betts, Anastacia Renee, C. Davida Ingram, Nikita Oliver, and Kyes Stevens for inspiring.

Thank you to my NYU MFA cohort and professors, in particular Matthew Rohrer.

Thank you Ashley Lucas and Justin Rovillos Monson, for your tireless support and brilliant words.

Thank you Benjamin Cloud, Bro. Truth, and Antonio Sanchez-Day (c/o Brian Daldorph), for generously allowing me to include your work in this book.

Thank you to the Prison Creative Arts Project at the University of Michigan, for launching me on this path and modelling fearlessness, faith, and ingenuity.

Thank you again to the late Judith Tannenbaum for paving the way.

Finally, and most importantly, thank you to all the artists currently or previously behind bars that inspired the poems and stories included in this book. Working with you fed our artistic identities and perspectives on creativity, presence, and justice. We can only hope we contributed the same to you.

Attributions

"Antonio Sanchez-Day," by Brian Daldorph, first appeared in *Coal City Review, Vol. 44* (2021)

"Janus Head," by Brittany Hailer, first appeared in *HEArt Online.*

"ALPHABET," by Helen Elaine Lee, first appeared in *Prairie Schooner, Vol. 85, No. 1* (Spring 2011)

"Tiger Lily Wants to Know About Freedom", by Caits Meissner, first appeared in *The Fourth River*, Iss. 16 (Words Without Walls, 2019).

"Showing Up," by Anna Plemons, first appeared in *Beyond Progress in the Prison Classroom: Options and Opportunities.* Copyright © 2019 by the National Council of Teachers of English. Reprinted with permission.

"Letter Pictures," by Rowan Renee, appeared as an earlier version in *Up River Syllabus*, a catalog to accompany the exhibition *Up River Studies: Carcerality and the American Sublime*, curated by Sofia D'Amico at the Hessel Museum of Art, CCS Bard.

"In the Very Essence of Poetry There Is Something Indecent," by Judith Tannenbaum, first appeared in *Disguised as a Poem.* Copyright © 2000 by Northeastern University Press. Reprinted with permission.

"La Paloma Prisoner," by Raquel Almazan, was programmed as part of the Next Door series with New York Theatre Workshop for a full theatrical run, directed by Estefania Fadul. Original dates were postponed due to COVID-19. Previous excerpt of *La Paloma Prisoner* excerpt and interview with Alessandro Clericuzio previously appeared in *Performing Gender and Violence in National and Transnational Contexts*, edited by Maria Anita Stefanelli, published by L.E.D. Edizioni universitarie di Letterature Economia Diritto, Milano, 2017.

"To Keep a Green Branch from Snapping," by Tara Betts, first appeared in *Poetry* magazine (2021).

"On Why "Prison Writer" is a Limiting Label: What Incarcerated Writers Want the Literary Community to Understand," by Caits Meissner with interviewees, first appeared in *LitHub* (2019).

"You Can't Have It All," by Caits Meissner, first appeared in *The Normal School* (2019).

Selections from *Exit, Civilian*, by Idra Novey, previously appeared in *Exit, Civilian: Poems.* Copyright © 2012 by the University of Georgia Press. Reprinted with Permission. "Recent Findings" first appeared in *Tongue: A Journal of Writing and Art.* "Riding by on a Sunday" first appeared in *Women's Studies*

"Women's Prison Every Week," by Jill McDonough, first appeared in Poetry Foundation Online Archive (2014).

"The Avenal State Prison & Larry Rivers Died Draft Two Blues," by Michael McLaughlin, first appeared in the *San Gabriel Valley Quarterly* (2003).

"Praise Poem," by Caits Meissner, first appeared in *Day One Literary Journal* (2015).

"A Cold and Trembling Thing," "If My Blackness Turns to Fruit," and "Malik," by E. Ethelbert Miller, previously appeared in *The Collected Poems of E. Ethelbert Miller,* ed. by Kirsten Porter (Willow Books, 2016).

"A Personal History of Breathing," by Joy Priest, first appeared in *American Poetry Review Vol. 45 No.5* (2020).

"Nightstick," by Joy Priest, previously appeared in *Horsepower.* Copyright © 2020. Reprinted by permission of the University of Pittsburgh Press.

"Saturdays at Reynolds Work Release," by Paisley Rekdal, previously appeared in *Imaginary Vessels.* Copyright © 2016 by Paisley Rekdal. Reprinted with the permission of The Permissions Company, LLC on behalf of Copper Canyon Press, www.coppercanyonpress.org.

"One of the Girls" and "Pink Painted Nails," by Amani Sawari, first appeared on *sawarimi.org.*

"Some Nights Like This," by Patricia Roth Schwartz, previously appeared in *Clackamas Literary Review* (2003) and *Planting Bulbs in a Time of War, and Other Poems* (FootHills, 2005).

"The Children in Their Little Bulletproof Vests," by Christopher Soto, appeared in an earlier version as "Los Padrinos Juvenile Detention Center, Unit Y2," *Hyperallergic* (2016).

"Hummingbird in Underworld," by Deborah Tobola, previously appeared in *Kalliope, A Journal of Women's Literature* and *Art* (2003) and *Hummingbird in Underworld: Teaching in a Men's Prison* (She Writes Press, 2019).

"Milk and Cookies," by Deborah Tobola, previously appeared in *Iron City Review* (2016) and *Hummingbird in Underworld: Teaching in a Men's Prison* (She Writes Press, 2019).

"From My Classroom Window at the Prison, Before Students Arrive" and "Teaching at the Prison in December," by Michael Torres, previously appeared in *An Incomplete List of Names.* Copyright © 2020 by Michael Torres. Reprinted with permission from Beacon Press, Boston, Massachusetts

"Homie," by Vachine, first appeared in *The Coiled Serpent: Poets Arising from the Cultural Quakes and Shifts of Los Angeles* (2016).

"Prison Letter," by Benjamin Cloud, first appeared in *The Sky is on Fire, After All, The Michigan Review of Prisoner Creative Writing, Vol. 6* (Dakota West Publishing, 2014).

Further Reading and Resources

(See Bibliography for full citations)

A Working Guide to the Landscape of Arts for Change: *Arts in Corrections,* by Grady Hillman (2011). https://animatingdemocracy.org/

Arts and Corrections. Community Arts Network. www.communityarts.net.

Arts in US Prisons, Justice Arts Coalition (2020). https://thejusticeartscoalition .org/

History: Then and Now, California Arts in Corrections (2021). https://artsincor-rections.org/history

Prison Arts Resource Project: An Annotated Bibliography, by Amanda Gardner, Lori L. Hager, and Grady Hillman (2014). www.arts.gov/

Theatre of the Oppressed. https://imaginaction.org/

What Curators Don't Get About Prison Art, by Zachary Small (2019) www.the nation.com/

Bibliography

Almazan, Raquel. "Interview w/ Alessandro Clericuzio in Rome, Italy." *Raquel Almazan*, February 25, 2016. https://raquelalmazan.com/interview-w-ales sandro-clericuzio-in-rome-italy/.

Almazan, Raquel. "La Paloma Prisoner." *Raquel Almazan*, Accessed May 24, 2022. https://raquelalmazan.com/latin-is-america/la-paloma-prisoner/.

"An Open Letter to Our Friends on the Question of Language." *CMJ Center*, July 2017. The Center for NuLeadersip on Urban Solutions. https://cmjcenter .org/wp-content/uploads/2017/07/CNUS-AppropriateLanguage.pdf.

"Arts and Corrections." *Community Arts Network*, n.d. http://wayback.archive-it .org/2077/20100906195054/http://www.communityarts.net/archivefiles /corrections/index.php.

"Arts in US Prisons—Justice Arts Coalition." *Justice Arts Coalition*, May 2020. https://thejusticeartscoalition.org/general-arts-in-us-prisons/.

Bennett, Joshua, Tara Betts, and Sarah Ross, eds. "The Practice of Freedom." *Poetry Foundation,* February 2021. https://www.poetryfoundation.org/poetrymaga zine/issue/155204/february-2021.

Blakinger, Keri. "Prisoners Are Setting Fires to Protest Pandemic Conditions." *The Marshall Project,* December 13, 2020. www.themarshallproject.org/2020 /12/13/prison-fires.

Charleston, Cortney Lamar. "It's Important I Remember That They Don't Have the Tools to Critique Me—." *Poetry Foundation,* June 2019. www.poetry foundation.org/poetrymagazine/poems/150049/its-important-i-remem ber-that-they-dont-have-the-tools-to-critique-me.

Coates, Ta-Nehisi. In *Between the World and Me*, 71. New York: Spiegel & Grau, 2015.

Dawes, Kwame. "Before Winter." *The New Yorker*, September 23, 2019.

Editors. "Prison Nation." *Aperture Magazine* no. 230, 2018.

"Fact Sheet: Trends in U.S. Corrections." *The Sentencing Project*, May 2021. www .sentencingproject.org/wp-content/uploads/2021/07/Trends-in-US-Correc tions.pdf.

Fleetwood, Nicole R. In *Marking Time: Art in the Age of Mass Incarceration*, 231–33. Cambridge, MA: Harvard University Press, 2020.

Gardner, Amanda, Lori L. Hager, and Grady Hillman. "Prison Arts Resource Project: An Annotated Bibliography," 2014. https://www.arts.gov/sites /default/files/Research-Art-Works-Oregon-rev.pdf.

Heawood, Sophie. "Grayson Perry's First Exhibition in Years Is Deliciously Provocative—and Utterly Brilliant." *British Vogue*, September 24, 2019.

www.vogue.co.uk/arts-and-lifestyle/article/grayson-perry-new-exhibition
-victoria-miro-super-rich-interior-decoration.

Hillman, Grady. "A Working Guide to the Landscape of Arts for Change: Arts
in Corrections." *Arts in Corrections | Animating Democracy*, 2011. https://
landscape.animatingdemocracy.org/resource/arts-corrections.

"History: Then and Now." *California Arts in Corrections*, 2021. https://artsincor
rections.org/history.

Kendrick Lamar. *Sing About Me, I'm Dying of Thirst*. CD. *Good Kid, M.A.A.D. City*.
Atlanta, Georgia: Interscope Records, 2013.

Kois, Dan. "Was Poetry Magazine Really Wrong to Publish a Child Porn Con-
vict in Its Prison Issue?" *Slate Magazine*, February 4, 2021. https://slate.com
/culture/2021/02/poetry-magazine-prison-incarcerated-writers-kirk
-nesset-child-pornography.html.

Lucas, Ashley, Natalia Ribeiro Fiche, and Vicente Concilio. "We Move Forward
Together: A Prison Theater Exchange Program among Three Universities
in the United States and Brazil." *The Prison Journal* 99, no. 4 (2019): 1–22.
https://doi.org/10.1177/0032885519861061.

Meek Mill ft. Jay-Z and Rick Ross. *What's Free*. CD. *Championships*. STREET-
RUNNER and Tarik Azzouz, Atlantic Records, 2018.

"MDOC Takes Steps to Prevent Spread of Coronavirus (COVID-19)." *Medium*,
April 26, 2022. https://medium.com/@MichiganDOC/mdoc-takes-steps-to
-prevent-spread-of-coronavirus-covid-19-250f43144337.

Nation, Carry Amelia. "Chapter VIII." Essay. In *The Use and Need of the Life of
Carry A. Nation*, 148–48. Charlottesville, Virginia: F.M. Steves, 1909.

Ransom, Jan. "A Look inside Rikers: 'Fight Night' and Gang Rule, Captured on
Video." *The New York Times*, January 13, 2022. www.nytimes.com/2022/01
/12/nyregion/rikers-jail-videos.html.

Rosal, Patrick. "Brooklyn Antediluvian." In *Brooklyn Antediluvian: Poems*. New
York: Persea Books, 2016.

Russian Federation. *World Prison Brief*, January 31, 2022. www.prisonstudies
.org/country/russian-federation.

Sawyer, Wendy, and Peter Wagner. "Mass Incarceration: The Whole Pie 2022."
Prison Policy Initiative, March 14, 2022. www.prisonpolicy.org/reports/pie
2022.html#covid.

Shakespeare, Willian. *Hamlet*. 1603

Small, Zachary. "What Curators Don't Get about Prison Art." *The Nation*, 2019.
www.thenation.com/article/archive/prison-art-shows-essay/.

"Special Edition: Covid & Incarceration." *The 24-hour Plays: Viral Monologues*.
Accessed June 3, 2022. https://24hourplays.com/viral-monologues-covid
-incarceration/.

"Theatre of the Oppressed." *ImaginAction.org*. Accessed June 6, 2022. https://
imaginaction.org/media/our-methods/theatre-of-the-oppressed-2.

Thompson, Gabriel. "Against Oblivion: Martin Espada on His Life in Poetry." *Poetry Foundation*, May 1, 2018. www.poetryfoundation.org/articles/146621/against-oblivion#tab-related.

Webster, H.R., and Demetrius "Meech" Buckley. "Poetry Is like Water: A Conversation between H.R. Webster and Demetrius 'Meech' Buckley." *The University of Arizona Poetry Center*, June 15, 2022. https://poetry.arizona.edu/blog/poetry-water-conversation-between-hr-webster-and-demetrius-%E2%80%9Cmeech%E2%80%9D-buckley.

Widra, Emily, and Tiana Herring. "States of Incarceration: The Global Context 2021." *States of Incarceration*: The Global Context 2021. Prison Policy Initiative, September 2021. www.prisonpolicy.org/global/2021.html.

Contributors

BUZZ ALEXANDER (1938–2019) was a political activist and a professor of English Language and Literature at the University of Michigan in Ann Arbor. His work in human rights, peace activism and social justice led to his founding, with Mary Heinen, the Prison Creative Arts Project at the University of Michigan. He is the author of *William Dean Howells: The Realist as Humanist* (Lenox Hill Publishing, 1981), *Film on the Left* (Princeton University Press, 1981), and *Is William Martinez Not Our Brother* (University of Michigan Press, 2010), as well as essays about film. He loved poetry and translated the poetry of Roberto Sanesi from Italian into English. *Fly Ball Snagger* is a collection of Buzz's poems, many of which were written in The Poet's Corner, a workshop he facilitated for many years at the Southern Men's Correctional Facility in Jackson Michigan.

RAQUEL ALMAZAN is an interdisciplinary performer, writer, director and educator (MFA Columbia University—Playwriting). Her career as artist-activist spans original multi-media solo performances, playwriting, devising-dramaturgy and filmmaking. She is the creator—facilitator of arts programs for intergenerational communities, with a focus on social justice and is a practitioner of Butoh Dance. Their work has been featured Off-Broadway, throughout the United States and internationally in Greece, Italy, Slovenia, Chile, Colombia, Guatemala, Canada and Sweden; including several of her plays within the (Latin is America play cycle), bi-lingual plays in dedication to Latin American countries. Select venues: Classical Theatre of Harlem-Lincoln Center, The Kennedy Center, The Signature Theatre, Bric Arts, The Playwrights Center. Recipient of the Map Fund, Doris Duke Foundation Grant, NYSCA Grant, National Association of Latino Arts and Culture LGBTQ Arch and Bruce Brown Foundation Playwriting Prize. Almazan has facilitated in incarcerated settings for over 15 years and is an essay contributor to Pen America's 2022 publication, *The Sentences That Create Us.* She is the artistic director of La Lucha Arts, which collaborates with organizations, social movements, and impacted individuals towards providing a platform for marginalized—abandoned narratives and people. (Community Partner Collaboration selections: Pen America, Close Rikers Campaign, Steps to End Family Violence, Brooklyn DA's Re-entry task force and The United Nations). See www.raquelalmazan.com

SARAH W. BARTLETT has brought two books into the world from *writinginsideVT* (https://writinginsidevt.com/), the year-round weekly writing program she founded in 2010 for Vermont's incarcerated women: *Life Lines: Re-Writing Lives from Inside Out* (Green Writers Press, 2019); and *Hear Me, See Me: Incarcerated*

Women Write (Orbis Books, 2013). She has authored two poetry chapbooks with Finishing Line Press, *Slow Blooming Gratitudes* (New Women's Voices Finalist #130, 2017) and *Into the Great Blue* (2011). Additional work appears in *Adanna, Ars Medica, the Aurorean, Chrysalis, Colere, Lilipoh, Minerva Rising, Mom Egg Review, PMS PoemMemoirStory, Women's Review of Books*; and numerous anthologies, including the award-winning *Women on Poetry*, (McFarland & Co. Inc., 2012). Word-midwife, grandmother and gardener, she celebrates nature's healing wisdom and the human spirit's landscapes. See https://sarahw bartlett.com/

ELLEN BASS'S most recent book is *Indigo* (Copper Canyon Press, 2020). She co-edited the groundbreaking *No More Masks! An Anthology of Poems by Women* and her non-fiction books include *The Courage to Heal* and *Free Your Mind*. A Chancellor of the Academy of American Poets, she is the recipient of Fellowships from the Guggenheim Foundation and the National Endowment for the Arts. She teaches in the MFA writing program at Pacific University. In 2012 Ellen Bass founded The Poetry Workshops at Salinas Valley State Prison in California. There are now several poets teaching at the prison and the program has expanded to workshops in the jails in Santa Cruz, California.

JOSHUA BENNETT is a Professor of English and Creative Writing at Dartmouth College. He is the author of three books of poetry and literary criticism: *The Sobbing School* (Penguin, 2016)—which was a National Poetry Series selection and a finalist for an NAACP Image Award—*Being Property Once Myself* (Harvard University Press, 2020) and *Owed* (Penguin, 2020). Bennett holds a PhD in English from Princeton University, and an MA in Theatre and Performance Studies from the University of Warwick, where he was a Marshall Scholar. In 2021, he received the Whiting Award for Poetry and Nonfiction. Bennett has recited his original works at various venues including the NAACP Image Awards and President Obama's Evening of Poetry and Music at the White House. He has also performed and taught creative writing workshops at hundreds of middle schools, high schools, colleges, and universities across the United States, as well as in the UK and South Africa. Bennett's writing has been published in *The Best American Poetry, The New York Times, The Paris Review* and elsewhere. He has received fellowships from the Guggenheim Foundation, the National Endowment for the Arts, MIT, and the Society of Fellows at Harvard University. His first work of narrative nonfiction, *Spoken Word: A Cultural History*, is out from Knopf.

TARA BETTS is the author of *Break the Habit* (Trio House Press, 2016), *Arc & Hue* (Willow Books, 2009), and the forthcoming *Refuse to Disappear* (Word Works Books, 2022). In addition to working as an editor, a teaching artist, and a mentor for other writers, she has taught at several universities. She was the Inaugural Poet for the People Practitioner Fellow at University of Chicago and founder of the nonprofit Whirlwind Learning Center. Her poetry has appeared in numerous anthologies and journals, including *The Breakbeat Poets*, *Poetry*, and *Essence*, which named her as one of their "40 Favorite Poets" in 2010.

DEBORAH KOFF-CHAPIN'S evocative images are created through the simple yet profound process of Touch Drawing. She has been developing the process it since discovering it in revelatory play in 1974. Deborah is creator of SoulCards 1 & 2, Portals of Presence: Faces Drawn from the Subtle Realms, and SoulTouch Coloring Journals. Deborah is author of *Drawing Out Your Soul* (Center for Touch Drawing, 1996) and The Touch Drawing Facilitator Workbook. She teaches internationally and online. Deborah offers Song Bath Sanctuary online weekly. See www.touchdrawing.com.

SHARON CHARDE, a retired psychotherapist and a writing teacher since 1992, has won numerous poetry awards, the latest being first prize in Story Circle Network's 2021 contest, second prize in the Connecticut Poetry Society's 2021 Nutmeg Poetry Contest and finalist in Broad River Review's 2021 Rash Poetry Awards. She is published over eighty-five times in journals and anthologies of poetry and prose, including *Calyx, Mudfish, The Paterson Review, Ping Pong, Rattle, Poet Lore, Upstreet* and *The Comstock Review*, and has had seven Pushcart nominations. She has also edited and published *I Am Not a Juvenile Delinquent*, containing the work of the adjudicated teenaged females she has volunteered with since 1999 at a residential treatment center in Litchfield, Connecticut. She has three first prize-winning chapbooks, *Bad Girl at the Altar Rail, Four Trees Down from Ponte Sisto* and *Incendiary,* as well as a full-length collection, *Branch in His Hand,* published by Backwaters Press in November 2008, which was adapted as a radio play by the BBC, broadcast in 2012. *After Blue* for which she won honorable mention in Finishing Line Press's 2013 chapbook contest, was published in September 2014 and *Unhinged,* finalist in Blue Light Press' 2019 chapbook contest came out that year. Her memoir, *I Am Not a Juvenile Delinquent: How Poetry Changed a Group of At-Risk Young Women* was published in June 2020 by Mango Publishing. *The Glass Is Already Broken,* her seventh poetry collection, was published by Blue Light Press in September 2021. She has been awarded fellowships to the Vermont Studio Center, Virginia Center for the Creative Arts, MacDowell, the Ucross Foundation and The Corporation of Yaddo.

EVA CHILADAKI was born in Germany in 1950 and moved to Greece in 1961. She studied and worked as an interpreter in Italy and performed with Kourelou puppet theater. She now makes dolls and props for theater, cinema, and television, and teaches at various schools and institutions, as well as the Gypsy craft program "Suvava" for Save the Children. A member of the AFI collective, Eva has also worked for Arsis Association for the Social Support of Youth. In addition, she has worked in the carpenter workshop of the open community Diavasi, a rehabilitation program. From 2001 to 2008 she directed the sewing workshop for the women of Korydallos Prison. Since 2008 she has continued to work with the same group in Thiva, where the women's prison was transferred, organizing shows to sell their work and bring the women a small income. The group consists of 20 women. With every woman released a new member joins the group, so over 600 women have come through the program since its formation. Some of the formerly incarcerated women are still participating from their homes.

PHILIP CHRISTMAN teaches writing at the University of Michigan and is the faculty advisor for the Prison Creative Arts Project's *Michigan Review of Prisoner Creative Writing*. His essays and book reviews appear frequently in *The Hedgehog Review, The Christian Century,* and *Commonweal*. His book *Midwest Futures*, about the ecological history and future of the Midwest in popular culture, and his collection *How to Be Normal: Essays* are available from Belt (published in 2020 and 2022, respectively)

BENJAMIN CLOUD writes as a means to escape and to maintain sanity. He finally embraces the craft and is honored when someone is able to relate to his finished work.

CHELLA COURINGTON taught at the Maximum Security Prison for Men in Columbia, SC, from 1980–1983. As a graduate student in English at the University of South Carolina, she taught first-year writing and sophomore literature through the University's Prison Program to students from solitary confinement. Those years were some of the most rewarding of her career. In an English Literature class from *Beowulf* to Aphra Behn, they read all of *Paradise Lost*, probing the themes of free will, obedience and justice. As a result of that intense month, she wrote "At the Maximum Security Prison for Men" more than twenty years later. Courington's poetry and fiction appear or are forthcoming in numerous anthologies and journals including *DMQ Review, The Los Angeles Review,* and *Anti-Heroin Chic*. She was raised in the Appalachian south and now lives in California. Her recent micro-chapbooks of poetry are *Good Trouble*, Origami Poems Project, and *Hell Hath*, Maverick Duck Press. Twitter: @chellacourington, Instagram: @chellacourington

BRIAN DALDORPH teaches at the University of Kansas. He has taught a Creative Writing class at Douglas County Jail in Lawrence, Kansas, since 2001. His most recent book of poetry is *Kansas Poems* (Meadowlark Press, 2021). With Mike Caron he co-edited *Douglas County Jail Blues* (Coal City Press, 2010), an anthology of prisoner writing. Brian's nonfiction book *Words Is a Powerful Thing* (University Press of Kansas, 2021), a chronicle of his 20 years teaching at Douglas County Jail, won a 2022 Kansas Notable Book Award from Kansas State Library.

IAN DEMSKY is a writer and poet living in Ann Arbor, Michigan. The poems included in this volume are examples of documentary poetry that stem from his days as a newspaper reporter. By recontextualizing snippets from publicly available law enforcement and prison records, the aim is to illuminate an often-unseen corner of societal storytelling.

BRIAN GILMORE Native of Washington DC, poet, writer, public interest lawyer, and author of four collections of poetry, including the latest, *'come see about me, marvin,'* (Wayne State Press, 2019), a 2020 Michigan Notable Books recipient. He has written for *The Crisis Magazine, The Washington Post, The New York Times, Jazz Times*, and is a long-time columnist with the Progressive Media Project. He has also been an NAACP Image Award nominee, a Hurston-Wright Legacy Award nominee, and runner-up for the Larry Neal Writers Award. He is a Kimbilio Fellow and a Cave Canem Fellow and currently teaches in the Law & Society Program at the University of Maryland.

KATE GLAVIN received her MFA in Poetry at UMass Boston. She taught writing and literature at Lansing Correctional Facility in Lansing, Kansas, and poetry at Bay State Correctional Center from 20112015. She currently works with Black Seed Writers, a writing group for Boston's homeless community.

RENNY GOLDEN worked with a prisoner led education program (PEP) at Walpole Maximum Security prison in Massachusetts. In the 1980s she and her Northeastern Illinois University students volunteered to work with women prisoners at Cook County Jail. In the 1990s Golden interviewed children and their mothers incarcerated in Cook County Jail and Dwight prison. She also interviewed mothers recently released from New Mexico prisons for her book *War on the Family: Imprisoned Mothers and the Families They Leave Behind*, (Routledge, 2005).

NANCY MILLER GOMEZ'S work has appeared or is forthcoming in Best American Poetry 2021, Best New Poets 2021, *The Adroit Journal, New Ohio Review, Shenandoah, River Styx, The Rumpus, Rattle, Massachusetts Review, American Life in Poetry, Verse Daily* and elsewhere. Her chapbook, *Punishment*, was published in 2018 as part of the Rattle chapbook series. She co-founded an organization that provides poetry workshops to incarcerated women and men in Santa Cruz County, California. She has an MFA from Pacific University and has taught poetry at Salinas Valley State Prison and the in the Santa Cruz County jails.

PAT GRANEY, a Seattle-based choreographer, has received Choreography Fellowships from the National Endowment for the Arts, Artist Trust, the NEA International Program, and the John Simon Guggenheim Foundation. Ms. Graney was also awarded the Alpert Award, a US Artists Award and the 'Arts Innovator' Award from Artist Trust and the Dale Chihuly Foundation. She was honored to receive the Doris Duke Performing Artist Award 2013–2017. Keeping the Faith (KTF), which Graney started in 1992, is an arts-based educational program that features dance, writing, ASL and visual arts, culminating in performances. KTF has been in over 20 prisons in the US and abroad. Ms. Graney was selected for a 'Crosscut Courage Award' from Seattle's Public Television Station KCTS in

Arts & Culture, for her 25 years working in US women's prisons. *Keeping the Faith/The Prison Project* is one of the longest-running prison arts programs in the US.

BRITTANY HAILER has taught creative writing classes at the Allegheny County Jail and Sojourner House as part of Chatham's Words Without Walls program and now teaches creative writing and journalism at the University of Pittsburgh. Her work as appeared in *NPR*, *Fairy Tale Review*, *Hobart*, *Barrelhouse*, and elsewhere. She is the director of the Pittsburgh Institute for Nonprofit Journalism.

DIANNA MACKINNON HENNING holds an MFA in Writing '89 from Vermont College of Fine Arts. Published in, in part: *Naugatuck River Review*, *Lullwater Review*, *The Red Rock Review*, *The Kentucky Review*, *The Main Street Rag*, *California Quarterly*, *Poetry International*, *Fugue*, *Clackamas Literary Review*, *South Dakota Review*, *Hawai'i Pacific Review* and *The Seattle Review*. Finalist in Aesthetica's Creative Writing Award in the UK. Henning has taught poetry for several years through California Poets in the Schools. She received several CAC grants and through the William James Association's Prison Arts Program which gave her the opportunity to teach poetry at Folsom Prison as well as at other CA prisons. Nominated by *Blue Fifth Review* December 2015 for a Pushcart. Henning's third poetry book *Cathedral of the Hand* published 2016 by Finishing Line Press. Teaching in the prisons has been the most rewarding work her life. She witnessed that once someone goes deep inside, there is no need to return to the inside of a prison. Art unlocks doors and dissolves bars. Poetry is a direct line to the soul.

MICHAEL G. HICKEY started a "Poetry-in-the-Prison" program at the Monroe Correctional Complex in Monroe, Washington, in 2017, where he worked as a volunteer for one year in the Special Offenders Unit (SOU). He also coordinated a book drive in which he delivered 63 boxes of books to the MCC library. In 2009, Michael volunteered for the Pongo Teen Writing Program in Seattle, WA as a poet/therapist for six months. The venue was King County Youth Detention. Since then, he has helped to train new Pongo volunteers and participated in promotional events such as poetry readings.

HELEN ELAINE LEE'S first novel, *The Serpent's Gift*, was published by Atheneum (1994) and her second novel, *Water Marked*, was published by Scribner (1999). Her recent novel, *Pomegranate*, is published by Atria Books (April 2023). Helen was on the board of PEN New England for 10 years, and she served on its Freedom to Write Committee and volunteered with its Prison Creative Writing Program, which she helped to start. She has written about the experience of teaching creative writing in prison in a *New York Times Book Review* essay, "Visible Men". Her stories about prisoners have appeared in *Prairie Schooner*, *Callaloo*, *Hanging Loose*, *Best African American Fiction 2009* (Bantam Books), and *Solstice Literary Magazine*. Her short story "Blood Knot" appeared in the spring 2017 issue of *Ploughshares* and the story "Lesser Crimes" appeared in the Winter 2016 issue of *Callaloo*. She was educated at Harvard College and Harvard Law School, and she is Professor of Comparative Media Studies/Writing, MIT, and Director, MIT's Program in Women's & Gender Studies.

YOU LI a lawyer and poet who was born in Beijing and lives in New Haven. Her work has appeared or is forthcoming in *Shenandoah, Asian American Writers' Workshop's The Margins, Narrative*, and elsewhere. A Bread Loaf Writers' Conference work-study scholarship recipient, she was a recent finalist for the AAWW Margins Fellowship. She has worked with incarcerated people for a decade as a tutor, advocate, and lawyer.

ASHLEY LUCAS teaches theatre at the University of Michigan, where she is also Director of Latina/o Studies, Former Director of the Prison Creative Arts Project (PCAP), and a founding member of the Carceral State Project. Her book *Prison Theatre and the Global Crisis of Incarceration* (Bloomsbury, 2020) examines the ways in which incarcerated people use theatre to counteract the dehumanizing forces of the prison.

KATHARYN HOWD MACHAN, author of 39 collections of poetry (in 2020, *A Slow Bottle of Wine*, winner of the Jessie Bryce Niles Chapbook Competition) has lived in Ithaca, New York, since 1975 and, now as a full professor, has taught Writing at Ithaca College since 1977. After many years of coordinating the Ithaca Community Poets and directing the national Feminist Women's Writing Workshops, Inc., she was selected to be Tompkins County's first poet laureate. Her poems have appeared in numerous magazines, anthologies, textbooks, and stage productions, and she has edited three thematic anthologies, most recently, with Split Oak Press, a tribute collection celebrating the inspiration of Adrienne Rich.

JILL MCDONOUGH is the author of *Here All Night* (Alice James, 2019), *Reaper* (Alice James, 2017), *Where You Live* (Salt, 2012), *Oh, James!* (Seven Kitchens, 2012), and *Habeas Corpus* (Salt, 2008). The recipient of three Pushcart prizes and fellowships from the Lannan Foundation, the National Endowment for the Arts, the Fine Arts Work Center, the New York Public Library, the Library of Congress, and Stanford's Stegner program, she taught incarcerated college students through Boston University's Prison Education Program for thirteen years. Her work has appeared in *Poetry, Slate, The Nation, The Threepenny Review*, and *Best American Poetry*. She teaches in the MFA program at UMass Boston and started a program offering College Reading and Writing in two Boston jails.

MICHAEL MCLAUGHLIN, A three-time $17,000 California Arts Council grant recipient, worked for twenty-nine years as an Artist-in-Residence at Atascadero State Hospital, a maximum security forensic facility, as a Contract Artist with the California Department of Corrections/the Federal Penitentiary in Lompoc, California, with what was formerly called California Youth Authority (with incarcerated adults & youth), and as San Luis Obispo county Area Coordinator for California Poets in the Schools. A graduate of The University of Southern California's Master of Professional Writing program and founding editor of their literary journal, *The Southern California Anthology* (now *Exposition*), McLaughlin has written two novels, *Western People Show Their Faces* (1987) and *Gang of One* and three books of poetry, *Ped Xing* (Creative Press, 1977), *The Upholstery of Heaven* (Don't Trip Press, 1996) and *Countless Cinemas* (University of Hell Press, 2016). Selected Poet Laureate of San Luis Obispo County in 2003, he orchestrated Santa Maria, California's Live from the CORE Winery poetry/performance series for over six years. Originally from San Francisco, McLaughlin, his wife, and their nine cats now reside in Prescott, Arizona, where he conducts weblive poetry workshops and ESL classes and is an English Instructor at Yavapai College.

CAITS MEISSNER'S poems, comics, essays and curation have appeared in *The Creative Independent, The Rumpus, [PANK], Harper's Bazaar, Adroit, Literary Hub, Split This Rock, Bust Magazine, The Normal School, Hobart,* and *The Guardian,* among others. In 2017, Meissner re-envisioned the concept of book tour for her illustrated poetry collection *Let It Die Hungry,* pairing public speaking engagements with opportunities to work with incarcerated writers across the United States. She spends her days as Director of Prison and Justice Writing at PEN America where she edited *The Sentences That Create Us: Crafting A Writer's Life in Prison* (Haymarket Books, 2021).

E. ETHELBERT MILLER is a literary activist and author of two memoirs and several poetry collections. He hosts the WPFW morning radio show "On the Margin with E. Ethelbert Miller and hosts and produces "The Scholars" on UDC-TV which received a 2020 Telly Award. Miller has conducted poetry workshops for incarcerated individuals at the Montgomery County Correctional Facility (MCCF) in Boyds, Maryland. Most recently, he was given a grant from the D.C. Commission on the Arts and Humanities and a congressional award from Congressman Jamie Raskin in recognition of his literary activism. Miller's latest book is *How I Found Love Behind the Catcher's Mask* (City Point Press, 2022). See Twitter @ethelbertpoet; Instagram: @eugeneethelbertmiller; and Facebook: @ethelbertmiller.

JUSTIN ROVILLOS MONSON, a first generation Filipino-American artist, was the winner of the inaugural 2017 Kundiman/Asian American Literary Review/ Smithsonian Asian Pacific American Center Mentorship in poetry and an inaugural 2018–2019 PEN America Writing for Justice Fellow. His work has been featured in publications including *Poetry, The Nation, Hayden's Ferry,* and more. His first collection of poetry, *American Inmate,* is forthcoming from Haymarket Press in 2024. He is currently serving a sentence in the Michigan Department of Corrections, from which he hopes to be released in 2027.

RUTH MOTA lives in the Santa Cruz Mountains of California on Ohlone land with her Brazilian/Tupinamba husband, lots of mule deer, and a recently sighted mountain lion. After a career as an international health trainer, she returned to her undergraduate focus on English Lit and began writing poetry. She facilitated poetry circles at the Rountree Correctional Facility in Watsonville and printed anthologies of the men's work. She repeated this process with veterans in the community. Her own poems have been published in many on-line and print journals, including *Terrapin Books, Quillsedge Press, Gyroscope Review, Tulip Tree Press, Hare's Paw, Black Mountain Press,* and *Cathexis Northwest* among others.

MARY NAOUM is a nonprofit professional who collaborates with organizations to move forward tangible, community-driven solutions that are boldly designed to transform local systems. She came to this work through the Prison Creative Arts Project (PCAP), an organization based at the University of Michigan, through which she co-created poetry, plays, and music with people who are incarcerated in youth and adult prisons across Michigan for over six years. Most notably she was a member of Poets Unchained, a writing group based out of Macomb Correctional Facility in New Haven, Michigan. She currently lives in Atlanta.

IDRA NOVEY'S novel *Take What You Need* will be out from Viking-Random House in 2023. She is also the author of *Those Who Knew*, a finalist for the 2019 Clark Fiction Prize and a New York Times Editors' Choice. Her first novel *Ways to Disappear*, received the 2017 Sami Rohr Prize and was a finalist for the L.A. Times Book Prize for First Fiction. Her poetry collections include *Exit, Civilian*, selected for the 2011 National Poetry Series, *The Next Country*, and *Clarice: The Visitor*, a collaboration with the artist Erica Baum. Her works as a translator include Clarice Lispector's novel *The Passion According to G.H.* and a co-translation with Ahmad Nadalizadeh of Iranian poet Garous Abdolmalekian, *Lean Against This Late Hour*, a finalist for the PEN America Poetry in Translation Prize in 2021. She teaches fiction at Princeton University.

NAJEE OMAR is black, queer, and making magic somewhere in Brooklyn. A multidisciplinary poet, rapper, and educator, Najee uses the arts to activate spaces of healing and community building. Named a New York Times '2018 Visionary' for his passion for youth activism, Najee is the Founder, Executive Director of Spark House, an arts education organization that champions black and brown teen voices by bringing poetry and performance programs to New York City public schools. In 2020, his commitment to art and home led him to become the Founding Curator for The Neighborhood Project: an initiative designed to propel emerging black artists further in their careers with the support of their neighbors. His residencies, fellowships, and features include BRIC & University Settlement's Intergenerational Community Arts Council, Callaloo Creative

Writing Workshop, The Public Theater's #BARS Workshop, Brooklyn Academy of Music, Lincoln Center, and Hi-ARTS.

GREGORY OPSTAD is a retired teacher and divides his time between Cloquet, Minnesota and Cochiti Lake, New Mexico. He is a member of Lake Superior Writers. He taught Adult Basic Education/ GED Prep and high school credit classes in English (creative writing/ poetry /expository writing) to men under civil and criminal commitment as Sexual Psychopathic Personalities and Sexually Dangerous Persons at the Minnesota Sex Offender Program in a medium security facility in Moose Lake, Minnesota from 1995 until retirement in 2005. He also taught beginning reading and facilitated therapeutic classes in reading/understanding therapy materials and the journaling process for treatment under the direction of the clinical director. Following retirement, he taught at an alternative school for at-risk youth through the Cloquet Public Schools (ISD#94) in Cloquet, Minnesota and at a reservation school on the Cochiti Pueblo, Cochiti Lake, New Mexico. His poems have appeared in literary journals and anthologies. His chapbook, *Lake Country*, was released by Finishing Line Press in 2013.

KATHY PARK (also known as Kathy Park Woolbert) is a sculptor, painter, writer, and martial artist. She taught incarcerated women and staff at FCI Dublin, California from 1990–1994, she taught incarcerated women and staff at FCI Dublin, California where she founded and administered the Prison Integrated Health Program, an all-volunteer holistic health program for inmates and staff. In its heyday there were classes in stress management, meditation, yoga, somatic bodywork, conflict resolution, creative writing, arts and crafts, theater, drumming, and parenting. But when the climate changed to the punishment model from the rehabilitation model, the program gradually got shut down. Kathy wrote about her volunteer work in prison in a homemade, self-published book in 2000 titled *Soaring Over the Wall: A Volunteer's Collection of Prison Freedom Stories*, but this was never "officially" published and probably topped out at 100 copies. Kathy is also the author of four books: a memoir about her 15-year apprenticeship with a stone sculptor entitled *Seeing Into Stone: A Sculptor's Journey* (Mercury Heartlink, 2011); a compilation of fiction, nonfiction and ten-minute plays entitled *Coyote Points the Way: Borderland Stories and Plays*; *Aikido Off The Mat* (Mercury Heartlink, 2015), a hybrid memoir about her forty-year experience with the martial art Aikido and how its principles of peaceful conflict resolution can help us stay sane in a crazy world; and *Bowing Into Sensei Glioblastoma* (2021), poetry and prose about dealing with aggressive brain cancer by using the principles of aikido. Besides doing artwork, Kathy teaches English print-based correspondence courses through Adams State University's Prison College Program where all her students are incarcerated.

JANIE PAUL is a visual artist and a writer. She is the co-founder, with Buzz Alexander, of the Annual Exhibitions of Art by Michigan Prisoners, a project of the Prison Creative Arts Project at the University of Michigan, now in its twenty-seventh year. She is an Arthur F. Thurnau Professor Emerita at the Stamps School of Art and Design and the School of Social Work at the University of Michigan. Her book *Making Art in Prison: Survival and Resistance* released from Hat and Beard Press in March 2023.

ANNA PLEMONS is the Associate Vice Chancellor for Academic & Student Affairs at WSU Tri-Cities and a faculty member in the Digital Technology and Culture program. Her research focuses on issues of educational justice both in higher education and the US prisons. Plemons' work with incarcerated students at California State Prison Sacramento is highlighted in her monograph, *Beyond Progress in the Prison Classroom: Options and Opportunities* (National Council of Teachers of English, 2019).

JOY PRIEST is the author of *HORSEPOWER* (Pitt Poetry Series, 2020), selected by United States Poet Laureate Natasha Trethewey as the winner of the Donald Hall Prize for Poetry. She is the recipient of a 2021 National Endowment for the Arts Fellowship, a 2019–2020 Fine Arts Work Center Fellowship, and the Stanley Kunitz Memorial Prize from the *American Poetry Review*. Her poems have appeared or are forthcoming in the Academy of American Poets' Poem-a-Day series, *Kenyon Review*, and *The Atlantic*, among others, as well as in commissions for the Museum of Fine Arts, Houston (MFAH) and the Los Angeles County Museum of Art (LACMA). Her essays have appeared in *The Bitter Southerner, Poets & Writers*, and *ESPN*. A Louisville, Kentucky native, Joy is the editor of *Once a City Said: A Louisville Poets' Anthology* (Sarabande Books, June 2023). Joy has facilitated poetry workshops with incarcerated juvenile and adult women, and she is currently an MD Anderson Fellow in the Literature & Creative Writing Program at the University of Houston.

PAISLEY REKDAL is the author of many books of nonfiction and poetry, including *Appropriate: A Provocation* (W. W. Norton, 2021) and *Imaginary Vessels* (Copper Canyon Press, 2016). She is a former NEA and Guggenheim Fellow, and the current Utah poet laureate. She has taught at the Utah State Prison for the University Prison Education Program and worked as a literacy volunteer for the Reynold's Work Release Program, King Country Correctional System, in Seattle, Washington, between 1992 and 1993.

ROWAN RENEE is a Brooklyn-based artist who addresses complex issues of harm, accountability and stigma within the criminal legal system. Their work draws from their own personal experience as a victim of a crime that was never adjudicated, the child of an incarcerated parent and a member of the historically criminalized queer and transgender community. Through craft processes—loom-weaving, analog photography, and kiln-fused glass—they use the labor of making as a way to reclaim the body and enact new pathways to healing. Their work has been exhibited in solo exhibitions at Smack Mellon

(2021), Five Myles (2021), Aperture Foundation (2017), and Pioneer Works (2015). In 2020, their project *Between the Lines,* supported by We, Women Photo, ran art workshops by correspondence with LGBTQ+ people currently incarcerated in Florida. Their installation, No Spirit For Me (2019), was included in the critically acclaimed exhibition *Marking Time: Art in the Age of Mass Incarceration,* curated by Dr. Nicole R. Fleetwood at MoMA PS1.

KARLA ROBINSON uses poetry, installation, and facilitation to support people caught at the intersection of multiple state institutions. A community-based arts educator, conceptual artist, and poet, her multi-media work spans discipline and medium. *Land Witness (Abolition Now!,* Asian Arts Initiative, 2019) is a poetry and photography collaboration. It explores the manner in which Black, Brown and Indigenous bodies have been segregated and detained on US soil and is a refusal to be complicit in the erasure of domestic terrorism. *Anxiously Awaiting Your Return: A Love Letter Altar to Children Detained Across Bridges and Boroughs* (Five Boro Justice Project, Hour Children, 2018) is a participatory public altar installation designed to support children, currently and previously, detained by carving a space to imagine a city without youth detention. Karla currently teaches at The New School and is a recipient of a Creatives Rebuild New York Artist Employment Program grant to start *Document.Dream. Disrupt.,* a multi-generational, Bronx based boutique press dedicated to nurturing youth voices.

ANTONIO SANCHEZ-DAY (1974–2021) was born in Topeka, Kansas. He was incarcerated for 13 years, released in 2015. He published his first book, *Taking on Life* (Coal City Review Press) in 2019. He worked as a class co-leader in the writing program at Douglas County Jail in Lawrence, Kansas, where he was previously incarcerated. He died in March 2021 and is buried at the Dancing Ground Cemetery on the Potawatomi Reservation in Mayetta, Kansas.

AMANI SAWARI is a graduate of the University of Washington with bachelor's degrees in Media & Communications and Law, Economics & Public Policy. Her interests lie in the connection between media and law as she explores the consequences that mass media representation has on the socioeconomic status of people of color in the United States, particularly for Black Americans. Sawari is a poet, photographer and reflective research writer. Her *Right2Vote Report* newsletter is printed and distributed among hundreds of incarcerated individuals across 33 of the United States. This trilogy was compiled during her work in Washington State as a Poetry Mentor to students incarcerated in Seattle's King County Juvenile Detention Center as a part of the Pongo Poetry Project during the 2016–2017 academic year.

MATTHEW SCHMITT recognizes that his experience serving as an improvisational theater facilitator at Western Wayne Correctional Facility in the late nineties was revolutionary to his understanding of humanity and modern societal injustices. Whether in his music (as mathyu djän), his writing, his ministry, or his nonprofit work, he draws from those memories and perspectives almost daily. After graduating from the University of Michigan in 1999, Matthew served as a sixth-grade teacher in New Orleans through Teach For America before going on to lead a nonprofit urban ministry in Los Angeles for eight years, intersecting the traditional mission trip with social justice, anti-racism, and anti-classism exposure and education. Matthew currently lives on Detroit's eastside with his children and works as the Director of Resource Navigation at Michigan Community Resources. He is a co-founder of The Table Setters, a nonprofit dedicated to promoting vulnerable and transformative discussions across division. He also sits on the development board of the Prison Creative Arts Project.

PATRICIA ROTH SCHWARTZ, who lives in the Finger Lakes region of New York State, holds a BA and MA in English and an MA in counseling psychology. She has worked as a psychotherapist in private practice and as an adjunct instructor in English and psychology for community colleges. Schwartz taught part-time in a prison college program for two years in Moravia, New York, until its demise, then served as a volunteer in Auburn Correctional Facility, a men's maximum security prison, in Auburn, New York from 2000–2014, where she facilitated a weekly poetry workshop with inmates. She is widely published in small press journals and anthologies, as well as with seven volumes of her poems, including *The Crows of Copper John: A History of Auburn Prison in Poems* (Foothills Publishing, 2017). She also edited and obtained publication for several volumes of poetry written by the poets at Auburn Correctional, including the anthology, *Doing Time to Cleanse My Mind.* Her full-length memoir, *Soul Knows No Bars: A Writer's Journey Doing Poetry with Inmates* (Olive Trees Publishing), was published in 2016. Her website, from which all her books, as well as the inmates', are available, is www.patriciarothschwartz.com.

CHRISTOPHER SOTO aka Loma is a poet based in California. He is the author of *Diaries of a Terrorist* (Copper Canyon Press, 2022), *Sad Girl Poems* (Sibling Rivalry Press, 2016) and the editor of *Nepantla: A Journal Dedicated to Queer Poets of Color* (Nightboat Books, 2018). In 2017, he was awarded "The Freedom Plow Award for Poetry & Activism" by Split This Rock. In 2016, Poets & Writers honored Christopher Soto with the "Barnes & Noble's Writer for Writers Award." He frequently writes book reviews for the Lambda Literary Foundation. His poems, reviews, interviews, and articles can be found at *The Nation, The Guardian, The Advocate, Los Angeles Review of Books, American Poetry Review, Tin House,* and more. His work has been translated into Spanish and Portuguese. He has been invited to speak at university campuses across the country. He is currently working on a full-length poetry manuscript about police violence and mass incarceration. He cofounded the Undocupoets Campaign and worked with Amazon Literary Partnerships to establish grants for undocumented writers. He received his MFA in poetry from NYU.

JUDITH TANNENBAUM (1947–2019) was a writer and teacher whose work focused on community arts and issues of cultural democracy. She served as training coordinator for San Francisco's WritersCorps program, and taught poetry in urban, rural, and suburban public schools through California Poets in the Schools, and at San Quentin and other state prisons through Arts-in-Corrections and the California Arts Council. Her books *Disguised as a Poem: My Years Teaching Poetry at San Quentin* (Northeastern University Press, 2000), a 2001 finalist in PEN American Center USA West's Literary Award Winners; two books for teachers—*Teeth, Wiggly as Earthquakes: Writing Poetry in the Primary Grades* (Stenhouse Publishers, 2000) and, with Valerie Chow Bush, *Jump Write In! Creative Writing Exercises for Diverse Communities, Grades 6–12* (Jossey-Bass, 2005); and six poetry collections. Her co-memoir with Spoon Jackson, *By Heart: Poetry, Prison, and Two Lives*, was published by New Village Press in March 2010. Judith wrote and edited: California's *Arts-in-Corrections* newsletter, and their book-length *Manual for Artists Working in Prison* and the *Handbook for Arts in the Youth Authority Program*. She also completed a feasibility study for arts programming in Minnesota state prisons, and participated in and chaired many panels on prison arts. She taught in prisons across the country and was the keynote speaker and on panels at many conferences on prison and prison arts.

DEBORAH TOBOLA is a poet and writer whose work has earned four Pushcart Prize nominations, three Academy of American Poets Awards and a Children's Choice Book Award. She graduated with high honors from the University of Montana with a Bachelor of Arts in English, and from the University of Arizona with a Master of Fine Arts in Creative Writing. Deborah taught poetry in California prisons for several years before taking the position of Institution Artist Facilitator at the California Men's Colony in San Luis Obispo in 2000. Her students in prison won writing awards, published their work locally and appeared on local and national radio. Each year, she produced original plays with music. In 2008, she founded Poetic Justice Project, the country's first theatre company for formerly incarcerated people. Poetic Justice Project is a program of the William James Association. Tobola's memoir, *Hummingbird in Underworld: Teaching in a Men's Prison* (She Writes Press, 2019), has won several awards in the US and was released in Taiwan and Hong Kong in 2020. She continues to teach creative writing and theatre in prison.

MICHAEL TORRES was born and brought up in Pomona, California where he spent his adolescence as a graffiti artist. His first, full-length collection of poems, *An Incomplete List of Names* (Beacon Press, 2020) was selected by Raquel Salas Rivera for the National Poetry Series and named one of NPR's "Best Books of 2020." Torres's work has won several awards, including grants from the Minnesota State Arts Board, and fellowships from the National Endowment for the Arts, the Bread Loaf Writers' Conference, CantoMundo, the Jerome Foundation, and the Loft Literary Center. Currently he is an Assistant Professor in the MFA program at Minnesota State University, Mankato, and also teaches in the Shakopee and Faribault Correctional Facilities through the Minnesota Prison Writing Workshop. See michaeltorreswriter.com

BRO. TRUTH, aka Bro. Hernandez Wiley, is a freedom fighter who mobilizes his visual art and spoken word to combat racism, misogyny and prejudice for all Americans. He has broken the chains of the mind to live free from oppression. He considers himself a political prisoner, due to racial bias by police that resulted in his wrongful conviction. He is a contributor to A.B.O. Comix, based in Oakland, California, which publishes work from incarcerated LGBTQ+ people, and he participated in *Between the Lines*, a series of collaborative art workshops by correspondence organized by Rowan Renee. His contributions have been exhibited in *The Power of We*, a large-scale public art exhibition, supported by We, Women. In 2021, his work was featured in the virtual exhibition *Freedom & Captivity*, a state-wide humanities initiative in Maine that asked contributors to imagine freedom in an abolitionist society. Bro. Truth's comics star himself as Katman, with members of the alien nation of Love Kats, from Planet Love. Their leader has given them orders to return to Planet Earth to help free humans from bondage and the tyranny of racist police, and to assure the victory of the largest civil rights movement in history. He dreams of an intergalactic future on Planet Love, where his artwork will help him raise funds for a lawyer to advocate for his exoneration.

VACHINE workshopped with prisoners at Watsonville State Prison, Watsonville, California. A third-generation American writer, Vachine is published in numerous journals and anthologies. An active open-mic-reader at venues from Cambridge, Massachusetts to Big Sur, California, he has featured at Los Angeles' World Stage, The Rapp Saloon, Cobalt Cafe, and Beyond Baroque, among others, his first book of poetry, *Stitches & Scars*, was published by Lummox Press in January 2021.

ERIN WILEY spent six years working with the Prison Creative Arts Project (PCAP), the majority facilitating open-format creative writing workshops at a men's facility in Jackson, Michigan. She enjoys writing poetry, a passion that started and continued to evolve as a participant in these workshops. Her work demonstrates the breadth and flux of topics and stylistic experimentation inspired by these writing groups. See Instagram @superboamagic.

About the Editor

A close-up, black and white photo of a petite White Jewish woman. The image is cropped around her face. Her hair is long and draped over her shoulders, and her chin rests in her hand. She is gazing indirectly beyond the camera.

Brandon Perdomo, 2021.

LEIGH SUGAR is a Michigan-born disabled writer. She was introduced to arts in prisons programs by Buzz Alexander and the Prison Creative Arts Project (PCAP) while in college at the University of Michigan. Through PCAP, she facilitated creative writing workshops (with contributor Erin Wiley) at Cooper Street Correctional Facility in Jackson, Michigan, from 2011–2014, and co-edited (with contributor Phil Christman) PCAP's annual *Michigan Review of Prisoner Creative Writing* (Vol. 4–6). A former movement artist, she trained with Yoga Behind Bars and taught yoga to children imprisoned at Echo Glen Children's Center outside of Seattle, Washington. Leigh holds a Master of Public Administration with specialization in Criminal Justice Policy from John Jay College, and a Master of Fine Arts in Poetry from New York University, where she served as a 2017–18 Veteran Writers' Fellow and facilitated free writing workshops for New York City-area veterans of the Iraq and Afghanistan Wars. In addition to the NYU Veteran Writers' Workshop and Cooper Street Writers' Workshop, she has taught writing at John Jay College's Institute for Justice and Opportunity, New York University College of Arts & Science, Poetry Foundation, Justice Arts Coalition, Hugo House, and more. Her own poetry and prose appear in *Poetry, Split This Rock, jubilat, Honey Literary*, and elsewhere, and she created and co-facilitates *Access Oriented Lit*, a monthly reading series by and for disabled writers. Her first poetry collection, *FREELAND*, is forthcoming (Alice James Books, 2025). See www.leighksugar.com.

On Book Sales

All author royalties from sales of this anthology will be donated to Dances for Solidarity, an organization that connects artists with people incarcerated in solitary confinement to co-create a movement sequence that can be done within the walls of a solitary cell.

Dances for Solidarity began as a letter writing campaign between artists and activists in New York and incarcerated people in Texas and Louisiana. Each letter begins with the same 10-step Dance for Solidarity as a means to initiate a conversation around movement. The project has been in correspondence with more than 200 people incarcerated in solitary confinement throughout the United States and has produced live performances created by currently and formerly incarcerated artists throughout New York City and New Orleans. DFS has been supported by A Studio in the Woods (New Orleans/Tulane), MAP Fund, Gibney's Moving Toward Justice Fellowship, Culture Push's Fellowship for Utopian Practice, PEN America, The Fortune Society, and more.

See www.dancesforsolidarity.org/.